River Rats

by

Ralph Christopher

authorHOUSE™

1663 LIBERTY DRIVE, SUITE 200
BLOOMINGTON, INDIANA 47403
(800) 839-8640
WWW.AUTHORHOUSE.COM

First published by AuthorHouse 05/10/05

ISBN: 1-4208-2690-5 (sc)
ISBN: 1-4208-2689-1 (dj)

Printed in the United States of America
Bloomington, Indiana

This book is printed on acid-free paper.

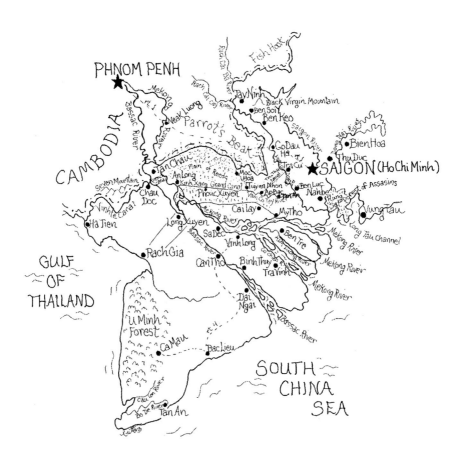

PHNOM PENH

CAMBODIA

Bassac River

Mekong

Neak Luong

Rach Cai Cay River

Rach Ba Bay River

Fish Hook

Parrot's Beak

Tay Ninh

Black Virgin Mountain

Ben Soi

Ben Keo

Saigon River

Go Dau Ha

Tra Cu

Bien Hoa

Dong Nai River

Thu Duc

SAIGON (Ho Chi Minh)

An Chau

Plain of Reeds

Moc Hoa

Tuyen Nhon

Ap Bac

Tan An

Ben Luc

Nha Be

Forest of Assassins

Seven Mountain

An Long

Kinh Xang Grand Canal

Phuoc Xuyen

Vinh Co Tay River

Cai Lay

Vam Co Dong River

Sat

Vung Tau

Chau Doc

Vinh Te Canal

Ha Tien

Cai Lay

My Tho

Vung Tau Channel

GULF OF THAILAND

Rach Gia

Long Xuyen

Bassac River

Mekong River

Sa Dec

Vinh Long

Ham Luong River

Ben Tre

Mekong River

Can Tho

Binh Thuy

Tra Vinh

Mekong River

Dai Ngai

Bassac River

U Minh Forest

Ca Mau

Bac Lieu

SOUTH CHINA SEA

Cua Lon River

Bo De River

Tan An

Cua Long

RECOMMENDED BOOKS

PAPA BRAVO ROMEO – Wynn Goldsmith
SLINGSHOT – Edward Vick
POINT MAN – Chief James Watson
GAMEWARDENS OF VIETNAM – unit history book
ALL THAT GLITTERS… Lester Westling

To purchase 30 minute RIVER RATS DVD, make a donation to the Vietnam Unit Memorial Monument, or purchase Gamewardens merchandise, contact Gamewardens of Vietnam – www. tf116.org.

PROLOGUE

I dedicate this book to all the Vietnam veterans who fought and won the war in Southeast Asia, only to have it taken away.

On January 27, 1973, the Paris Peace Accords were signed, ending U.S. participation in the Vietnam War. On March 29, 1973, the Naval Advisory Group and Naval forces of Vietnam were disestablished and sent home. Saigon fell on April 30, 1975, two years later. To say we lost the War is ludicrous. It would be more accurate to say that the group of Americans who protested and voted for the Congress and Senate that tied the American fighting man's hands and imposed unfair rules of engagement on us throughout our time in service, and the South Vietnamese, lost the War. To put it on the shoulders of our brave and noble troops, who distinguished themselves time and time again and tried desperately to deliver the people of Vietnam from the suppression and terror they encountered in their daily lives, is merely continuing the abuse and pain of a generation.

We who marched off proudly when our country called, in a time when many chose not to, were continuing the legacy of the American Liberators and attempting to deliver freedom to far-off nations and people who had never known it. The American Armed Forces have never been the aggressor and have always answered the call to arms from the weak and helpless.

I encourage all Veterans to hold your heads high and overturn this wrong. The Vietnam Veterans were ordered to war and when their time was over, they were ordered home. When the South

Vietnamese government fell in 1975, we weren't even there. If South Korea falls, does that mean the Korean Vets lost the war? I certainly hope not. The American fighting man has fought proudly alongside the starving and suppressed people of the world. We fight terror, abuse and starvation and we do so willingly. This falls upon us because our forefathers had the insight to set our country up in a way that we are the most blessed nation on this planet. Our conscience won't allow us to sit idly by and watch our neighbors be raped and killed. I would like to say to all American Veterans: You are my heroes, especially the Vietnam Veterans whom I had the honor to have served alongside. Thank you, and God bless you for what you tried to give this world.

I am not claiming this book to be history because it is impossible to get all the names, times, dates and places one-hundred percent accurate. I had to piece stories together from many accounts, although many of the words and stories in this book are true and from the men who were there. My personal story is only a vehicle used to deliver them to you. In many cases it has been painful for both the author and the Veterans to revisit these places that live only in our hearts and minds. But I have felt it was important to record a little piece of the past that has been for the most part forgotten.

Please forgive me for what I may have left out, for it was a long time ago, and for many years I tried to forget. Thanks to my wife Deb and my family for standing by me in this time that I have dedicated to the past, and to the many advisors and Veterans who stood alongside me and contributed greatly. I couldn't have done it without you and I hope you will find some pride and satisfaction in leaving a peace of our legacy behind. I am especially grateful to Larry Bissonnette, Eldon Fry, Dan Backus, Kirk Ferguson, Al Deroco, Tom Anderson, Al Maxson, Robert Wilson and the many others who got involved and believed that this story was worth telling. I salute all the families, and especially the children, of the men and women who made the ultimate sacrifice. I pray that you, too, will find some comfort in what your loved ones have given us.

PRELUDE

It was a warm summer's day with the breeze blowing across Mission Bay in the year 2000, when the brown water veterans of three Naval Task Forces met at the Naval Amphibious Base on Coronado Island, California. It had been thirty years since we had marched on her fields and studied in her classrooms. U.S. Navy sailors, in their dress whites, greeted us with warm smiles and looks of admiration as we departed the buses that delivered us to the base. The sailors passed out schedules of events and seated us with our families in our perspective units on the grassy field in front of the Vietnam Unit Memorial Monument. We had joined back together for the dedication ceremony of three of our crafts that had been restored and mounted on stands next to the long gray wall. Ralph Fries, the father of the monument, and many others had worked long and hard to complete the memorial, but money was still needed. My wife Deborah, and daughter Kayli, sat by my side as I stared into the crowd looking for faces of men that I had served with. I glanced over at a young sailor and whispered to my wife. "Some of them don't look old enough to be in the Navy." Then I recalled how young I was when I first arrived. We were all in our fifties, sixties and seventies, and had become the grandfathers of river warfare. It was nice to see someone had remembered us and the job we had performed so many years ago. Vietnam was not a popular war and had been forgotten by most of America, but not by us. We few would never forget. The names of our fallen brothers had not yet been engraved across the wall, but we knew someday they would be etched in for future generations to see.

One of our unit chaplains, Lester Westling JR., gave the benediction and then a few of our unit commanders took the podium and recalled those days of duty, honor, and sacrifice. We had all recently lost our spiritual leader, Admiral Zumwalt, who had planned to speak at the ceremony. But we were still happy to see each other and the fact that we weren't the only ones turning gray and getting a little chubby around the mid section. Suddenly, the sound of a helicopter approaching overhead drew our eyes to the sky. Damn, where would we be if it hadn't been for those guys? How many times had they flown in under fire to secure our safety? It must have been thousands, but now it was just another fading memory that lived only in our hearts and minds. A strong wind lifted skirts and blew off old hats, as I flashed back in time to when I was a kid, and America was at war.

CHAPTER ONE - THE BUNKER

It was about dusk when the first mortar round hit Advance Tactical Support Base, Ben Keo. Men began to come alive as they scrambled to gather their weapons and get to their battle stations. The second round hit moments later near the tactical operations bunker, just outside the fence. Awakening the village was the sound of shuffling boots and boat engines turning over. The base siren screamed, water buffalos ran, screen doors swung open and slammed. Sailors were leaping from the barges as the ropes were being cleared away to push off and move deeper into the River of Death. The dirty brown water slapped against the hulls as the crafts got up to speed, while we donned our flak jackets and jacked rounds into our guns. By the time the first fiberglass patrol boat had reached the bend in the river, the Viet Cong had gotten off four mortar rounds, all of which had fallen short of their targets.

Guns were opening up from both sides as the river patrol boats' twin .50 caliber machine guns started tearing into the camouflaged mound of mud and logs. All hands were on deck and firing to port as the two boats planed pass the bunker at full speed on step. The Vam Co Dong River was so narrow that the boats had to continue pass the bunker and perform high-speed turns by reversing the flow of their jet pumps and turning around in their own back wash. Sailors jumped to the opposite side of the boat, swinging their guns 180 degrees to fire to starboard. Throttling full ahead, Chief Ramsey yelled, "Let'em have it!" Small palm trees were falling as the thunder of the .50s began chopping down the jungle around the mound of clay.

Still, the enemy persisted as green tracers zipped over our heads. The smoke and smell of gunpowder filled the air. Empty, hot, brass shell cases were scattered over the deck and rolling to and fro as the boat maneuvered in and out of the choppy river to turn for yet another firing run. Men were yelling and screaming obscenities as the adrenaline flow reached a feverish pitch.

Catching up was a green monster, resembling a far-gone relic of a Civil War Ironclad. A tough, seasoned crew hurriedly prepared to enter the kill zone. As she neared the tree line, rocket propelled grenades were released against her, tearing into the outer bars protecting the wheel house and creating the most awful sound of steel hitting steel. It was a classic duel between two big boys. An old-fashioned slugfest, and whoever hit the other the hardest the most, was going to win. But it was clear from the first exchange that the bunker was too heavily fortified for even the sixty-foot battle wagon. With guns answering, the heavy assault boat withdrew as the thirty-one-foot patrol boats cut back in to take up the fight and allow the heavy time to move to safety. Chief Ramsey radioed back to Lieutenant Barnhouse at the firebase. "The mud and logs are too thick, sir."

Appearing around the bend in the river, a second assault boat, equipped with high pressure water cannons, moved in to engage the enemy. Buried in the smoke of Chinese and Russian weapons, the Viet Cong were throwing everything they had at the water cannon boat. A rocket came burling out like a great bird seeking to disable a giant before she became to close to her nest, BOOM! Then a second and third, BOOM! BOOM! The deformed boat was covered in smoke and debris. Its crew was thrown to the deck and hastily recovered to their feet. The heavy was taking a brutal pounding, but never wavered from moving forward.

Thankfully, we had been lucky, due largely to the chief and the quickness of the lightly-fortified patrol boat, although chunks of fiberglass were now missing and holes of daylight appeared through the hull. CA-PLINK, CA-PLINK. If they hit us with a rocket, we're dead. The sound of the twin Detroit engines roaring as the boats got up out of the water, in combination with all guns in a thunderous return of fire, was deafening, as we raced past the bunker, making firing runs again and again. Men's faces were distorted with looks of fear and anger as they stood in the open, firing, as rounds ricocheted and whistled by. Time stood still. The sound of my heart thumping in my chest, I labored for breath. I couldn't recall how long the firefight had lasted, only that we were in a life-or-death struggle with a determined adversary. Minutes seemed like hours as the enemy stood his ground in defiance of our firepower and the courage of the men manning the green boats.

As the water cannon boat neared, she opened up with her cannons propelling water at the thick mud, and the curtailing sound of drowning rats sang through the valley. Still, there was no let-up of the blistering fire raining down on us. Finally, the Navy's Seawolf attack helicopters showed up to rescue us. I was glad we were backing off to give them a wide berth. The two UH-1B Huey gunships circled and ran along the middle of the river at tree-level to give their door-gunners a chance to open up on the bunker. Then they rose and swooped down like two birds of prey, spraying the jungle canopy with M-60 machine guns and white-tailed rockets. CHITCHITCHIT! CHITCHITCHITCHITCHITCHIT! PHOOST! PHOOST! PHOOST!

The Seawolves cleared away a city block of jungle, repeatedly diving in under fire, releasing their anger on the dense tree line. The tracer's could be seen hitting the belly of the choppers as they rose back up to avoid hitting the tall swaying palm trees. BANG, KLINK, BANG, KLINK! KLINK!

After what seemed like an eternity, the Lieutenant ordered us to return to the firebase. Command had seen fit to order fire support from Tay Ninh Army base ten miles down the road. The 25th Infantry and 11th Cavalry's Black Horse Division were there, preventing the ancient city from falling into enemy hands. The Army had mounted an artillery battery on top of Nui Ba Dinh, Black Virgin Mountain, and the howitzer rounds could reach the jungle surrounding our small navy outpost.

We could hear the sound of the rounds as they bellowed overhead, like runaway locomotives, and then sucked up the air, crashing and exploding into the earth. Trees that had stood for a hundred years tumbled down around the bunker as the Lieutenant, in the tower, determined the exact location and spotted the rounds through field glasses, walking them in.

"Up one hundred yards, left fifty," he called out to the radioman next to him, who in turn communicated the coordinates to the artillery battery on the mountain. Again, the shells were released within a few seconds of each other, slamming into the jungle around the mound of logs and mud. The ground shook under our feet, even though we had moved a mile down river. By now it was so black out we couldn't see our hands in front of our faces. Each time a round hit, the entire valley lit up like heat lightning on a summer's night. The sailors in Ben Keo's mortar pit kept the 60- and 81-millimeter tubes going continuously as they pounded the jungle with high explosives, and dropped illumination flares, which drifted down slowly on small white parachutes, allowing the men in the tower to spot any movement in the rice paddies across the river.

The artillery bombardment went on for quite some time as the sailors gathered and marveled at the money being spent trying to unearth the enemy from their fighting holes in the ground. No matter what the cost, we all agreed it was better than sacrificing one of our lives for a war that nobody seem to care about back in the States. The sailors stood atop the sandbag wall near the M-60 team adjacent to the river and cheered as each round exploded, chipping away large chunks of the jungle.

"Wow, did you see that one," yelled out a wide-eyed teenage sailor.

As the shelling was called off, the patrol boat returned to the base and rejoined the group. Just then the radio broke its silence.

"YOU MISSED, GI," eerily the Viet Cong's words echoed over the air for all to hear.

"GODDAMN!" Chief Ramsey cursed as he tossed me a hot Carling Black Label beer.

"I hate those fucking Gooks," Ramsey said as he stomped off.

I set back on the hood of the warm engines and sipped my beer, trying to stop my body from shaking, with the sound of the guns still ringing in my ears. Chief Ramsey and the other boat captains looked to their men, taking inventory, making sure they were all present and in one piece. Several of the Vietnamese sailors on the heavies were pretty shaken up after receiving multiple rocket hits. It's a wonder that any of them survived as we viewed the twisted and mangled steel on the boat. They were right about the outer bars and C-ration boxes; they had broken up the initial hits and slowed the shrapnel as it entered the hull. Several of the men had been helped out and were lying in the yard, recovering from the shock of the battle. One Viet sailor was bleeding, and had temporarily lost his hearing from the shell blast that almost took him out.

There was a commotion at the front gate as the villagers were trying to convey some sort of emergency. The medic passed me as he went running by.

"What's up, Doc?"

"One of the hooch's in the village was hit."

After unlocking the front gate, he and a Vietnamese interpreter proceeded into the village to administer first aid. Arriving at the hooch, they could see that those inside had been lucky; the mortar round had hit just outside the front door. A few more feet and it would have been devastating, killing everyone inside. As it was, only the small children of the family suffered mostly superficial wounds. The medic stayed behind to patch up the kids, while concentrating most of his time on one little girl who was bleeding from a wound on her leg. The parents of the girl were looking on as the father tried to console the mother, telling her the child would be okay.

Back in the yard, sailors were moving around, trying to shake off the battle that had just occurred. Dusting off the debris from their uniforms, there was a feeling as if we had just ducked a big one. Making eye contact around the compound we all looked at each other differently. Faces were more drawn as the fear of the moment was receding and a few smiles from one buddy to another started to appear. Hugs and embraces were being exchanged between men who up to a few hours earlier were not even friends. The relief that we had all made it was a great feeling.

I journeyed out to the hooch to check on Doc.

"How's she doing?" I asked.

"She'll be okay."

The father grabbed my hand and shook it as he bowed.

"Thank you, thank you." He obviously was scared out of his wits.

"It will be all right, my friend," I said, trying to calm him down.

We waved as we retreated back to the base. Yeah, it would be all right, okay. What a joke that was. It would never be all right for these poor rice farmers as long as the Peoples Army and the Americans dueled for control of this valley. The Lieutenant appeared out of the radio shack door after getting off the horn with command.

"Good job, men, we hurt 'em," he said as he moved around the base, encouraging the men.

I looked up to see if he was serious. Maybe the Seawolves and artillery had hurt them, but I doubted seriously if we had. We were just bait to draw them out into the open. It was a gallant charge, but had it not been for the superior firepower, we most likely would still have been out there slugging it out with those guys, and somebody definitely would have gotten hurt. At times I almost felt sorry for those poor bastards at the receiving end of such awesome firepower. But then I remembered what they had taught us at Coronado, that without it they would have overrun the base and killed us all.

For a long time we had felt we were up against a determined crack squad of men. Intelligence had captured a wounded freedom fighter in another battle, and through interrogation had discovered that they were sending in a fresh squad of men each time they reoccupied the bunker. They would rebuild and fortify, waiting for the opportune time to start the battle all over again. We had been chopping them down for months and never knew it, and yet most of the South Vietnamese sailors seemed reluctant to commit themselves to battle without their American counterparts beside them. The enemy seemed to have the determination and fire in their bellies and the South didn't. Most of us had lost the notion that we were going to make a difference; we were now fighting for each other and the right to return home and go to school like other kids our age. Looking around, it seemed as if we had all awakened to a new day. All the while, I was thinking back to what our instructors had told us in my counter-insurgency course. Somehow it did not seem the same, but then how could it, the war had changed. This fucking war was never going to end. I thought back to Coronado and the beginning.

CHAPTER TWO - CORONADO

The rain trickled down the window as I peeked out into a dark cloudy sky; it was raining cats and dogs as the drops splashed, bouncing off the choppy waves of the bay. It was 1700 hours and I was about to report to the Naval Amphibious Base on Coronado Island, California. It was early February of 1970 and the town was jumping. San Diego across the bay was lit up and growing right up the hillside. I took a bus and they dropped me off at the front gate. After checking my orders the sentry directed me to my barracks.

CISM (Congress, International, Sports, and Military) Field was amidst a group of small grey buildings not far from the crashing waters of the shore. I was awed by the sight of sailors running up and down the beach, carrying telephone poles on their shoulders while instructors yelled in their ears, "You hear me puke?" The whole company would answer in unison, "Yes sir, drill instructor sir." Who the hell are these guys? Another class came around the corner, running in step, double-time, and stopped in front of the galley. The instructor jumped up the steps and ran into the hall leaving the trainees standing at parade rest in the pouring rain. These must be the SEALs (Sea, Air, Land), that I had heard so much about, the U.S. Navy's highly-trained counter-insurgency teams. Trained in unconventional or para-military operations and equipped to train personnel of allied nations in such operations. As well as underwater demolition men, they were qualified parachute jumpers, proficient in at least one foreign language and expert in all types of hand-to-hand combat and self-defense measures. The navy's elite commandos were still a secret in those days, but the stories were starting to leak out about the job they were doing in Southeast Asia. I had originally volunteered to sign on for their program, but was informed I would have to extend my tour, which was a bit much for me to swallow. After almost three years in, I wanted to get home before my twenty-first birthday and pick up my life where I had left off. I knew then that I was not going to make a career of the navy. Besides, I had heard the training was the most intense in the armed forces, and if I washed out, I would have to finish my two-year extension commitment. I could not take that chance. I was so homesick it was about to kill me. I picked up my pace and hurried on down the wet sidewalk as the rain increased and the chill of a foggy night started to close in.

At 0600 the next morning, we were awakened. "Reveille, reveille, drop your cocks and grab your socks, reveille, reveille." After breakfast I reported to formation on the parade grounds with a company-size group of sailors like myself. All rates were represented, even airmen, or Air Dales as we called them, but the bulk of us were engineering or electronics technicians. We were instructed to fall in and dress our ranks. Then a salty-looking sailor, sporting a heavy mustache stepped forward and shouted out.

"Look to the left, look to the right. One of you guys ain't coming home. What you will learn here at counter-insurgency orientation will save you and your buddy's life." Well, he had gotten my attention mighty quick. I was not planning on coming home in a box. I was going to follow this guy around like a puppy and learn all I could in the short time that I had been given. He marched us to a warehouse where the storekeepers were waiting to issue us our new olive green uniforms. They visually sized us up from across the room and threw the clothes at us. I got straight leg pants and short sleeve shirts with narrow pockets. Next they piled on socks, boxer shorts, and tee shirts, the same uniform the Seabees construction battalion wore. Finally, they gave us a brand new boot designed for Vietnam, called jungle boots. At first I thought they were being cheap by putting canvas in the leg of the boots, but I overheard a sailor explaining that it let the water drain out and helped the boot dry faster. Then I thought they were a bit heavy until the instructor informed us they had a thin piece of steel in the sole so the punji stakes wouldn't penetrate. What's a punji stake? I opted to go back for a larger pair. I thought it would be better to flop around a bit than tiptoe through my tour with blisters.

Our uniforms were a combination of what the guys had worn in World War II in the island campaigns, and what the navy had found to work in the jungles and swamps of Southeast Asia. I was glad to be out of the spit-shine navy; I was tired of pressed uniforms and military inspections. I would be too busy for all that marching and saluting; besides, I wouldn't have to wear the little white cap I couldn't seem to keep on my head. We now had green baseball caps with a brim to shade our faces from the sun. It was one of the few articles of clothing that we were allowed to show a little self-expression. I started forming the brim to make it look a little hipper, while eyeing the room to see what other sailors were doing with theirs. You could round it off like a baseball player, or square it like the marines. You could flip it up or down, or maybe just turn it around. Better not do that, as I folded the hat in two and stuck it in my back pocket.

That night I wrote to my aunt Rachel, my mother's sister back home in Virginia. She had lost her fiancé in the South Pacific in World War II and had taken a special interest in me. We often wrote as if we were sweethearts and spoke about music and cool-ones which was our code for beer. She worked alongside the rest of my family in the cigarette factories in Richmond, Virginia.

Dear Rachel   12/Feb/70

Well I finally started school today. I want to hurry up and get it finished. I want to get over there as fast as possible. I have 351 days left in the Navy. I received your letter today it was the first one. It was very nice. Tell Ann I said hi. I sprang my ankle and now I'm down here for training and it hurts like hell. I drew my greens today and they are too big for me. I think they will shrink or at least I hope so. I sent Grandma forty dollars and told her you wanted to pay the rent. I dropped that seventy dollars you use to owe me.

Tell everybody I send my love. I went to see Quick Silver the other night. They are really good. They had some wild bands there. I'm just setting around right now. I think I'll go and take a shower in a little. I didn't tell mom because I didn't want to worry her but they said something big is happening in Vietnam and that only half of our class would probably make it back. Well I'll write later, you be good and take care.

Love Chris

The next morning I limped into formation as our instructor informed us why we were going to South Vietnam. We go to fulfill one of the most solemn pledges of the American nation. Four Presidents - Eisenhower, Kennedy, Johnson, and Nixon - for more then fifteen years had promised to help defend this small and valued nation. Strengthened by that promise, the people of South Vietnam have fought for many long years. Thousands of them had died; thousands more had been crippled and scarred by war; and we could not now dishonor our word or abandon our commitments, or leave those who believed in us and trusted us to the terror and repression and murder that would follow. This is why we were in South Vietnam.

President Johnson had once stated the reason why. "To keep this country free so millions of children can grow up to go to school and live in a world of peace. Freedom from subversion, slavery, and Communism, for a people who have seen nothing but war and deprivation for decades and are faced with a new threat to their existence. Americans have always been known for rallying to a cause and none draws them more quickly than freedom."

The instructors then walked us through counter-insurgency orientation, as specialists were brought in to train us in the many lessons we would need to know to survive our twelve-month tour. We studied the Vietnamese language and customs, as well as the enemy's tactics and how to counter them. We disassembled and reassembled Communist weapons and learned how they would be used against us, as well as how to use them against our enemies, the Viet Cong (VC) guerrilla's of the south, and the Peoples Army, better known as the North Vietnamese Army (NVA).

Our instructors told us stories about being captured and kept in small cages for long periods of time. You couldn't stand in these monkey cages and your legs would lose circulation after an hour.

"Don't worry, you'll pass out after two hours or so, and when you wake up you won't feel a thing," he pronounced.

The enemy had kept people in cages for years and when they finally let them out they no longer had use of their legs. Now the class was looking around at each other. I know I was scared; I had made up my mind not to be captured at any cost. I would rather go down fighting. They had all kinds of wonderful stories to fill our heads. Like the one about the gentleman who escaped the Iron Curtin with his family by eating out of trash cans across Europe. Upon arriving in the United States, he wanted to fight against Communism, so he joined the navy and flew jets. During a mission over North Vietnam his plane was shot down. So what does he do? He escapes and eats out of trash cans. The lesson of the story was mind over matter. If you can get over the fact that the food came from the trash cans, you can survive. They called it Americanized. If you thought like an American back home and underestimated the Viet Cong, they would use it against you, and you would die.

A perfect example was their usage of children and booby traps. A young boy would approach you on the streets with a shoe shine box.

"Shoe shine, mister?" as the small smiling boy came running over. As soon as you set your boot on the box, he would run away leaving you standing on top of a bomb. They also used young men on motorbikes that would try and catch several Americans congregating on a corner, then pitch a grenade at them as they sped away. We called them Saigon Cowboys, and they were deadly.

During SERE (Survival, Evasion, Resistance and Escape) training they told us how to trip up the enemy and escape being captured. I was surprised to hear that the Viet Cong had been holding prisoners of war down south in the Mekong Delta for years. They taught us how to eat bugs and bark off of trees. Where to look for edible roots, plants and berries, and how to catch small game and birds. Maggots were especial high in protein. We all lined up for seconds on that one.

"Stay alive no matter what," they preached to us.

When we were not in the field, we got time off and received mail back at the barracks. I went to see the rock band Quick Silver Messenger at the San Diego Civic Center on a pass. They were great. Mail was huge for me. All my family and friends were back home in Virginia.

Dear Mom   27/Feb/70

Well today I got back from five days in the jungle. You wouldn't believe how much dirt I had on me. I had to eat all kinds of weird stuff; they don't give you any food while you are up there. They captured me and interrogated me and all that weird stuff. I thought I was going to starve to death. I came through with flying colors.

Sunday I start my gun training at Camp Pendleton Marine Base. That will be the last of my training. They offered me seven days leave but I turned it down. Too much money involved. I'll be home soon enough. Tell Jo Ann thank you for the picture. Tell her and Phillip I send my love. I'll write later.

Love Chris

After SERE, they turned us over to the marines at Camp Pendleton, California, for small-arms familiarization. Regardless of the unit, be it construction, amphibious, public works, or maintenance, we all were given infantry training by the marines. They housed us in tents and marched us to the field and chow hall to give us a sense of being in the bush. It felt like I had stepped back into an old John Wayne movie. The boots that had marched through those tents had freed the world many times over. I must admit, seeing the marine instructor hit bull's eyes at a thousand yards with an M-14 rifle was very impressive. They were everything they said they were, tough bastards. They had us at firing ranges every day, rain or shine. We fired rifles, handguns, machine guns, and threw hand grenades. Then they demonstrated grenade launchers, LAW (Light Anti-tank Weapon) rockets and mortars. Claymore mines were a big hit, right across the front was written, Front, Toward Enemy.

The marines sneered and looked down their noises at us. They thought of us as weekend warrior's since they had very little jurisdiction to discipline us. We were not marines; we were your regular fleet-type sailors. I had one Vee under my Crow, pay grade E4. One thing was certain; we were heading to Southeast Asia just as soon as they could get us ready. Our navy instructors were good guys for the most part. They knew we had volunteered to go over and serve as river sailors. They tried their best to instruct the class well and instill the idea that we could all make it and return home to live long lives.

Whenever they didn't have a sailor's complete attention, they came out with some catchy little phrase like "Your mom is going to cry when you come home in a box." It was very effective in a room full of eighteen and nineteen-year-old boy-men. Our training was not nearly as physically demanding as the SEALs. They had them swimming and humping all day and half the night. Ours, on the other hand, was mostly classroom with short field trips to the marines and naval survival instructors. The class kept quiet and tried to absorb whatever was being taught each day. There wasn't any grab assing or kidding around; we were all deadly serious. The instructors seemed to be well informed, as if they were speaking from experience, which I believe was the case. We were lucky to have them. I wasn't too sure about those guys yelling at the SEAL Wannabe's, and I say that only because less than half of a SEAL class graduated. The same was not true for us. We all moved on and received orders to report to our next duty station. For me, that was Naval Support Activities Detachment, Saigon, South Vietnam.

CHAPTER THREE
THE UNFRIENDLY SKIES

It was another beautiful California Dreamin' day with the sun shining when I left Coronado. My orders read to report to Travis Air Force Base in Northern California, where I would board a flight to Vietnam. They issued me money for transportation and food, so I jumped on a Greyhound bus and let them do the driving. At times I thought I should have changed into my civvies, but it probably wouldn't matter, it was easy to see I was in the military. I had a regulation haircut, and at twenty years of age I still couldn't grow a mustache. In those days, most young men in California had long hair. I felt young and old at the same time and knew that wearing my uniform could be asking for trouble. I had heard the stories of soldiers returning home and being heckled by flower children hippies at the airports. I was going off to war for my fourth tour with the knowledge that not all of my countrymen supported the efforts and sacrifices that were being made by American serviceman in this so called "police action."

Much had changed since 1967. The veterans saluted us, and the college kids threw dog shit and called us baby-killers. I saw Vietnam through different eyes now; I had heard the stories of bravery. Men wouldn't be doing these things if they didn't believe in what they were doing, even though parts of America had lost faith. It felt as if we were playing in the biggest game of our lives, and halfway through, the crowd got up and left.

Our government flew thousands of servicemen over on chartered yellow Braniff International Airline flights, complete with hostesses and meals. The yellow banana express was full of army, marines, air force, and there were a few navy and coastguard men. Most of us had your usual service ribbons displayed. A few pimply-faced teenager boots had just graduated basic training, wearing only the national defense. Sprinkled among us were a handful of guys loaded down with a whole chestful. Sitting across from me was a marine gunny sergeant with ribbons stacked five rows high. This guy must have been some kind of legend. He had hash marks signifying his years in service half the way up his arm and campaign ribbons dating back to World War II. He looked up at me and I quickly looked away. He had to be on his second or third tour. Why would anyone go back after seeing the action he obviously had? Did he have a death wish or was he John Wayne?

The sun had just disappeared into the western sky as the plane taxied down the long runway joining the formation. Transports full of servicemen were in front and behind; it seemed like one nonstop column headed into uncertainty, going to meet the enemy. I sat back in my seat, closing my eyes and thinking how the money line America was spending must be staggering. I could not clearly see what we had to gain from a war so far away. There was no oil or natural resources, unless you counted rubber trees and rice, or was there? I rejected the idea that we were fighting for tennis shoes or Uncle Ben's Instant. I heard the rumors that we had some interest in this small poor farming country. It was good for our economy. All the money being spent on Bell helicopters and other war machines that were being sold to the government, etc. I didn't buy into it. I had been training to fight the Communists. I was going to support a little peasant rice farmer who had lived in the Mekong Delta for hundreds of years and simply wanted to raise his family in the ways and traditions of his ancestors. This was hard to do with the Viet Cong stealing his rice and abducting his young men against their will to serve as freedom fighters. I didn't know much about politics and democracy. I had never voted, but I truly believed that if we stopped Communism in Southeast Asia, we would prevent it from spreading to Thailand and the rest of the world. We had the best men in the United States Navy serving in newly formed Task Force units throughout South Vietnam. The stories were filtering back to the fleet of gallant battles that were being waged by the navy for control of the rivers and canals. We were beating the enemy soundly, and it had to end soon.

The crowded plane crept forward as I looked out the window to view a cloud-covered moon. The runway was lit up like a Christmas tree during the holidays and you could see the planes stacked up ready to depart. It was like one continuous convoy of ships with hundreds of planes taking off every day. Anxiety, anguish, and the fear of death filled the coach as the pilot throttled forward, launching us into a windy sky. By the time we got to Hawaii to refuel, we seemed to be alone. It wasn't to be a long layover in Honolulu, but I did depart long enough to try and phone a Hawaiian shipmate of mine. We had sailed together on my first tour of Southeast Asia in 1967 aboard the USS Vega, AF-59, a refrigerated cargo ship in the Seventh Fleet. I recalled how I had come to join the armed forces and my first year of service to my country.

CHAPTER FOUR
THE LOSS OF INNOCENCE

I was the eldest of three children born to Ralph W. and Delores B. Christopher. My parents had separated after my tenth birthday and I started developing problems soon after. My sister Jo Ann, brother Phillip and I lived together with our mom in Mechanicsville, Virginia, near old Cold Harbor. I grew up playing in the trenches where the Confederacy repelled the Union attacks in the Seven-Day Battle. My grandfather, Allen E. Ball, would take me fishing in the swamps and tell me stories of his exploits with Blackjack Pershing in the "war to end all wars." He also taught me about my great, great grandfather who rode with Jeb Stuart's cavalry under General Lee. His stories were so vivid that I could almost visualize the horses pulling the cannons through the thick pine trees, as AP Hill's infantry formed a trench line along the Chickahominy Bluff.

I remember once, we had just finished one of those big Southern fried dinners. The heat of a hot summer's day was starting to turn into the coolness of a promising evening. Grandma and Aunt Rachel were clearing the table and preparing to wash the dishes. Uncle Bubba was resting his eyes as he settled into his favorite easy chair about to take a little cat nap. The TV could be heard in the background as the play-by-play announcer gave a report of Mickey Mantle swinging at the plate. I was out back feeding the dogs the scraps from dinner when I caught grandpa through the side of my eye. He was sneaking out the back door. He waved me over while raising his index finger to motion for me to be quit. On the way he grabbed two fishing polls on the side porch along with his tackle box.

"Come on Chris, lets me and you go catch some fish," Grandpa said as he lightly closed the side gate and we tip toed to the old grey Dodge parked in the front of the house.

"Don't be late Pa," Grandma shouted.

"We have to get up early for church tomorrow."

"All rite, Ma," then he looked at me and chuckled.

"That old woman is part hound dog."

His shrunken crippled hands inserted his key into the ignition. After a couple attempts the old Dodge sputtered and spat but started as always.

"Where we goin Grandpa?"

"I thought we go down to the Chickahomy and catch that pike."

"Okay," I said with a smile across my freckled face.

I knew the fishing hole he was talk'n about. Him and everybody else in the county had been trying to catch that old fish for years. As the Dodge coasted slowly down through the bottom land, I stuck my head out the window to blow off the stickiness of the humidity. I loved that time of day. There was a light fog trying to form over the pockets of water through the swamp. Peaking through the pines was an orange light reflecting off the clouds mixing with the blue gray of the sky. Sunset, it couldn't get much better, and I was with my favorite person in the whole wide world, my Grandpa. He was the greatest story teller of my life and I never tired of hearing his tales of the good old days.

"Tell me what it was like when you were grow'n up Grandpa."

"I was born in the early 1900's in the Great Smoky Mountains of North Carolina."

His Grandfather had taught him to be a woodsman and a hunter, but unlike him, he could not harm the deer of the forest. He claimed they were his friends when he was growing up. Describing colorful stories, of a slim boy in bib overalls, shoeless, running and jumping through the trees and briers. Along side of him would be a group of young deer who would challenge him who was the fastest. Each day after finishing his chores, it was his time to go off and fish and hunt. He did shoot the little varmints of the woods, since they would sneak under Great Grandmas fence and eat her vegetables. Grandpa claimed he could walk up on a rabbit, setting in his bed. Take out his slingshot and with a stone, bean him on the head. Before he was ten years old he could put a musket ball in a squirrel at the top of a bristling tree.

"My mom could make some of the best rabbit stew you'd ever 'et. And Daddy would take the skins and make little caps like Daniel Boone."

"Once while playing, we wandered into a hollow. Smack into a big old Hillbilly with a long barrel rifle. His long beard smelt like Hickory, and in the back woods you could hear the crackling of a sizzling fire."

Just then, there was a strike on the line as Grandpa picked up his pole and jerked. Grandpa hooked the great fish as the line tightened till the poll bent in two; the fish was running for the log. Grandpa pulled with all his might, causing his feet to slip under him into the muddy bank. Falling back he struggled to hold on to the pole and catch himself at the same time. I dropped my pole and was scrambling to get to him when I saw the line slacken as the fish turned and ran toward us. Suddenly the pike jumped a foot out of the muddy water surprising us both. He must have been three feet long, the legend was true; he was a giant, as big as me. I grabbed a hold of the pole as Grandpa released line while getting back to his feet. Then he slowed the reel down with his thumb as we both pulled with all our might holding the great fish just short of the stump.

"He's tire'n out Chris."

Grandpa battled back and forth with the monster and then released the pole to me. The fish pulled me two feet through the mud before he grabbed the pole back and started taking control of his old adversary. Gradually the fish began to weaken and Grandpa started the slow process of reeling him in. Again he jumped in the air, head twisting, tail flapping, trying desperately to free himself. His eyes bulging, he looked up at me and I could see his fear as if he knew his days were up. There would be no more setting on the old log, listening to grandpa talk about the big one that got away. We'll take him home to grandma and she'll finally believe us, and then she'll fix him for dinner. The fish could no longer resist as grandpa pulled him into the shallow water. We could see him clearly now.

He had pieces of broken line hanging out of his cut mouth from the times he had been snagged and broken free. We jumped into the pool; I went for the tail as Grandpa slipped his hand into the side of his gill, carefully avoiding his sharp teeth. His mighty tail flapped in my arms. I tacked to and fro hanging on, as if he was a small hog at the county fair. Exhausted the fish stopped struggling; Grandpa lifted the great pike's head to the surface and started to speak to him softly as his old friend relaxed. I couldn't understand what he was saying, but there seem to be a moment of compassion between the two old warriors. Pulling his pliers from his back pocket, he reached down removing all the hooks from the pikes mouth, then whispering, "goodbye my old friend," he released the great fish. I too released my hold and backed off, but the fish did not run, instead he slowly turned and disappeared into the deep water of the Chickahomy. I smiled up at Grandpa recognizing his tenderness and compassion for all of God's living things. I learned so much from Grandpa in those early days.

When I was sixteen years old, I rebelled, not wanting to go to school anymore. So my mother called my father and he came over to talk to me.

"So you think you're a man now," said dad standing toe-to-toe with me.

"Yes sir, I do." I looked up to the man who had fifty pounds on me.

"Well, you have two choices, son - military school or military." Dad did not want me to end up working in a tobacco factory like the rest of our family.

"You don't tell me what to do any more," I said, clinching my fist in front of the man whom I feared most.

"Would you like to go out in the backyard with me, son?" "Sure," I said, knowing I was in big trouble.

The dust stirred as we wrestled for position. Bam, he hit me. Bam, he hit me again, and I picked myself up off the ground. "What branch do you think I should go in, Dad?" I asked quietly, brushing the dust off my clothes.

My father was a tank sergeant in the famous Blues National Guard Unit of Virginia. He knew young men were being crippled and dying in Vietnam. He thought the navy or air force were better choices for his very young, high-spirited son. We signed the navy papers when I was sixteen under the kiddy cruiser program, which would release me from service before my twenty-first birthday. I was sworn in and placed on a train shortly after my seventeenth birthday, along with twenty other recruits from Virginia. I believe I was one of the youngest men in the United States Navy for a few days or so.

Dear mama

I started my training officially today. I took 6 classes, washed myself, clothes, floors and every other thing. We had our heads shaved and our teeth brushed with fluoride. Mr. Gooch is our Company Commander. We eat 3 meals, which aren't the best in the world, and we drill for 4 to 8 hours, rest of time go to classes and clean. We have to keep notebooks and memorize things. It is raining up here. I've got guard duty tonight from 2 to 4 so I get 4 hours of sleep. I take a test once a week and you can't fail or you get set back. We have inspections and if you have piece of lint on clothes it counts off. I've got one hit for leaving lock off drawer. If you get 5 hits, you get one happy hour. I don't know why they call it happy hour, all you do is run, push ups and stand at attention on your face. Too many happy hours and you get set back. If you get sent back two many times it's the brig and then dishonorable discharge. A boy beside me fainted and I caught him, we are all dead tired. I went to sickbay with 102 temperature and they gave me some pills, one boy had a nervous break down. To put it lightly, it's Hell up here. I will make it, they are putting muscles and weight on me. I have 2 buddies named Barry and Bennie, we bunk beside each other. They are from Virginia and we help each other everyday. I'll be glad to get out of here, I'm telling you. Say hi to everybody and if Grandma or Grandpa asks why I'm not writing to them, explain I'm just to plain busy. Well 9:30 lights out, so I'll say goodbye.

Your Son
Seaman Recruit Christopher

P.S. Jo Ann, tell people at school to write me.

21

After graduating boot camp at Great Lakes, Illinois, in one of the largest classes ever assembled, I took a thirty-day leave and went home to show off my uniform. I reported to the USS Vega at the pier of the Naval Air Station in Alameda, California, in July. Two weeks later, we were on our way to Southeast Asia.

I was the baby of the ship for nearly a year. I volunteered to change rates from seaman apprentice to fireman apprentice and was assigned to the boiler room, the toughest job I ever had. The first week, they had all of us boots looking for left-handed monkey wrenches and cut-off valves for the cooling water system to the handrails. The boiler men were a rowdy, crazy bunch of hell-raisers and prided themselves as being the toughest sailors on the ship. Two of my new buddies would kiss each other smack on the lips, or one would open his mouth wide while the other spit in it, then return the favor by spitting it back. At first I thought they were queer for each other, but then I saw them on liberty with two girls who were just as crazy as they were. On one drunken occasion, one of them threw up and the other grabbed a piece and ate it, just to gross us out. He succeeded.

The only bar room brawl I ever witnessed was in the Philippine Islands between a squad of marines and the Vega's boiler tenders. An argument over a girl started fists swinging and chairs flying as I ducked under a table, when suddenly the shore patrol grabbed me by my ankles and dragged me out into the streets of Olongapo City.

I was a virgin when I first went in and wanted desperately to give it away. When USS Vega arrived in Yokosuka, Japan, I went out on the beach with another boot and lost all my money to a Japanese bar girl, buying her house teas. After being cheated, I wanted nothing to do with Japan. USS Vega sailed southwest from Japan through the Formosa Straits and I got my first taste of underway replenishments.

Following a month in the Tonkin Gulf and South China Sea with lines extended over to aircraft carriers and destroyers as we cut through the water, replenishing the Seventh Fleet, we pulled into Kaohsiung, Taiwan, to restock with fresh fruit and vegetables. While there I was talked into going out on the beach with a bunch of the black gang. The first bar we passed, a group of bar hogs ran out and grabbed our hats and ducked back in, forcing us to follow. The next thing I knew, we all were heading to a hotel for a party. There were five sailors and five girls as they split off and went different directions after playing a few hands of poker and downing cold beers. I was left staring at a woman I didn't know and had no attraction to, but being seventeen and pretty stupid at the time, I didn't realize it.

After she undressed and removed her padded bra, we jumped in bed. Then she started reminding me of a traffic cop ordering me to go this way or that. Frustrated, I set up on the side of the bed, questioning my manhood, and then got up, dressed and left the hotel.

Feeling depressed and rejected, I walked down the streets of the city, shopping for bootleg record albums of pop groups back in the States. The yellow, red, and blue vinyl albums played a bit faster than the original recordings, but cost only pennies. I was approached by an old woman who darted out a bar, saying she had number-one girl for me.

"Baby-san, you come in I have special girl for you," the old mamma-san persisted as she pulled me into the bar.

"No no, I don't want a girl," I tried to break free.

"No you see, you stay here." She pushed me into a dimly-lit booth in the corner and went into the backroom.

When she returned, she brought out a young, beautiful half-Chinese, half-Polynesian girl. The slim, long hair beauty had very little make-up on and was wearing a cheap, homemade dress. Her name was Susie Q. She spoke no English and I couldn't speak Chinese, but we hit it off great. I asked the mama-san how much to take her out of the bar. I paid the amount and took her to a movie with subtitles as we snuggled and shared popcorn and a Coke all night. Later, I kissed her at the doorstep. She smiled and asked if she would see me again. I returned to the ship alone.

This went on for a couple of dates, as it soon came time for us to leave and return to Market Time and Yankee Station off the coast of Vietnam. I wanted to get closer to her, so I approached Senior Chief Machinist Mate Druce and explained that I wanted to spend the night with a woman for the first time. Since I was seventeen I had to request permission to stay on the beach overnight in a foreign port. I asked for advice and Chief Druce told me to write on a special request chit the same story that I had conveyed to him. Later I wrote, I respectively request an overnight pass for I have never slept with a woman. Little did I know the whole ship was laughing and Chief Druce was playing a joke on me.

The next morning at muster, Captain D.W. Alderton slid over next to Lieutenant Bowman and whispered in his ear as Mr. Bowman pointed me out. They then turned and smiled at me, as if they both were my uncles.

"They approved my pass," as I looked up and caught Chief Druce laughing.

That night everything was perfect as we stayed up all night crossing unexplored boundaries together, hugging and kissing, and then I fell in love.

I woke up to the present day by a loud noise as I hung up the phone and turned to leave. My friend, Eddie Arquitte, was not to be found. He wasn't in the phone book and the operator found no listing. He must be out on the beach having a luau, I thought. I pulled out my handkerchief to wipe the sweat off my face. The humidity was worst than Virginia on the Fourth of July and my tailored dress white uniform felt thick and too heavy for tropical conditions. Now I knew what I had to look forward to in Vietnam. We boarded back up and took off for the last leg of the flight, to Saigon.

Wow! We had a movie with our meal "Paper Lion," a real all-American football movie with the Detroit Lions. I felt like a kid on a family vacation headed to Disneyland, only no one was laughing or celebrating like we would do on such trips. Everyone kind of stayed to himself; it was sort of the calm before the storm. The flight attendants wore mini-skirts and were very attractive, but none of the usual flirting that accompanies lonely servicemen and pretty girls seemed to be present. Maybe these men knew something I didn't. The older servicemen were normally more aggressive, but not this time. The flight attendants were probably shell-shocked that they weren't being given the time of day. I wondered how they saw all of us. They seemed nice enough, but maybe it was a bad idea to get close to a young serviceman headed to war. It was also possible these ladies didn't like us. By 1970, most people did not agree with our country's policies in Southeast Asia and the American servicemen were being forgotten.

We finally started to descend on Tan Son Nhut Air Force Base, South Vietnam, thanks to the United States Air Force, which had fortified the landing strip with sand bags and machine guns while also performing the maintenance and upkeep on the runway, which received frequent mortar and rockets attacks. As the wheels touched down, we all looked out the windows at a strange new world. The structure of the buildings and landscape were different from anything I had known.

The door opened after the plane braked slowly to a stop. The airmen rolled a portable staircase over, allowing us to depart after the boring thirty-five-hour trip. Everyone stood up in the middle aisle, calmly collecting his carry-bags and stretching, anticipating leaving the plane and starting their tours. When it was my turn, I stepped out through the doorway to take a hit of fresh air.

Holy cow...it was hot! It was so hot and humid it almost took my breath away. The sun shone intensely bright, causing me to block my face with my hand so I could see. I had left the States in the cold of March, and now I was landing in the hottest climate I'd ever known. It must have been 120 degrees in the shade, and the humidity reading had to be off the chart. I wanted to turn around and go back into the plane with the stale cabin air. I looked up at Air Force jets flying overhead. Tanks were positioned along the runway, U.S. soldiers marched in formation, Huey's choppering around the field. Descending down the walkway, I thought to myself, I hope I see you again Mister Braniff Airlines.

CHAPTER FIVE
ANNAPOLIS HOTEL

After picking up my seabag, I was directed to a bus stop outside of Tan Son Nhut Air Base. The United States Navy was nice enough to send over an old gray school bus with chicken wire and metal bars over the windows. There I was, soaked in my long-sleeve whites, dragging my bag behind me, when the door opened and a burly giant of a man dressed in jungle greens yells out.

"All aboard!" he called out, flicking his cigarette out the doorway into the street, just missing me. I pitched my bag into the doorway.

"Thanks, where we going?"

"Annapolis Hotel," he replied as he pulled another Lucky Strike out of the pack with his mouth. I leaned forward and gave him a light with my Zippo.

"They're putting us up in hotels?" I asked, surprised.

"Naw, that's just what we call her. It's a naval support detachment for incoming and outgoing personnel," he pulled the door closed and floored the gas, almost knocking me down and kicking dust and rocks up in the air behind us.

I stared in wonder out on a sea of humanity on the crowded chaotic streets as the driver maneuvered through Saigon, dodging motorbikes, cyclos, pedestrians and taxis, without benefit of stoplights or street signs. He hit the horn often and the brakes rarely as he cursed the traffic and the war in general. He was the biggest hog on the road and they'd better get out of his way or he'd run them over. We circled and turned, in and out, up and down little streets. Still, he had not run anybody over. We passed the Cholon market, a bee-hive of activity. Women were selling dogs to eat and beggars filled the streets. Finally, the driver stomped on the brakes and we came to a screeching halt in front of a group of small buildings connected together. There was only one entrance through a narrow opening in a fortified sandbag wall. The whole corner of the block was surrounded by fifty-five-gallon barrels filled with concrete and dressed with barbwire and claymore mines. The windows and doors on the first floor were sealed shut, and the second-floor windows were protected with bars and chicken wire.

I stepped down out of the bus into a dusty, dirty street. Jumping over a mud puddle, I entered the compound through the gateway. I muscled open a very heavy door and entered the fortified building. There was no entrance to the first floor, only a staircase leading up to the second. A petty officer, dressed in green fatigues, greeted me from behind a wall with a protective window shielding him. He asked me for my papers through a hole in the window, then stood and read them silently. I felt as if I were standing in a line to buy a ticket for the matinee. Turning, I looked up and down the small, dark, dirty hallway. The wall was burned as if an explosion had gone off there recently. I couldn't help but think that this place had to have been hit hard to warrant all this protection. It was fortified like a forward firebase in the jungle, only this was Plantation road in the Cholon district of Saigon. All the same, it must be one of the hottest corners in the city. Every Viet Cong in the area must have known right where we were.

I was waved to enter through a second door to the secure area of the building, where I was greeted by the Master-at-Arms who was putting a pile of gear together for me. I got yet more green fatigues and another pair of jungle boots. The whole experience sort of reminded me of boot camp. He didn't bother to ask me what I wanted. He just handed me what the United States Navy had decided to issue me. It was a little ironic that here I was entering a war zone without a weapon to protect myself. Adorning a big smile, he handed me my first gun, or piece, as we called it in the navy. It was very different from the M-14 rifle I had trained with at Great Lakes, or the Browning automatic I was assigned during repel borders on USS Vega. It was an M-16, and I would never forget mine. It almost looked like a toy; the plastic stock was made by Mattel. The sight could also be used as a handle to carry the weapon. I dragged it everywhere I went. It kind of felt as if I had gone back to the old west and was packing. Hell, everyone was packing, even the women and children.

"Read me the serial numbers, son," he commanded.

They hand you an automatic weapon and call you son, par for the course. I had completed three West Pac tours off the coast of Vietnam with the Seventh Fleet and was heading into the jungle on my fourth, couldn't buy a beer or vote, but I now have a gun and had been trained to kill. Last but not least, I got a bandoleer with six clips, each containing sixteen rounds of .223 bullets. Now I was feeling a bit more secure. It was somewhat intimidating, walking around, surrounded by people that had guns and I didn't. Guns were the great equalizer. You might not respect the man, but you had better respect his gun. The smallest child could be deadly.

I dragged my bag and my new gear into a dark, hot room full of racks, the Navy's equivalent of bunks, and plopped down on the bottom. I had been in-country only one hour, and every time I stopped, I left a puddle of sweat. My uniform was soaked and I had to keep wiping my face so I could see where I was going. What's the name of that creek I was up?

After taking a few minutes to get oriented, I started to change into my new olive drab fatigues. I was approached by a couple of sailors who had arrived a few days before and were waiting for orders to rotate out to river divisions. Although they did not know me, they invited me to go next door for a steam and cream.

"A what?" I asked? They smiled at each other and assured me that I would enjoy it. I'd had enough surprises, so I thanked them and declined, reminding myself of my promise to a girl back home.

"Now you be good," she had said, bestowing a little kiss on me.

"Okay," I had responded, sincerely.

What the heck, I'd done enough of that in Subic Bay on my first tour to last me a lifetime. I had one more year left and I wanted to get through it and return home without too many more nightmares. In Coronado they had taught us that the enemy would use women. Ho Chi Minh called his women soldiers "Long-Hair Warriors" and he used them very effectively against us. The two patrolmen skipped off to have some fun as I lay down to take a nap.

Nobody talked much to me that night; it was as if no one wanted to know me. They were probably going to send me off somewhere in a few days, anyway, so why bother.

I didn't have a clue where I was going or what was in store. All sorts of thoughts ran through my head that night. I was secretly hoping for the bush, but I was scared of what that might mean. The navy was in a slugfest in the Mekong Delta, and although they said there were no front lines, there were definitely some pretty shitty places you could end up. People were being blown to pieces out there. If you weren't careful, the tiger would eat you. Saigon, on the other hand, had way too much brass. With my attitude and luck, I probably would end up with a bunch of deadbeat rear-echelon and get ever shit detail there was, or blown up standing on a corner of Tu Do street in the red light district. Face it, there was no safe place in the whole damn country. Hell, they had overrun the United States Embassy in 1968 during the Tet Offensive. If they had wanted to come and get us, they would have. They would pay a hell of a price, but they had proved they could do it. I slept pretty well that night, thanks to the security that Annapolis personnel supplied.

I arrived in Saigon on March 5, 1970 and started this letter to my mother. The letter was written in segments and not mailed till I was settled, since I was at a temporary duty station.

Dear Mom

Well here it is Sunday and everybody is working just like any other day. I had a 35 hour trip getting here. I got to wait a couple of days before I get my permanent duty station. I should be leaving Tuesday. Boy it is really weird over hear. I don't like what I've seen so far. I got some more greens and another set of boots. I'm supposed to be stationed at one of the Naval Support bases. They said there were about 16 of them, so they sent out a message seeing which one needs me the most. I hope it is not out in the wilderness. I'm not going to tell you to much of anything I do, because I don't want to worry you. Don't worry though, I haven't really done anything dangerous and I probably won't. I'm not going to mail this letter till I get to my mailing address of my permanent duty station so I will write this letter in chapters. I'll write more latter.

The sound of the busy street in front of the hotel woke me the next morning and I rolled out of my sweat-stained rack to take a shower and dress for a new day. I was given directions to the galley, which was several blocks into the Cholon district. This was the Chinese side of town and very much controlled by the Viet Cong. I followed a group of men heading in the same direction down the dusty road, and filed into the Montana mess hall. I jumped into a line composed of army, air force and navy. The food was laid out in steaming hot trays, served by American personnel in white jackets and shined boots. It was just as if we were back in the States. You had your choice of bacon, sausage, scrambled eggs, hash browns, toast, coffee, milk, juice and sweet rolls. Hmmmmmm, maybe this won't be that bad after all. Uncle Sam sure knew how to take care of his troops. I grabbed a tray and jumped in behind a well-groomed soldier. He had spit-shined jump boots and a pressed uniform, with his trousers bloused sharply. I thought to myself, that he must have a great job somewhere. A lot of soldiers would probably kill to switch places with him. Or maybe I'm being unfair and should not prejudge the man; things are not always as they appear. He could have earned the right to be here. The silence continued. I don't think I had said more than a few words in the last forty-eight hours.

The chow hall looked to be an old warehouse of some type. The Vietnamese had cleaned it up and given the high ceiling a fresh coat of paint. The room was filled with long tables and chairs with white linen cloth. Scattered about were a few pockets of soldiers, talking. There also were a few Viet laborers eating at a table off to the side. I sat down alone and thought of everyone back home. They were probably all going to bed right about now. "The food was great," I said to the cooks as I cleaned my tray.

I then returned to the Annapolis, where I was informed that I was moving to a room near the galley. After receiving directions, I gathered up my belongings and journeyed back down the busy street to the address. It was just a block off the main drag, behind a bar with French Viet B-girls standing in the doorway calling me over. Beggars held out their hands but seemed to know not to press. A child cried out in fear of me. I looked up to see a tall, white building, obviously built by the Vietnamese. On the first floor, a sailor sat behind a desk with a small fan blowing in his face. His rifle was leaning against the wall as he puffed on his Camel and twirled his Zippo between his fingers. The room I was assigned was on the second floor. I climbed up the twisting staircase, all the time looking down at a disfigured man, dragging himself along the street. I walked down the narrow hallway to a room without a door. It was a small, white room with a tile floor and open window. For furniture there were bunk beds, a table, a chair and a fan. There seemed to be no doors anywhere. Not downstairs, not upstairs, not to my room. What's to keep somebody from coming in and taking my stuff, I wondered. The window had no glass, blinds or bars to protect me. I must have pissed somebody off; maybe I snored in my sleep. Wait a minute, I don't snore.

After breakfast, I received my first payday. I was paid 295.00 a month. Fifty dollars was allotted for hazardous duty pay for being in a combat zone. Many men volunteered to go to Vietnam for the extra money so they could send it home to help their families. I was one of them.

That night I reported back to the muster bay at 1900 for a movie. Halfway through, I got up and left. I couldn't understand why they kept showing us all those old war movies. You would have thought the Three Stooges or Laurel and Hardy would have been better. I went back to my room and continued writing my letter.

Tell Jo Ann to take Crystal that Navy sweatshirt of mine. I told her she could have it. I have 275.00 saved up so far. I just drew 20.00 for expenses. I ordered a box of roses for Crystal for Easter but don't tell her so. I guess you are mad and worried because you have not got a letter. I'm sorry, but I don't know my return address. I'll write more latter.

After 48 hours without sleep and sweating profusely with my gun by my side, a small monsoon blew in, and both I and my gear were drenched. Not to fear, the sun appeared the following morning and I hung out my clothes over the chair, bedpost and table. Everything was dry by lunch. I folded my clothes and packed them back into my bag. By now I was ready to be assigned anywhere, as long as there was someone to talk to. I didn't know if they were giving me time to get acclimated to the heat or what, but I was ready to go.

After five days of musters, in-country security briefings and lectures on the hazards of venereal disease and marijuana use, a seaman finally was sent to inform me that my orders had arrived. Halleluiah! I was being assigned to the YRBM 21, (Yard, Repair, Berthing, and Messing), most commonly used in World War II to support crews while submarines were undergoing overhaul. Nobody knew much about her, some kind of floating repair barge out on the Cambodian border, a Naval Support Activity Saigon Detachment.

The Naval Support Activity (NAVSUPPACT), Saigon, was commissioned on May 17, 1966, and her many detachments were established to support the ever-growing U.S. Navy effort to prevent the enemy from using the waterways as highways to infiltrate men and equipment into the Republic of South Vietnam. The two major operations being supported were Operation Game Wardens, which prevents resupply and counter infiltration along the rivers and canals of the Mekong Delta and Rung Sat Special Zone, and Operation Market Time, whose efforts were aimed at preventing enemy infiltration of men and equipment by sea. All U.S. Naval Forces in the II, III, and IV Corps areas of South Vietnam depended for their logistic support from NAVSUPPACT, Saigon.

On my last night in Saigon, I still couldn't sleep. I lay in a puddle of sweat, listening to the sound of the street merchants, peddlers, and whores pitching their wares at the busy intersection. I will never forget the smell of Saigon; I had never smelled anything like it. I never could quite put my finger on it, the smell was somewhere between a garden and a dump. There were little markets offering everything from strange-looking vegetables to small birds, like your Aunt Alice had as pets, only people would eat them. The people were definitely starving and would eat cats, dogs, rats and any kind of bird or fowl they could get their hands on. The smell of steaming rice and exotic seasonings lingered in the air. Women squatted behind small trees or used blankets to hide themselves as they answered nature's call. The men didn't care; they just pulled it out and urinated on a fence or in a corner of a building. Thousands of motor bikes and cabs zoomed up and down the chaotic streets, racing the bicycles and cyclos and leaving their exhaust fumes and smog to choke the pedestrians, who wore bandanas around their faces to block the fumes and sicknesses being passed around the city. The hundreds of little wooden fires the peasants used for cooking on the sidewalks or the aroma from the corner restaurants preparing their duck and fish dishes. I could never describe it to anyone and I have never smelled anything like it since.

CHAPTER SIX - YRBM 21

After a week of misery, I reported back to the Annapolis to pick up my papers and say goodbye. I was uncertain if I would ever see the hotel again, but I knew that I would never forget it. They placed me back on the bus and delivered me to Tan Son Nhut, where a seaman and I were shuttled onto a Jolly Green Giant helicopter along with the movies and mail, the latter of which I believe was top priority. Seems there were few roads to get where we were going. Most traveled either by boat or helo. They fired up the engine and the blade turned so slowly I questioned if we would have the power to lift off. After a few minutes we rose above the dust of the busy city. The scenery was beautiful, I thought of how it must have been before the war. The pilot flew only a few hundred feet above the trees, so we had a good view. The farmers wore their black pajamas and bamboo hats, following water buffalo with plows through the muddy fields. Small hamlets made up of grass and bamboo huts with women washing cloths in tubs ran along the river banks. Children playing and helping were hanging the laundry over tree branches and makeshift lines. Five million South Vietnamese lived in the Mekong Delta. It was a flatland of rice paddies and miles of connecting rivers and canals, surrounded by mangrove forests, full of nipa palm and banana trees overflowing with vines and tall grass that reached for the sky. In better times the rich soil provided rice for all of Vietnam, with large quantities remaining for export. Then thousands of Viet Cong guerillas undermined the political and economic order. Production had been choked to a fraction of pre-war levels.

After more than an hour, of watching bomb crater after bomb crater go by, I began to realize we were headed into the boonies. I couldn't believe what the war had done to this country. There didn't seem to be a single acre that hadn't been burned or scared. Finally, we started to descend and I couldn't believe the beauty I was seeing. There was a grand river and the river community was filling its dirty brown water with junks, water-taxis and sampans, racing in the mornings silver dawn. For centuries the people had lived on this river, in these rice paddies. A strange-looking green vessel anchored in the middle of the river came into view. I had never seen anything like it. Then I read the letters on her hull - YRBM 21.

YRBM 21 had a boom and winch aft, and a helo deck with two Hueys forward. She had the hull of a ship, but no real bridge section. Antennas extended thirty feet out on both sides of the helo deck, parallel to the murky water. Ammi pontoon barges, housing additional buildings, were secured alongside, both port and starboard. A floating dock with a shack and walkway system was moored to the aft. Tied to the pontoon barges were several groups of green boats. Some looked surprising like the heavy iron-clad river boats of the American Civil War that I had studied in Virginia history. Others looked like converted pleasure craft turned into naval vessels as one pushed off and streaked across the water in a hurry to get up stream. I could see that the boats were heavily armed. The larger boats seemed to have combinations of machine guns, and cannons. The choppers also had heavy firepower as I observed their rockets and mini-guns. YRBM 21 had a few .50 caliber guns stacked over 81 mm mortar tubes, but no cannons. I guess she didn't need them, what with choppers on her flight deck and patrol boats moored alongside. She was a small city, an oasis for the United States Navy, ninety miles from Saigon and the sea.

There was a constant movement of logs and floating plants rushing by her quickly in and out of the river's fast-moving current. The helo deck was full, so we touched down in a clearing near a little hut on the left bank. After landing, I helped drag the mail over to the river bank. The door gunner wished us luck and returned to the helo, which promptly lifted off and disappeared over the tree line. My new friend looked over to me as we pulled our M-16's off our shoulders.

"Hope someone comes to get us soon. Think they saw us?" the seaman spoke as he nervously looked around.

"I'm sure they did," guessing they were informed by radio. The first ones to reach us were a group of kids from the nearby hamlet. I couldn't understand them, but when they held out their hands, I got the message. Searching through my pockets, I remembered I hadn't brought any gum or candy. I did have some C-rations which appeared to be left over from the Korean conflict. I grabbed my P-38 can-opener and opened the pound cake; it disappeared. I then opened the butterbeans and ham, which also vanished.

After relieving us of all our C-rats, the children started back to the huts, all except one little girl who had a pretty nasty cut on her leg. She trusted me enough to pick her up and set her on a little log near the river. I pulled out my first aid kit and began cleaning and bandaging her infected leg. Turning, I heard the sound of a landing craft backing down as the belly of the foc'sle slid onto the muddy shore line. I set the girl back on the ground just as her older brother appeared through the doorway, calling her name.

"Lin, Lin," we both waved as I retreated to the Mike boat and she limped back to her family.

"Hey, pitch me up the mail bags will ya?" I grabbed the bags and threw them on the deck. "Here, let me give you a hand." I was pulled aboard by a tanned, shirtless young man wearing cut-off shorts and jungle boots. He looked as if he was eighteen years old and belonged on a beach somewhere in California. He had natty blond hair with love beads around his neck and peach fuzz covering his face. We both turned, holding out our hands to help the seaman. I took one last glance over my shoulder at the young girl standing in the doorway of the little bamboo hut. Then the boat reversed off the muddy bank and turned toward the green vessel in the middle of the river.

"What's your name," as a big wave splashed against the bow of the boat, spraying us with the mist of the silt-laden water? "Chris",

I replied, turning into the wind and enjoying the feel of the cool spray.

"I'm Ellsworth." We grabbed hold of the boat to keep our balance as the Mike-6 rocked up and down in the wake of a departing fifty foot grey gun-boat.

"Does YRBM 21 take care of the river boats?" I asked, holding on so I wouldn't fall over the side.

"Yeah, we're here supporting border interdiction operations with Game Wardens.

"What are all those boats?" I asked, knowing I was witnessing history as we pulled up to the green fleet.

"Well, the sixty-foot green heavies are with Task Force-117, the battleships of the Mobile Riverine Force. The fifty-foot grey Swift boats are from Task Force-115, the Coastal Surveillance of Operation Market Time. And the thirty-one-foot green patrol boats are with Task Force-116, Operation Game Warden, river patrol.

"I didn't realize there were so many different types."

"Oh, this is nothing. Down the canal in the Plain of Reeds they have cat-eyed, shark-teeth hovercraft that can go right up over the banks and across the marshes at sixty knots.

"Plain of Reeds?" I asked, trying to learn all I could in a short time.

"Yeah, it's the wilderness that separates Cambodia and Vietnam. That's Cambodia over there," he pointed up river.

"The Cambodians and Khmer Rouge Communists are sitting up there, watching us as well as the VC and the NVA."

"Damn, I really got myself in it this time," I said, turning to look at the seaman who was sweating buckets.

"Its okay guys, that's why the Seawolves are here, if the enemy sticks their necks out, than the Seawolves will chop'em off," said Ellsworth.

"Seawolves," responded the young seaman who had just left his mama's house.

"Yeah, the Huey gunships on the flight deck."

As we neared YRBM 21 I knew I had found it. This was the brown water navy at its best. The two Hueys on the flight deck looked like hawks poised to pounce on their prey. We pulled alongside one of the barges and threw a line over. All the men on the dock were young, strong and tanned, with conditioned bodies from working long hours in the sun. We dragged our bags up the gangway and down to the lower level to enlisted berthing below the waterline.

"Grab a rack, guys."

Racks were made of canvas, rope and aluminum frames with thin mattresses. They were stacked on top of each other four and five high, in multiple rows. Each sailor had added his own "touch" to his space. There were pictures of bikes, cars, state symbols, peace signs, and of course, Miss January, Miss February, or whatever month you had fallen in love with. Reel-to-reel tape decks were wired to speakers, sitting on homemade bookshelves against the bulkhead, and gas masks hung from the stems of cut-off valves on pipe lines running through the decks. Boy, the officers must be a great bunch of guys to allow this much freedom, I thought as I admired Miss February of 1968. "Damn, are those real?"

I climbed up to the top rack in the deepest, darkest corner of the berthing compartment. It was choice; I couldn't believe it wasn't taken.

"Oh, that was Fallows," Ellsworth informed me. "Did he go home," I asked plopping in for a test ride. "Yeah, only he didn't make it." There was a moment of silence as I looked down. Four of the crew was shot down in a helicopter a couple of weeks ago. I noticed a picture taped on the side of the locker. "That's Red there." Ellsworth pointed to a thin, red-headed blue-eyed boy that I had to look closely at to tell it wasn't me. "He was from North Carolina." Damn, now I had the hook in me. Same job, both Southern and we looked like brothers. I grabbed a hold of the top of the rack and lowered myself down. "Which one's my locker?"

Lockers were stacked six feet high with polished aluminum so bright you could see your reflection in them. Other than that, they were standard navy issue. You take a three-foot-square area, pile everything in your bag into it, slap a lock on it and you're home.

"Come on its time for chow," We ran up to the mess deck and jumped in line. When it was my turn, I grabbed a tray and started helping myself. I was happy to see beef with all the trimmings, freshly baked rolls, real potatoes, gravy, beans and a deep pan of apple cobbler. To drink there were pitchers of instant milk and Kool-Aid.

After lunch I was taken to meet the Engineering Chief Petty Officer Catorie. He was a large, tanned man with a pin-line mustache. He looked a little like a chunky Clark Gable. I believe his family was Cajun French ancestry. He was polite and offered me a seat; but I stood at parade rest. After reviewing my service jacket he called in a first class engineman by the name of Bailey.

Bailey was the guy who kept us busy each day; he would see that we were all working; if we weren't, he would find us something to do. He didn't care what we were working on, just so the repairs were getting done. Bailey walked into the room, extending his hand to welcome me aboard.

"Bailey, this is Christopher, show him around." The Chief went back to sorting a pile of papers on his desk.

"Machinist mate... well we can use you. Come on, I'll give you the nickel tour." We stepped out of the chief's office and across the passageway into the chiefs' quarters.

"This is Christopher." A group of chiefs looked up from their card game and gave me the once-over.

"Come on, let's go aft." Bailey led me down the passageway and out a hatch to the rear section.

Secured at the aft of the repair-barge was a chain of small pontoon walkways linked together for the smaller boats to tie to. There were boats everywhere, with some units joined together as many as six abreast. Fifty yards astern was a small pontoon fuel barge anchored alone with the very flammable JP-4 aviation fuel for the helicopters.

There also were three large water tanks, each capable of holding several thousands of gallons of water.

Mekong River water was pumped into each of the tanks as they emptied and allowed to stand. The silt dropped rapidly out of the water to the tank bottom and was drained off. The water was then treated with an alum-like compound, which caused other suspended debris to drop to the bottom. Then came several liberal dousings of chlorine compounds to kill all of the microbes and pollution that had permeated the river water. At this point we had crystal-clear water with a terrible taste. Then the water was run through a little black box called an Erdilator. The Erdilator was a Godsend. As if by magic, through a system of ion exchangers, the bad taste disappeared and we were left with nothing but sweet, clean water to drink. Hard to believe but we drank, cooked and showered with that muddy water that came down from the Himalaya Mountains.

On the aft deck aboard YRBM 21 was a gunk tank full of acid for dunking engine blocks. Below deck was the compartment housing the two 12V71 diesel generators that produced electricity.

The starboard aft room was the internal combustion shop with sliding doors and fans. Inside was a dynamometer, which was a motor mount, we secured the 6V53 and GM 671 engines to, then connected the fuel, water and exhaust and tested them under battle conditions. As you passed you could often hear E4 Dave Staercke cursing the engines as if they were women who had mistreated him, while lifting the engines out of the boats with a hand-pulled, chain-driven winch set up on a roller system attached to steel beams overhead. Staercke was normally covered in diesel oil and puffing on Salem Menthols as he worked his butt off, sweating buckets. He was introduced to me as a firecracker of a worker and one of the best enginemen onboard.

The patrol boats could tie-up alongside and he and his guys could lift an engine out and replace it with a rebuilt in a matter of a few hours. The internal combustion snipes always had four or five rebuilt 6V53's stored, ready for issue. Next door was the injector shop, where I first met Lenny Walzak, a big, burly, good-natured boy from Wisconsin who spent his days overhauling the fuel injectors. Across the passageway was the electrical shop. The port aft compartment was a small machine shop with a lathe and a drill press. Down a ladder, below deck, was the engineering office, where I was introduced to Chief Warrant Officer Dan Backus, the Engineering/Repair Officer and my boss. He was a very "squared away", even-tempered, all around nice guy. He always dressed to military standards and was in charge of all engineering personnel aboard. At the ripe old age of forty-two he was nearing the end of his career in the navy and was respected by all aboard. Dan had the ability to take a hunk of brass and cut it into a bolt and nut; there was nothing he couldn't fix on YRBM 21. This also was the storage area for replacement parts and was maintained by Richard "Sleepy" Schliep, who was a Nebraska farm boy. Sleepy ran the storage area like a Chevy parts department at a State-side dealership, only he carried parts for gun-boats. Repair and maintenance of the boats was our primary job. Across the passageway was the storekeepers' office and storage compartments.

On the bottom deck in the center was enlisted berthing. Ships Company berthed to the starboard compartment and boat and helo crews to the port. Climbing up the ladder to the center deck you reached the galley, which also was used as a movie theater and card room. Just off the passageway outside the mess were the barber shop, head, and ship's store, run by the Ship Servicemen and stocked with cigarettes, candy, gum and miscellaneous items such as coffee cups, Zippo lighters and toiletries. Far forward was the boatswain locker and a pump room for moving water, oil and fuel, with two York compressors for air conditioning. I can't tell you how important it was for the boat crews to rotate back to hot meals, showers and air-conditioned racks for a day after spending a week washing in the canals and setting up all-night ambushes in the rain, heat and humidity, all the while being attacked by mosquitoes and giant horseshoe flies. It really helped morale when the guys got a break to write home and have a beer.

Climbing up to the top deck inside aft you come to sickbay and the radio shack with its giant radios from the floor to the ceiling. Next to the shack was the ship's office, where a second class yeoman did most of YRBM 21's paperwork. He was a great poker player. On one of his all-night poker games, I won the largest hand of my life, but usually he took all of our money. Forward, behind a wooden door, was officer's country, with a wardroom complete with two Filipino stewards. Across the passage way was berthing for the ship's officers, pilots and division commanders.

Outside, on the second deck aft, was an area with a boom and winch for pulling boats out of the water. The damage control men set them on mounts so they could patch their fiberglass hulls, which needed twenty-four-hour drying time, but didn't always get it.

Lieutenant Junior Grade William C. Green Jr., the Assistant Officer in Charge, commanded the outside areas.

The helo deck was the roof of YRBM 21, with a ladder and sunken observation tower. On the other three sides were nets to catch the helicopters if they encountered problems, which had happened a few weeks before my arrival. The crew said the engine of the chopper sputtered and spit and then went into failure, sending the Huey into the water. Luckily all four crewmen survived. Moored on the port side forward was a large ammi pontoon barge with an EOD (Explosive, Ordinance, Demolition) shack for storage of our demolition divers' gear. The shack also was a good place to grab a beer if you had made friends with the divers, who were independent and governed themselves. Moored aft port was the diesel fuel barge, where the boats pulled alongside to fill up.

On the starboard side of YRBM 21 was moored another ammi, with a small beer bar named the "Last Chance Saloon." In front of the saloon was an open area for musters and working. Both ammis were connected by gangplanks declining down from YRBM 21. After showing me around and introducing me to a few of the guys, I began to realize that there was no boiler or propulsion room.

"How you move this thing?"

"This is a non-propelled repair vessel," said Bailey "We're anchored here with a sea anchor. We have a pusher boat with two 671 diesels on the aft for moving. YRBM 21 truly was a mobile America-owned island, set up halfway around the world from home and safety. She had been configured specifically to support the operation of river patrol boats. Except for the fact that it had no propulsion plant for emergency moves in a hostile environment, the vessel fitted requirements quite satisfactorily. It had modern command and control spaces; up-to-date messing and berthing, office, and communication spaces; binned storerooms; good work shops; and sufficient boom-lifting capacity.

"Come on, it's time to meet Mr. Fry," said Bailey as he ran up the ladder staircase to officers country.

Lieutenant Junior Grade Eldon J. Fry, Officer in Charge, was an Annapolis graduate. A well-groomed gentleman with a pressed, bloused green uniform and spit-shined jungle boots, he was the epitome of what the brown water navy was all about, a young man with a "can do" attitude. There was no job above or below him. He would often pick up a hammer or pin and do whatever it took to complete the task at hand. He would see to his men's safety and what they needed to get the job done. Mr. Fry and Mr. Backus went to battle more than once in defense of the men and the harsh working conditions we endured on a daily bases. Mr. Fry also held Captain's mast and supervised discipline of the crew; I only worried about him because he was a small, dark, island boy, and without his uniform could be mistaken for the enemy. He held out his hand after returning my salute and welcomed me to the crew with a big warm smile. I felt good things about Mr. Fry; I could see why the crew was so happy. He enquired about my duties on USS Vega and where I was raised, while sharing his own stories about the islands. We then got down to the business of what my job was to be.

After reviewing my service jacket, he walked me down to the forward pump-room and introduced me to a good old boy from Lewisburg, West Virginia, who seemed to be a nice enough guy and reminded me of my grandpa, a hillbilly from the Smoky Mountains. We exchanged pleasantries and were happy that we would be working alongside someone from the good old South.

"You'll be working here in the pump room with Robert. Here's a key to the freezer, and you and I have the only copies. Guard it well. If anything is missing, you're responsible." Mr. Fry made sure I understood.

"Yes sir," Mr. Fry smiled, opened the hatch, and climbed through.

The freezer was ten feet high and ten feet deep. You could walk into it standing up. Inside, it felt as if you had died and gone to Alaska. It looked brand new and ran even better. I knew I didn't need to touch it, so I didn't, except to let Don Rypka, the cook, in or for a little ice cream run for me and the boys once. That night, after dinner, I watched an old John Wayne Western movie on the mess deck and wrote a few letters.

Hi Sweetheart

Well here I am in sunny Vietnam. I have a tan already but I will get a better one. I'm stationed on a YRBM. It is a barge setting in the middle of the river. I don't even know what river it is. All I know is that I am way down south on the Mekong Delta about two miles from Cambodia. We are a support for the river boats and attack Helicopters. There is nowhere to go on liberty and some of the guys haven't seen a girl in a year so I guess I won't either. I've been or rather they have been keeping me pretty busy, but I guess that's pretty good because it will hurry the time on. I have a pretty good job right now, but they said it's possible I'll ride the gun boats, but don't worry. I made up my mind I'm coming back. Besides, I'm to good looking to get killed! All the girls back home would be cheated. All kidding aside, I'm in no danger.

There isn't a whole lot for me to do so all letters will be answered. If Ann wants to write then tell her I would sure like to hear from her. My return address will be on the outside of the letter. Boy, I'm kinda lonely already and I've just started. I gave first aid to some kids in a village on the way here. They were in bad shape. I think I fell in love with one of the little girls. We had a date, but I couldn't keep it. She was only six years old. 307 days left in the Navy. Can't wait. Well I'll write more later so take care of yourself and I'll see you soon. Give everybody my love.

Love Chris

P.S. We have a beer barge tied to us and its open three hours a night. I'm a regular already!

After breakfast the next morning, I turned my attention to helping Robert in any way I could. It was fun working with a good old boy from West Virginia. He was a second class machinist mate and a good one. We overhauled every pump there was and then turned our attention elsewhere. I started going wherever I was needed. I could have sat back, watched my tour go by, been safe and gone home. But

I did not volunteer to go to Vietnam to work in a pump room. I could have done that on Vega.

I wanted to be outside on the deck, working with the combustion mechanics and the boats. The snipes working in 38C, outside engine repair, were good, so I started making friends. Staercke was training a Vietnamese sailor named Hung, whom he called Ralph, and often was joined by Walzak, Odie Colon and Dwight Cabella. Several of the mechanics were navy reserve draftees from the Great Lakes region who had worked hard the eight months they had served aboard and received Ho Chi Minhs. A Ho Chi Minh was slang for a battle field promotion after doing well in a combat zone for six months without taking the test, which I did. They all were funny guys and in the thick of things, so I started to help out and they let me tag along.

Periodically, the boats were brought aboard for overhauls and necessary repairs. The damage control men would whip up their compound for patching the fiberglass hulls, the electronic technicians would go through the two VRC-46 FM radios and the radar. The electricians would repair the damaged wiring, starters, and generators, while the enginemen rebuilt the bilge, raw and fresh pumps and the 6V53 engines. From time to time one of the boats would limp in with a blown or shot-up engine, which was promptly changed out, returning the boat back to service the same day. Normally, the boats tied to the aft and the mechanics went aboard with their tools, setting racks, and made the necessary repairs under the hot delta sun.

The enginemen tested the 6V53 engines on the dyno until they produced 2,800 or better revolutions per minute, while watching the oil pressure and water temperature gauges for leaks. Often the sound of the 6V53's, 220-horse power, roaring at 3,200 rpm under a work load, echoed through the vessel. We also were able to rebuild and test the GM 671 diesels on the dyno.

We judged the performance of the boats by their speed and how well they could maneuver in the water. When the boat's engines were not performing well, their speed was cut and the boats would not get up out of the water on step, which was a term used to describe the boats planing on top of the water at flank speed. Poor performance ultimately put the sailors that manned their decks in harm's way.

After rebuilding back to specifications the boats returned to top speeds and we all took pride in the job, marveling at how well the little beauties had been built. Taking care of the patrol boats and their crews was the most important thing to us, and the boat crews really appreciated it.

We worked long hard hours in hot, dirty conditions, wearing little clothing and sweating profusely. Hell, if we had worn full uniforms, we would have had run out of clothes after the first month. The laundry was already bitching about washing our oil-stained pants, so we often wore the same pair till they rotted off of us. Even though we took long soapy showers, most of us never lost the smell of diesel fuel during our tours.

But who cared, it was great to be an American working on the best small boats ever built, watching them speed down the river, taking the fight to the enemy. Besides, there were bragging rights for the mechanics. Back home most of us had worked on hotrods and attended local drag strips, so it was not unusual to soup-up the performance of the boats and watch them race.

The famed river patrol boats, PBR's as the sailors called them (Patrol, Boat, River), were divided into two classes. The thirty-one-foot Mark I was first to arrive in 1966 and was still on patrol, doing a hell of a job. They had to be reworked, but other than that, were the same as their younger sisters the Mark II. The fiberglass hull PBRs were equipped with twin Detroit diesel engines and jet pump propulsion systems that could pick the boats up out of the water and propel them at more than thirty knots with a draft of only nine inches. Then just as suddenly reverse its pumps by dropping a U-shaped gate over the water jets and turning 180 degrees, coming around in their own backwash as they reversed direction at full speed in one length. The legends of the river could stop dead in the water in three lengths, but the muddy water was laden with silt, sand, salt, plants and debris, so we spent a lot of time unclogging pumps.

The armament of a PBR consisted of a twin .50 caliber Browning machine gun mount forward and a single-mount aft, with an M-60 machine gun and a Mark 18 hand-operated or the Mark 19 high-velocity automatic 40 mm grenade launcher amidships. There also was a wide range of personal weapons that the crew carried along, including Communist AK-47s.

The PBRs usually operated in pairs, each boat with a four-man crew. The patrol officer was the fifth man on one of the two boats, and often a Vietnamese maritime policeman rode along on day patrols, as interpreter to check papers. The ratings of the crew varied. In addition to boatswain mates, enginemen, gunner's mates and radiomen, other rates who had volunteered could also be found on river patrol. Every man on the boat was interchangeable and they all had to be qualified gunners. No one knew where he might be if the boats came under attack. The boat captains normally were high-ranking senior petty officers. By 1970 engineman were getting to be few and far between, so they started drafting machinist mates to fill the billet. Also, junior petty officers who had proven themselves were promoted to boat captains. It was not unusual to see an E4 petty officer as boat captain, making life or death decisions.

The river patrols worked seven days a week, averaging sixteen hours a day. If they were lucky, they would get one or two days off a month. During most of their tours, they lived under the stars, catching a few hours' sleep in the afternoons along a river bank or at a naval support detachment. They usually ate C-rats and rarely got hot meals. The patrolmen were all fiercely devoted to the little green boats and many had been decorated for distinguished conduct in battle. In spite of working long hours in hazardous, hot, humid conditions, the morale was high and many extended their tours in country. The Viet Cong tried to stop the river boat patrols, but in spite of booby traps set in the waterways, nets strung across the canals and mines floating downstream, they couldn't break their spirit. The boats truly earned the reputation of being, proud, brave and reliable. We on YRBM 21 had nothing but respect for them, and tried to see they had whatever they needed to get the job done.

The PBRs resulted from urgent appeals by field commanders for action to control the waterborne infiltration of enemy men and material. The need was so great that there was no time to design a special boat. Instead, the Navy quickly searched America for a craft that might be suitable. It settled on the hull of Uniflite's 31 foot cruiser. Rudderless and propellerless, the swift craft could negotiate the shallowest streams and go virtually anywhere in the river system. Their fiberglass hulls were impervious to rot, rust, corrosion, marine borers and other dangers of the rugged marine and tropic environments. Importantly, they required virtually no maintenance, including scraping and painting. The boats were extraordinarily strong. In collisions with floating logs and submerged rocks, they withstood blows that would have shattered wood and ripped open metal. They were as much at home on the sea as a stream.

With its modified V bottom and hard chines, the hull seemed ideal for the need. Furthermore, Uniflite had worked for the Navy previously on many demanding projects. These were the first of the United States Navy's River Patrol Boats. Fighting its first full scale river conflict since the American civil war, the Navy had turned to waterjet propulsion craft for the first time in its history.

The first PBRs were designed and constructed at Uniflite's shipyard in Bellingham, Washington, by Art Nordtvedt and his team. The next 120 Mark I PBRs were completed within three months and boats were tested in the bay by Bob Moors. Since the early PBRs had to be slightly modified, Uniflite started building a new version that was a foot longer and wider. Uniflite named this version the Corsair 32. The Navy knew it as the Mark II. Perhaps no craft designed for general purpose inshore and offshore patrol activities, search and rescue operations and law enforcement and logistics activities was as well conceived. The elements of the Corsair comprised a system ideally suited in its simplicity, to its mission.

Thanks to the bow's high deadrise angle, entry in a chop or swell was soft and dry. The hull's relatively flat stern section provided exceptionally efficient weight carrying capability at high speed, and gave a soft ride in moderate seas. Because of these design characteristics, the Corsair's crew could carry many more rounds of ammunition and other supplies while maintaining design speed much higher than that of any other hull on the market at that time. The Corsair had to maintain 25 knots fully loaded in Navy test.

The Corsair had the most effective noise attenuation system ever developed for a small diesel engine craft. Elements were complete engine room insulation, air tight hatches and highly effective mufflers. This had contributed to the Corsair's ability to enter a contested area undetected because of noise. Considering the craft's durability and maintenance free qualities, the ready availability of parts, the ability to take on a large number of jobs in all kinds of water, the Corsair was an extraordinarily low investment. Probably no other patrol-rescue-logistics craft with as many capabilities has ever been developed for such a modest investment.

By 1970 there were more than 400 PBRs being used by the Navy and Vietnamese forces. They were the main tools in the Navy's "Game Warden" project to reduce infiltration. They also patrolled the dangerous waters of I Corp with Task Force Clearwater, and served with the Army's 458th Transportation Company.

On my second night aboard YRBM 21 I was startled awake by the sound of a loud, pulsating horn bell. Thinking it was battle stations, I jumped into my boots and ran out on the deck, my heart pounding. Sailors were climbing up the ladders to the flight deck as they carried along their gear. There was a fire and rescue team in silver fire-resistant hoods and suits, resembling spacemen in an old Sci-fi movie. They crouched silently, holding their water hoses in anticipation of a flight deck crash. An E5 boatswain, a trained and appointed Landing Signal Officer, walked around the deck with two red flashlights in his hands. The pilots ran past me in long jumpsuits, wearing side arms and discussing what types of conditions they would be flying into. The choppers became hot and rotor blades started turning as the crash crew disconnected the sparker cable and stored it away. The door gunners were slipping on their safety harnesses and jacking their guns extended out the doors. YRBM 21 was being turned by a sailor steering a diesel-powered pusher boat on the fantail to allow the pilots to launch into the wind. The attack helicopter's turbines were barely up to speed when the first Seawolf lifted off the deck, tilted forward and dumped the helo towards the river, then the second Huey followed suit. Just missing they skimmed a few feet over the waves till the engines built up enough revolutions per minute to rise and disappear over the tree line. The sky was so beautiful, full of stars twinkling in the heavens, hiding the helicopter's running lights as the great birds rushed into danger under a half moon.

The whole process took only a few minutes and they were gone from sight. The crash crew took off their suits and I realized they were 21 personnel. Some of the same guys who had been working inside the shop that afternoon were now handling hoses. I stayed up with them, monitoring the attack choppers on the radio as they pulled away into the distance, headed to aid a river patrol boat on a canal in the middle of a firefight. We lay in the safety nets lining the helo deck, looking up at the bright stars as we listened to the voices of the crews and machine guns echoing over the headset, as they slugged it out with the Viet Cong.

"Smoke-eater Four-seven, this is Seawolf Nine-eight, where do you want it? Over," as the pilot prepared to fire his air-to-surface rockets.

"Seawolf Nine-eight, put it on the north bank." The boat captain yelled over the thundering .50s and cranking M-60. BAMBAMBAM! BAMBAMBAM! CHITCHITCHITCHITCHITCHITCHIT!

The attack chopper's engine screamed hard as they pulled up and then dove down on the enemy positions, drawing fire off the patrol boat and onto them, as the pilot released a volley of rockets.

PHOOST! PHOOST! PHOOST! PHOOST!

The Seawolf door gunners were opened up as one of the patrol boat crewmen fired a LAW rocket, burning a hole into the jungle nest. PHOOST--------------------------------BOOM!

The chopper's turbine screamed again, pulling up, avoiding the canopy over the canal, as the door gunners pinpointed their fire on the flashes of enemy muzzles and tracers, which were now hitting the chopper. KLINK! KLINK!

I could hear it all over the radio as the flight deck crew gave me a blow-by-blow report.

"That was a Condition One scramble," meaning American forces were in trouble, the young fireman explained to the newbie, which happened to be me.

It was early morning before the VC retreated back into their jungle sanctuaries, ending the firefight on the far-off canal. I said goodnight and climbed back down the ladder, noticing the sailor on the pusher boat balled up with a blanket, sleeping on the boat deck. Going below, I climbed into my rack to catch a few hours shut-eye as I revisited the sound of the radio in my head.

The next morning I got up, wiping the sleep from my eyes, and slowly headed up to breakfast, thinking back to the firefight the night before and wondering if everyone had made it back okay. Entering the chow hall, I was surprised and happy to see the crews of the Seawolves sitting at a corner table in the back of the mess deck. A Seawolf pilot had joined them and was speaking in a tired voice as they sipped their coffee and flicked their cigarette ashes into an over-flowing ash bucket. The door gunners sat across the table, listening attentively as they all chuckled at a comment made by the pilot, who was making hand gestures toward one of the gunners. All of their withered, tired faces were blackened by smoke, and their half-shut eyes were swollen from lack of sleep. They sat quietly, sharing their stories from the firefight that had taken place a few hours earlier. I thought to myself that I knew who they were now. I had finally seen the men that were fighting this war, and the stories I had heard about them were true. They were the best, and I knew from then on that I would never see them in the same way.

I slipped into a seat at a table near by, hoping to overhear some of their conversation, but did not want to disturb the space of the tired crews that I now admired. They grabbed their trays and walked past me as I stopped eating and stared up like a star-struck school boy at his teacher on the first day. I marveled at their humble bravery and wondered if they had been scared during the firefight, or if they had done it so many times that they had lost their fear. I wanted to be them, or like them, to know how it felt to go in and pull other men out of trouble and return to base as if it were all in a day's work. My eyes followed them as they left the mess deck when the pilot stopped in the hatchway and looked back at me as if he recognized a young admirer. He smiled and winked as he disappeared into the passageway.

Helicopter Attack (Light) Squadron Three, HA(L)-3, Seawolves as they called their choppers and themselves, were assembled to support the PBRs and river forces in the Mekong Delta. They were on a twenty-four-hour-alert basis, and could scramble in minutes. Their Bell-manufactured, UH-1B Huey gunship was one of the most feared units of the river patrol force, and Detachment Nine was a welcome sight aboard YRBM 21.

The lead bird of the fire team had a .50 cal in the right door and an M-60 free gun on a bungee cord in the left. The trail bird was equipped with a mini gun in the right door and an M-60 hard mount in the left. They both had forward-firing mini-guns and two seven-round 2.75 rocket pods externally mounted on each side. They normally fired their Zuni rockets a mile or less from their targets. Each rocket was armed with either ten or seventeen pounds of high explosives or phosphorous. Although they were "free flight rockets," without radar or guidance systems, and lacked pinpoint accuracy when fired in salvoes of ten or more, they could saturate a wide area with shrapnel or phosphorous. The mini-guns, especially the door gunners', could be fired with deadly accuracy. They generally cruised at one hundred miles per hour or better. They could rearm and refuel quickly and return to the battlefield with an endurance of ninety minutes in the air. The war birds often stayed aloft of the battle areas all day and truly earned the reputation as being the Cavalry of the Mekong Delta.

After breakfast I reported to Mr. Backus as I walked into his office and saluted. The enlisted normally saluted the officers in the morning and the rest of the day was more relaxed. Mr. Backus assigned me the job of helping the snipes out on the dock repairing a GM 671 diesel engine. I was glad. I wanted to become more a part of this great team of men pulling together to support the boats who patrolled the brown water, day in and day out. I became a gopher at first, another pair of hands passing wrenches and fetching parts. The next thing I knew, I was pulling heads and replacing burnt values alongside two enginemen working out of the boat repair shack.

Steve Rickman and Stew Churchwell were two of the best mechanics I had ever worked with. Everyday was like a lesson, learning more about the boats and their engines. Both men were close to going home and wanted nothing more to do with going out on the rivers, so they started breaking me in. We had a small boom and winch to help pull the heavy GM 671 diesel engines. We could pick the engines up and set them on the deck for overhaul. But usually we would remove the compartment cover and straddle the engines as we tore them apart, replacing components and reassembling, all the time sharing cigarettes and cutting up.

We worked all day in the hot sun and my skin was beginning to turn more than a little red. You have to keep in mind I was a redhead, freckle-faced, ruddy boy. I started putting on lotion and taking salt pills as we worked, breaking only to eat or go to the head. We were usually covered in oil and grease, so we sat at a table by ourselves when we ate, not stopping until our night showers or movie call.

Ever Tuesday, Thursday and Sunday was mail call and we would receive letters from back home. I got a letter from my Aunt Rachel informing me that my boyhood friend with whom I had been raised had died. Johnny Christopher was born the same year as me, with a heart condition, and we had spent our days when little at Grandma Balls' house playing while our parents were at work. Johnny never had a chance to live like a normal person; his heart would not allow it. Here I was in Vietnam, but it was my beloved cousin Johnny who had lost his life. After reading the letter, I headed down to the barge for some air.

Across from the boat repair shack was a gray beer hall that had been assembled by the navy. It had a bar, shuffle board table, wooden panel walls, and a window air conditioner. No alcohol was allowed on YRBM 21, but by housing a bar alongside the barge, it had become permissible. Hanging over the door was a sign that read "Last Chance Saloon" with a depiction of Andy Capp, the same little drunk guy that we used to read about in the funny papers. Andy was chugging a mug of beer, saying this ain't no beer hall while leaning against the bar.

In truth of the matter, all the saloon had to sell were a few kinds of beers. I believe a Miller was a nickel, and Budweiser or the house favorite, Pabst Blue Ribbon, was fifteen cents in Military Payment Currency. MPC was funny money issued by the military to keep greenbacks out of the enemy's hands. There was no discrimination against underage sailors who couldn't buy a beer in the States. I guess somebody figured that if we could serve in a combat zone, we could handle a few beers. The bar was opened between 1600 and 1900 hours and was the last place to get a cold beer before crossing the Cambodian border. They also served sodas. Once the bar ran out of everything but the soft drink Wink, that was a lot of fun.

In early 1970, YRBM 21 was in support of the Green Beret, Special Forces Base at Thuong Thoi Village on the Mekong, two miles south of Cambodia. One day while sipping a Pabst with my buddy Sleepy, I asked my boss Dan Backus how the bar had acquired its name and he started telling us this little story.

It seems that at that time, the barracks ship USS Benewah was anchored twelve miles south at the village of An Long. A couple of the young sailors from River Division 592 had made up an excuse to take their patrol boat north to enjoy some liquid refreshment at the beer barge moored to YRBM 21. Predictably, the short stay turned long while drinking with a couple of river assault crewmembers, who asked for a ride back to Benewah at dusk. What none of the young sailors knew at the time was while they were enjoying their refreshments, the ocean tide had worked its way up the Mekong River far enough to turn the repair barge around 180 degrees in the river.

During the spring and summer, the melting snows in the Himalayas flood the Mekong and its tributaries, causing the water to raise twenty to forty feet, flooding the rice fields throughout the Delta. During the fall and winter, after the summer monsoon rains have ended, the rivers drop back down, and the previously-swift current drops from ten or more knots to zero. There were occasions when the current actually reversed itself and there was a tide traveling upriver due to the effects of the South China Sea. Although spotted by a Swift boat commanded by Lieutenant Elmo Zumwalt III at the border, it took the PBR only a few minutes to be moving at full speed into Cambodia, while a few grenades lay next to the magnetic compass. It didn't take long for several Cambodian gunboats to intercept and capture the PBR and its surprised crew.

Of course, the division leaders aboard Benewah were unaware of these events, other than for the slow moment of the sea tide. The PBR was reported missing the next afternoon, and at that time radio contact was made with YRBM 21. Although the personnel on the beer barge knew that they had left, they did not know where they were located. Later that night they received a report in Benewah's command center from Saigon indicating the Cambodian government had reported capturing a river patrol boat on the Mekong which was headed upriver from the Vietnamese border. Early the next morning, Benewah was advised that Vice Admiral Zumwalt was enroute to the ship in his helicopter. About mid-morning the lookouts sighted the Admiral's helicopter with several chase helos. The Benewah's skipper and several patrol boat and river assault craft squadron commanders greeted the Admiral as he stepped onto USS Benewah. He asked the skipper if he could sit down with all of them in the ships Wardroom to discuss the missing patrol boat. Of course the skipper said yes, knowing how many senior officers would have flown into a rage, castigating everyone and threatening court-martial with such events as this, but not Zumwalt. He wanted to know from the boat's

Squadron Commander the details of the boat's loss, or as much as he knew.

The Admiral indicated that the Cambodian government hadn't yet placed any demands for the return of the PBR crewmen, but he felt the demand would be heavy equipment and farm machinery. They found out three weeks later that Zumwalt was correct when a shipload of farm machinery and heavy earth-moving equipment was offloaded at Phnom Penh in exchange for the PBR crewmen. The patrol boat was never returned. Vice Admiral Zumwalt appointed Lieutenant Commander John Kirk Ferguson investigating officer to inquire into the facts of the incident and report them back to him, along with his opinions and recommendations. They both knew without being told that an international incident would cast a poor light on the U.S. government and that a river boat man was responsible.

"What happened to the sailors," I asked?

"We never saw them again," said Backus, taking a long swig.

"Scuttlebutt has it that the Cambodians beat and incarcerated them in a motley jail until the ransom was paid and then released them in Phnom Penh to the U.S. authorities, who then flew them to Saigon. The two sailors from River Division 592 were court-marshaled, convicted and received some non-judicial punishment of some kind, but I'm not sure what."

"Damn... all because of a couple of beers." I said, taking my last swallow, then stopping.

"Are you pulling my leg, Mr. Backus," I questioned.

"Nope, that's the truth. It wasn't long after that the crew dubbed the beer hall the Last Chance Salon." Then he took one more swallow and set the can down on the bar.

"Can I buy you another, sir?"

"No thanks, think I'll hit the sack," Backus said as he started toward the door, then stopped and turned.

"On another occasion, a sailor leaving the Last Chance fell overboard," there was a short pause. "We never saw him again, either." He disappeared out the doorway into the cool breeze of an enchanting Mekong night.

Ralph Christopher

HI sweetheart,

    I received your letter today and was very happy to see it. Sometimes a fellow can get kind of lonesome around here. I hope everybody back home is feeling better. I'm doing just find. I'm trying to grow a mustache, it will probably take a long time. I'm sorry to hear about Johnny passing, I liked him a lot.

    I guess you have all ready read in the paper about us so I'm not going to say anything about that. Besides, I'm not suppose to if you know what I mean.

    I looked at the stereo equipment I want to buy. It comes to around $500.00. I'll buy it later on and send it home. You said you wanted to send me a package. If you don't have the money then don't send anything I rather you spend it on Grandma and Granddad. If you do have it send me some can foods like peanut butter and jelly. Boy it is hot here and the flies are pretty bad too.

    Did I tell you that I got a letter from Larry Talley. Yeah, well I did. I am waiting to receive another one from him. Tell Ann I said hi. I have been receiving a lot of letters from Sherry, a friend a mine. I haven't heard from Crystal this week but tomorrow I receive mail. If you want to buy me records, I like groups like Quick silver, Grand Funk, Grateful Dead, Blind Faith, Creedence and all of the weird music. I sound like a hippie don't I. My hair is getting a little long. Well, I'll sign off here and wait until later to write again.

Love you,
Chris

P.S. Tell my mother to send my tennis shoes if she sends me a package, love you.

CHAPTER SEVEN - THE CANAL

I was awakened by the sound of the Box Top's hit, "The Letter." There was no morning muster due to the fact that many of the crews were up all night. YRBM 21 never really slept, sailors had to stay on watch all hours, protecting her from attack. Although mortar and rocket attacks were possible, she was anchored a bit far from the river bank for attacks to be accurate. Most of the YRBMs before the 21 had been hit, so there was good reason to believe they would attempt to hit us. Security was a real concern. The Viet Cong would love to blow us up with twenty or thirty boats alongside. We were a prime target for them, a floating supply house with a complete repair facility for their dreaded nemesis the PBR. We were reminded that YRBM 16 had been heavily damaged by a swimmer-carried mine. Onboard, we rotated watches every six hours through the night. Sentries threw concussion grenades over the side all night long, keeping everyone awake. Patrolmen circling in Mike boats towing chains, throwing grenades and firing into floating plants and debris and sentries stood watch on the forecastle, where there was a defensive position with machine guns, mortar tubes and search lights.

I was still a little tired from my midnight watch as I slowly bent over to lace up my boots. Then I stumbled into the head to splash some water on my face and run a comb through my hair. Ready to face a new day, I headed up to the mess hall for breakfast. Climbing the ladder, I could see through the porthole that it would be another hot, sunny Delta day. The river patrol divisions were returning from their night ambushes and hurriedly tying to the docks as they raced each other up the gangway to the chow line.

Rypka, the grave shift cook, had been up all night, baking fresh pastries, pies and breads, and the sweet smell of them all mixed together greeted us as we entered the chow hall in the morning. Crews were scattered in pockets around the mess deck, devouring instant scrambled eggs and fried potatoes. There were large pots of coffee going day or night and normally some form of Tang or Kool-Aid in pitchers. I jumped in the rear of the line and waited my turn with the rest of the hungry sailors. Finally making it to the front, I grabbed a tray and chose the creamed chipped beef over toast, or as we called it back then, SOS - shit on a shingle. It was one of my favorites and I had never had it before entering the navy. I sat down with some of the 21's crew at a table off to the side, where we often set together. Not all the boat crews were friendly with us, some thought of us as "Support Pukes". The crews mostly stayed to themselves and were often rotated back to the bush, so we rarely got to know them well.

"Hey Christopher, how would you like to volunteer to go on a little river-ride for me?" Bailey, my boss, appeared through the doorway and approached me smiling.

"What kind of river-ride?" I asked inquisitively, having been told never to volunteer.

"I need an engineman who knows how to hook up a freezer." He smiled knowing I was the only refrigeration man aboard.

"Okay," I answered sarcastically. Besides, what choice did I have, I knew I was had.

"Better go down below and get some things together, you could be gone a while," he said patting me on the back and sounding like a mother hen.

"What? Right now?" I asked as I jumped up realizing I was about to leave on my first boat trip.

"They're waiting for you back aft on the Mike boat," he said, twitching his nose in the air and walking over to steal a sweet roll. I ran below and threw some of my things in a bag and headed back to the fantail to rendezvous with the rest of the crew. Waiting on a green flattop Mike-6 minesweeping boat were Pena, from New

York, and Steve, a tanned boatswain from South Dakota. You had to have at least three sailors on a Mike boat crew - one to steer and the other two to fire the .50 caliber machine guns and handle the lines. One of the three had to be an engineman or machinist mate, which was called a snipe. All boat crews had to have an engineer aboard and I was it.

Of the seventy engineering personnel stationed aboard YRBM 21, half were assigned indoors in repair facilities, working for Mr. Backus. They normally wore full uniforms with tee shirts; they had air conditioning and hot meals all day and seemed to be happy at their work. The other half of us snipes were out on the decks, pulling boats apart. We were tanned and covered in oil, usually without shirts and some wearing cut-off pants. Of those men, only a few wanted to ride the rivers. You could be gone for days, eating out of cans and getting fried by the sun. It appealed to some of us because we got out of shipboard watches and an E4 petty officer could be in charge. There were three Mike boats attached to the 21, so we needed several crews.

Jumping aboard, I noticed secured to the deck was a brand new shiny Detroit diesel power generator on wheels. Next to it was a crated refrigeration unit with a freezer box. Also, two fifty-five-gallon drums of diesel fuel, frozen steaks, ammunition and assorted supplies. At the aft of the boat was the coxswain's flat protected by a splinter shield with two .50 cal guns mounted separately on poles. Along the wall of the coxswain's station were rifles that had been drawn from the armory, crates of hand grenades, additional .50 cal rounds, C-rat boxes and a three-gallon thermos jug of ice water. There were flak jackets and helmets hung over the .50s and a portable tape deck playing "Willie and the Poor Boys" tied to the rail, holding up the coxswain's roof.

Inside the coxswain's station was a wheel for steering and two hand-operated throttles, one for each of the two GM 671 cubic inch diesel engines. By twisting the throttle arms, you accelerated the engines. You could throttle forward on one engine and reverse on the other at the same time, while turning in a circle. The Mike boat was equipped with only oil and temperature gauges, so you had to keep a close eye on the big power-horses and check levels regularly.

There was a long wooden pole that we inserted into the fuel tank to check the fuel level. If everything was good to go, then we did a radio check, fired up the engines and untied the ropes. We were just about to push off when Charlie C, a clean-cut kid from Pennsylvania, jumped aboard.

"They sent me over to keep you guys company."

"The more the merrier," Steve replied as he cut the wheel and snorted the engines.

We reversed off, throttled forward and headed downstream on the mighty Mekong River. I felt like a kid on my first date, hoping she would like me and everything would go well.

"What's that smell?" I asked not recognizing the putrid aroma. "That's the nuoc mam factory, blowing off VC Island," Steve answered. "An old papa-san owns the factory and pays the VC to leave him alone."

"What the hell is nuoc mam," holding my nose and hoping it would go away. "It's a Vietnamese sauce made by percolating water and soy sauce through large vats of salted, decaying fish. It's like ketchup to these people, they season everything with it," the smell and Steve's colorful description churned my stomach. "Does it always smell like this?"

"Yup." Damn, as if being in Vietnam wasn't bad enough.

We passed An Long village on our left, a thriving community. It was a small village that seemed to have been there for a long time. The river movement was constant; the boats filled the water, always on the go. Suspended over the river, along the banks of the village were little shacks and thatched huts on stilts, made of wood and straw. The galvanized metal roofs reflected the sun and kept them dry during the monsoons. The children stood along the bank, waving. Two old men were sitting and talking beside the river. Fishermen threw their nets from dugout canoes. We turned to the left into the Grand Canal entrance almost hidden by the river bushes, which were full of hardy stems of red and white flowers. As we entered, we came alongside the back entrance to the village. Junks and sampans with entire families living onboard were tied abreast, docked to makeshift piers. An old papa-san and young boys fishing off the junks with strings rapped around their fingers. Wooden poles sticking up out of the water, supporting fishnet traps below the water line. We passed under a long, high, homemade bicycle bridge with little children looking down, calling out in English as we held our breath, praying they were friendly and no one would drop a grenade. Steve throttled forward into the open canal, rocking all the little boats as we passed, swamping a sampan with the waves of our backwash.

The Grand Canal was built by the French to cut through Kien Phong Province and connect the upper Mekong with the Vam Co Tay River into Saigon. The canal was a sixty-mile straightaway with one small turn through the thirty-by-seventy-mile marshlands known as the Plain of Reeds. It wasn't very wide; you could throw a rock across if you had a good arm. During the dry season, the canal was low for the Mike boats. The EOD divers went in with two and three hundred feet lengths of detonation cord and blew it open. The locals loved it as they gathered up all the fish and snakes. During the wet season, the water level would rise six feet or more over the bank, flooding the rice fields and hamlets, causing the enemies reliance on the canal to be unnecessary. Straw-like reeds flourished everywhere and were interrupted only occasionally by tree lines. The canal was a main through-way for the people and farmers to move their rice, fruit, and grains to the market places of Saigon. It was like a highway with sampans, junks and water-taxis traveling east and west, powered by four-cycle Briggs and Stratton lawnmower engines. Occasionally, we would pass a river patrol boat checking the water traffic for contraband; it was part of their Daytime Resource Control program.

The patrolmen would signal the sampans alongside, verifying cargo manifests and checking ID cards. If everything was okay, they sent them on their way. Often the patrolmen bartered or gave the kids C-rations or candy. If they ran, then they were most likely the VC, so the sailors fired warning shots, then gave pursuit. Some of the long boats had two outboard motors and could outrun the patrol boats, but they couldn't out run the guns. The patrolmen were the police of the waterways and the local farmers had come to know them as such. The brown water navy had taken the canal away from Charlie and cut his supply lines.

61

At the west end of the canal, the south bank was dotted with small farm villages, rice paddies and very little foliage. There might be an occasional tree or a few bushes. As you continued eastward, you would enter areas with bushes, bamboo and thick reeds stretching ten feet high out of the water. East of Phuoc Xuyen village, it was very thick with heavy foliage along the banks. Water buffalos grazed and worked in the fields. At night the farmers would protect their buffalos by putting them in little sheds on the high ground near their hooches. All of the little hooches had bunkers inside so the families could hide when "the shit hit the fan." If they left a lantern burning outside of their hooch at night, the patrolmen were instructed to leave them alone.

The river divisions were assigned to patrol the waterways and to stop the flow of men and guns to Saigon and the Mekong Delta. The majority of crossings occurred at night in the dry season, when the melting snows of the Himalaya Mountains were gone and the water levels of the rice paddies had dropped. Vice Admiral Zumwalt, Commander U.S. Naval Forces Vietnam, had dubbed the canal, "Operation Barrier Reef" and was building another naval support base in the middle of Indian country.

It was going to take us half a day steaming down the canal with a heavy load in the hot morning sun to get to the base. You could have fried an egg on the deck, and the only wind was from the boat, cutting through the water at six knots. On the north side of the canal were vast fields as far as the eye could see. Farmers and water buffalos pulling carts full of grains and melons were everywhere. There also were hills and hidden spider holds that were being used to conceal enemy infiltrators, who would wait for the opportune time to attack the boats or cross the canal. The dug-out irrigation ditches along the banks traveled miles up into the fields, allowing the water to reach the rice and grain crops. They made a perfect trail for the enemy to hide in as they advanced down to the canal from their sanctuaries. At times a dense tree line, leading into a jungle that made up no-man's-land, was visible in the distance, marking the Cambodian border. A quarter of the way down the canal we came upon a little Viet regional outpost.

The small compound was made of mud walls, with four corner bunkers and straw huts in the center. The single entrance was fenced in by several layers of concertina wire and claymore mines. Entire family armies, comprised of men, women, and children, were dressed in jungle tiger-striped uniforms and were carrying weapons. They waved us in and we decided we would take a chance and check them out. I jumped off the back of the boat onto a five-foot high-bank, and the little children ran to me, holding out their hands. All I had with me was chewing gum, so I started handing it out in little pieces as they crowded in around me. I was six feet tall. The Vietnamese men came up to my chest and the little children came up to my waist. I sat on a log and I felt little fingers touching me all over. They were grabbing my hair and hugging my pale legs as they tried to rub the freckles off my skin.

"I don't think they've ever seen anybody like you before," Pena chuckled.

"I think you're right," I replied, almost laughing from being tickled by the little fingers. I picked up one tiny boy and sat him on my leg while rubbing his very fine black hair. The texture was very different from my thick red locks. The regional soldiers looked on with approval as they sized me up and watched me curiously play with the boy. His big brother and his ten-year-old friends came over and started hitting me up for cigarettes and beer, wanting to trade. Suddenly the biggest rat I had ever seen appeared out of a hole on the side of the river bank a few feet from us. I jumped back to grab my gun when two of the little boys ran by me almost knocking me over. The rat was as big as a small dog weighing more than twenty pounds. When it sat up on its hind legs, it was two feet tall with a three-foot tail hanging behind it. It saw the kids and ducked back into its hole, but not before one little boy dove and grabbed it by his back legs. Digging furiously with its front paws, the rat tried to pull away as the rest of the kids jumped in to grab hold. They managed to pull it out of its den. A second little boy grabbed a spear and spiked it in the back several times, as the giant river rat twisted and tried to escape. It was all over as they tied its feet to a pole and hung it upside down over their shoulders. Laughing, they carried it back into the compound, anticipating a big dinner that night. The old women dressed in their pajamas and turbans, greeted them at the front gate with songs and praise of their great hunt. I was a little embarrassed at my fear after witnessing the kids' brave attack on the giant rat. Some of the Viet soldiers looked to be fifteen or sixteen years old. I could beat two or three of these guys in a fist fight, but there were a lot more than that. You could tell they were a little scared of us big Americans; I pulled out my pack of Marlboros and passed them out to the boy soldiers. In return they offered me opium, which I declined. One of the older men held up a World War II-era bayonet and wanted to trade for food. I looked back on the Mike boat and found half a box of C-rations and offered them to him. Much to my surprise he took it. It was a good trade and everybody was happy as we shook hands and bowed politely. I felt I had learned a little about the river people along the canal and now I knew that the concertina and claymores were not to keep us out.

We jumped back on the boat and throttled away as I ran my belt through the sheath of the bayonet. I was still astounded by the constant beauty I saw around me. I could plainly see the curvature of the earth. The heat and the humidity were overwhelming. I wondered about the nickname "River Rats" and where it originated.

Support base Phuoc Xuyen was in the early stages of being built when we arrived. Navy Seabees were busy in the hot sun and mud, digging post holes and stringing miles of concertina wire. The new firebase had merely a few emplacements of wooden walls filled with sand to protect the Seabees and NSA sailors from "incoming," as enemy ordnance was called. The Seabees had already dredged the canal and dug into the bank, anchoring three pontoon barges.

The Seabees in South Vietnam had often been exposed to enemy action and their wounded-in-action totaled more than those in World War II. In fact, the killed-in-action rate per total men deployed was four times that of World War II.

Across the canal were three green heavies of River Assault Squadron 15. They resembled Ulysses S. Grant's boats on the bank of the mighty Mississippi below Vicksburg during the American Civil War. The green sixty-foot armored troop carriers, called Tangos, were built to carry and disembark the U.S. Army's 9th Infantry and South Vietnamese troops into battle along the thousands of rivers and canals, busting up enemy strongholds and bunkers in the Delta. The Tangos were made of metal and were protected by outer steel-bar armor around the hull and wheelhouse. Between the armor hull and the rebar, the sailors had stuffed C-rat boxes to absorb the initial blast of the enemy's rockets. Since they were heavy in weight they were inherently slow at eight knots, I could see that the Tangos were more heavily equipped with cannons in round, rotating turrets, with numerous machine guns sticking out of holes in the armor. As we neared the three heavies, we saw their crews sitting on the aft decks of the boat and hanging in hammocks, resting in the shade. Duty on the big boats was brutal. There was very little air circulation and the heat inside could be like an oven.

The Tangos had dug into the bank to intercept any attack on the sailors building the fire-support base. The Tangos were part of a River Assault Division, made up of modified World War II landing craft, with exception of the Alpha Assault boat, which was designed and constructed for Vietnam. There were two divisions to a squadron and each division was composed of thirteen Tangos. Most were equipped with canopies and some with helo decks. Others were comically termed Douche boats, with their two high-pressure water-cannons propelling 2700 gallons of water a minute at 250 pounds of pressure, disintegrating mud and cement bunkers along the waterways. One Tango was converted into a refueler, allowing the division longer stays away. In addition, there were eight Assault Support Patrol boats; nicknamed Alpha. Several heavily armed and armored Monitor Assault boats, named after the Civil War ironclad. Equipped with either a 105 mm howitzer or an 81 mm mortar tube and a Monitor Assault Napalm flame-thrower, dubbed the Zippo. Also, one Monitor was normally a Command Communication Charlie Boat, code name Romeo, being used for a Tactical Operation Center. Armament varied on the heavy assault craft, but usually consisted of combinations of 20 and/or 40 mm cannons plus .50 and .30 cal machine guns, and whatever else the crew could drag aboard.

The North Vietnamese troops and Viet Cong guides came down the Ho Chi Minh Trail with arms and supplies from the North. Our river boats on their Waterborne Guard Post were the first contacts they encountered. The Communists had to swim or board sampans to cross the waterways between Cambodia and Vietnam. Vice Admiral Zumwalt and his staff devised a plan to barrier off their entry routes to Saigon and the Mekong Delta and urged their commanders to use initiative and improvisation.

From sunset to sunrise along the rivers and canals, hidden in the little irrigation ditches or in the mosquito-infested reeds and bamboo, hundreds of combatant boats manned by crews of four to six sailors were positioned just south of Cambodia. Guard posts were changed nightly in order not to establish a pattern that the VC spies could exploit and ambush. There was a two-hundred-mile barrier of operations that started and extended from the Gulf of Thailand through the Vinh Te Canal to the Bassac River, called Tran Hung Dao, named after a famous early Vietnamese warrior sailor. Continuing from the Bassac River at Chau Doc, northeast to the Mekong River at Tan Chau, was a barrier on the French Canal. The barrier from the Mekong east to the Vam Co Tay River was the sixty-mile-long Grand Canal called Barrier Reef. The Vam Co Tay had a sister over to the east, and these two rivers ran south, where they joined, forming a slingshot. This was another barrier that was established. It was called Giant Sling Shot. The Vam Co Tay skirted west of the Parrot's Beak area, which is a land mass of Cambodia that projects fifty miles south into Vietnam and then swings back up again to the north. The Vam Co Dong skirted east of the Parrot's Beak deep into Tay Ninh Province. The combination of all these Barrier Operations was code-named Operation SEALORDS. Southeast Asia Lake, Ocean, River and Delta Strategy, and it had severed the enemy supply lines. The enemy was no longer able to move his men and supplies with impunity from Cambodia into III and IV Corps areas. A Naval "tariff" had been imposed on those shipments, measurable in terms of men and supplies captured or destroyed, but incalculable with respect to what was deterred from ever being sent. Vice Admiral Zumwalt was winning his brown water war.

In late 1969, crews of Strike Assault Squadron 20 (STABRON 20) having been cross-trained and without their boats, were split into duffel bag crews and assigned to PBR and Assault Craft units. Riding along with the crews of several river patrol divisions and the heavies of River Assault Squadron 15, the combined forces surprised the enemy on Christmas Eve 1969 attempting to cross the western end of the Grand Canal in a large formation disguised as bushes. Along with the Seawolf and OV-10 Bronco gunships, they mauled the enemy badly and forced him to change his tactics. After receiving shipment of their twenty Strike Assault Boats, called STABs, at Dong Tam in January 1970, the crews quickly assembled the boats and traveled back up river to the Grand Canal, where they would be involved in a series of firefights as a squadron in the next few months. On March 18, 1970, they caught the Peoples Army again trying to cross in a large formation. Contact was made up and down the canal as the enemy had split into smaller groups and many of the boats were involved in firefights. Just below An Long Village, Seaman Daniel C. Case was mortally wounded on Racing Danger One-one when a bullet passed his flak jacket, entering his body under his armpit and causing him to be air lifted out.

The STABs, along with the heavies and PBRs, were integrated together to form a barrier wall to cut off the enemy's approach.

Because their high frequency, FM communication radios were line-of-sight. It was impossible to talk to all boats along the canal's sixty-mile length from the command ship Benewah on the Mekong. The support base at the village of Phouc Xuyen, which was thirty miles east of the Benewah, would be able to communicate with all the boats within ten miles of the base. The headquarters aboard Benewah would communicate with Phouc Xuyen, and the boats on the eastern end of the canal could communicate with the support base at Tuyen Nhon. Phouc Xuyen would have a forward landing pad for rearming the Seawolf gunships, making it quicker to get the choppers back in the air and on the attack. The base also would provide showers, meals and racks for the crews to rest so they could combat the long tedious nights on ambush. The NSA sailors attached to the base would supply the fuel and ammunition to replenish the boats on the canal, as well as stand the watches and man the guns in order to repel any enemy attack on the small vulnerable support base.

We landed and tied alongside the pontoon barge. There to meet us was an old Chief Petty Officer dressed in his khaki fleet uniform, wearing a duck-billed hat. The legs of his pants were tucked into his half-tied jump boots and a big cigar was hanging out of his mouth. He strutted around his newly acquired firebase with his protective flak jacket on, yelling orders to anyone that wasn't moving.

"Give a hand there sailor, secure that line. Goddamn, it's about fucking time," he said admiring the brand new generator sitting on the Mike boat. "Hey Dave, get the Seabees over here. Tell them to bring that backhoe."

Senior Engineman Chief Lloyd A. Murphy was as salty as they came; his gravely voice was full of colorful metaphors from having been in his beloved navy for thirty years. Forty-eight didn't seem old to most, but it sure was a long way from nineteen and twenty, which is what the majority of us were at the time. In the background I could hear AFVN with their back home country survey, playing George Jones on the chief's battery-powered AM-FM radio. Hanging on a wooden pole over the galley was the Stars and Strips. Proudly displayed under it was an Alabama State flag. It might be President Nixon's War, but it sure as hell was Chief Murphy's firebase, and if you forgot it, he'd put a foot up your butt to remind you of the fact. He looked us over pretty closely and did not seem to approve of our lack of uniform.

"What's your rank, sailor," he spat at me.

"Machinist Mate Third Class," I answered.

"Does your Commanding Officer allow all his sailors to dress this way?" He asked, looking us up and down and shaking his head.

"No Chief, only the ones that work out in the heat." I said, noticing a Seabee dressed in the same attire approaching on a backhoe.

"Where did you get that old contraband bayonet?"

"I traded for it, Chief," standing my ground with my arms along my side. "Can I see it," he asked politely so I responded "Sure," I pulled it out of the sheath and handed it to him with the blade toward myself. "What's your name, sailor?" he said, bending over and unevenly cutting the bottom legs of his pants off.

"Christopher." I watched with a surprised look on my face.

"Thanks, Christopher, that feels better" he handed back the bayonet. "You're right, it's too fucking hot out here," he said, laughing at the sight of his lily-white legs that hadn't seen the sun in years.

The Chief was a crusty old bastard and navy through-and-through. Other than that, he was a great guy and I could have listened forever to his tall tales about the good old days. He offered me my first taste of Carling Black Label beer. The beer was hot and I almost threw it up. Wanting to appear older, I sipped it slowly and laughed at the Chief's stories as if I understood what he was talking about. Back in the world we probably wouldn't see eye-to-eye, but here, we were good ole boys stopping the Communist threat. Besides, it was nice having a Senior Chief as a buddy.

We untied the Mike boat, backed off and ran aground at the closest point to the river bank. All under the watchful eye and command of Chief Murphy, who yelled out orders as he paraded up and down the bank of the canal like a traffic cop during rush hour. There was a three-foot gap from the deck of the Mike boat to the bank of the beach so we all jumped in the canal, and along with the backhoe, dragged the generator and crates of refrigeration equipment up and over a ten-foot bank in mud up to our knees. By the time we finished we were covered in mud, so we all dove into the canal to rinse off. The mosquitoes and flies were eating us alive as we watched a water buffalo drain his bladder in the dirty malaria-infested water that we were all standing in.

After off-loading the diesel fuel and supplies, we tied back up and opened the crates containing the refrigeration equipment. I started connecting the refrigeration lines as the Chief went over to inspect his men, who were prepping and fueling the power generator. The first time the Chief hit the start button, it fired up and purred like a kitten.

"Those boys back in Detroit sure know what they're doing,"

"Fucking A, bubba," commented one of his men. Within an hour the Chief had the whole base lit up and I had started the freezer.

"God Bless Admiral Zumwalt," the Chief shouted. I just stood there with a shit-eating grin on my face, not knowing the Admiral myself. It was too late for us to head back that night; darkness would soon be upon us. The canal had too many hazards; they would be setting ambush positions right about then. So we decided to bed down with the Chief and his boys for the night. After radioing back, we stepped into a small wooden galley built on a floating barge. The cook had lit the barbecue and thrown on the frozen steaks, charring them, as the men lined up for their first hot meal in some time. The sailors out in the boonies had to make do the best they could. Cans of C-rations was the norm and what they lived on through the long nights.

"Y'all help yourselves." A deep black Southern drawl filled the room.

"Thank you, sir," I answered with a smile.

"Sir, I ain't no officer; I work for a living, you can call me Brown."

"Thanks Brown."

After we finished, we all lay back to digest.

"Brown I feel like an old hound dog, all I need is a shady tree to lie under." He chuckled at the sight of us. Then we all settled into a friendly poker game, sipping hot beer and telling tall stories and listening to "shit-kick'n" music. The Chief piped the music over the loud speaker. "The VC hate this shit," he said as he chuckled.

There were only twenty or so sailors with the Chief and Brown, and some of them were Seabees, so they welcomed the company as we passed around the Black Label and placed bets with Pall Mall and Camel non-filter cigarettes. Around dusk, the Chief called sentries out and the men headed to their night guard posts on the walls of the base.

Hiding behind the wooden walls of sand with the sentries and guns, I looked across the field at the flashes in the distance as a mortar flare opened and drifted down slowly, illuminating the plains in that forgotten place on our planet. The sentry on the ammi threw his talc grenades into the canal and fired his M-79 rounds over to the field. Death could come to anyone in that place, I thought. Our patrols were filled with it, both ours and theirs. In a time when men were walking on the moon, young Americans were manning the walls in small outpost in far-off jungles. I took one more drag on my Marlboro, thinking that place had to be one of the most dangerous spots on earth for a boy like myself. Still the insufferable heat plagued us as our bodies stunk with the smell of sweat and bug juice. I snuffed out my cigarette and retired to the hooch, knowing I needed to catch a few winks before dawn.

The sound of the swamp was all around me as crickets and frogs delivered their nightly songs. The dampening of mufflers against the water echoed off the bank as one of the Tangos slipped out and disappeared into the darkness. The generator purred in the background as it supplied power to keep up the lights around the base. I tossed and turned in my rack as the concussion grenades exploded in the canal, and the sheets stuck to my skin. I was miserable as the humidity and mosquitoes tormented me and would not allow me to sleep. I sat up in my rack, shooing them and rubbing lotion, while listening to the rain trickle and dreading tomorrow's sun.

That night, all along the canal the guard posts of Operation Barrier Reef was being set into motion as the elements of three river divisions were digging in. A flotilla of green-man-of-wars, spaced roughly a half mile apart, sat quietly hidden on the banks of the canal, waiting for the enemy to come down the trail and cross their path. The STABs dispatched their crews onto the beach to search out the enemy. Their men had been trained to conceal electronic sensors and set up land-based ambushes, booby traps and demolition. It was standard operating procedure for them to patrol the beach and check the area for fighting holes and bunkers. In many places, the banks of the rivers were too high, so boat crews stationed marksmen on the beach or on a patrol boat's canopy to have eyes out ahead.

At 2200 hours, Boatswain Mate First Class, Al "Boats" Maxson sat in the coxswain's chair of Racing Danger One-two on his assigned guard post. The lightning flashed in the distance, for the rain had come and gone on a dark windy, dreadful night. He thought back to earlier in the month when he had shared a few cans of C-rations with a six-year-old orphan girl who lived on the bank of the canal. She had built her own little shelter out of wood and straw under a small overhanging mound of dirt near Phouc Xuyen. He had only wanted to help her, it was sad that she was caught in the middle of this war and was having to live alongside the rats of the river. A few cans of food for a little girl couldn't hurt anyone he thought. That was until the night the Viet Cong tax collector came to the village. The VC had found the cans and knew the little girl had talked to the Americans. She would have to be punished; they would use her to set an example to the rest of the village.

It was Gunners Mate Third Class George Crabtree from Tennessee who had noticed that the little girl was missing. Boats pulled the STAB onto the beach of the village and jumped out with Crabtree, Baker and his Viet interpreter, leaving Johns, the new kid from Kentucky, behind to watch the boat. He instructed the interpreter to go into the village and inquire about the girl. The Viet interpreter refused, admitting he was afraid the VC might still be there. Again Boats insisted as he gripped his gun tightly. The interpreter reluctantly entered the village. After an hour of speaking to the scared villagers, he returned and walked up to Boats with a look of horror.

"Where is she?" Boats demanded.

"Viet Cong come in night and take her," the interpreter spoke with his head bowed. "What did they do to her?" Boats asked, straining to hold back his emotions. The interpreter shook his head, but Boats knew.

What kind of men could do this kind of thing, he thought as he wanted more than ever to finish this war and let these people go back to living the way they had for a thousand years. What kind of animal could do this, as the rage built up inside of him and boiled over as he thought of what he would like to do to this kind of men? Every man on the boat secretly thought of what he wanted to do to the enemy to revenge their little shipmate, as each one walked back to the boat with a feeling of depression. That night, Boats looked up into the sky and made himself a promise to never get close to the locals again. The river patrolmen were hated by the enemy and the VC retaliated against the indigenous people if they were friendly with Americans.

"Racing Danger One-two, this is Tango One-five-one-six requesting illumination over." The radio broke the silence as Boats grabbed the mike. "Tango One-five-one-six, roger that." He signaled to Baker, the engineer standing on the aft, to pop a flare. The flare illuminated the northern side of the canal as it drifted down slowly, and then fireman Joseph Johns "popped" a second flare more to the east. Still they saw nothing as it drifted down, exposing the Strike Assault boat's position. Chief William Spencer the Patrol Officer aboard picked up movement through the starlight scope across the canal, seventy-five yards to the east.

2215, "Romeo, Romeo, we have movement north. Requesting immediate fire clearance. Over," Boats radioed back to the Charlie boat, requesting permission to initiate fire. "Negative One-two there are friendlies in your area. Wait."

"Romeo this is Racing Danger One-two. Roger." Boats and the chief looked at each other, shaking their heads in agreement that it didn't look like friendlies. Baker and Crabtree waited behind the M-60s staring out into the reeds on the north bank as Chief Spencer spied through the night vision glass at the silhouettes of men moving in the thicket. Thirty minutes had passed since they had heard back from the Charlie boat. The Chief motioned Boats to pass him the mike.

"Romeo, Romeo, this is Racing Danger One-two, requesting fire clearance. Over." Boats looked over at Crabtree, Baker and Johns. He knew his crew was ready for a break - five days living on the side of a river setting up all-night ambushes and one day back at the Benewah for the last few months had racked up thirty firefights and more than twenty enemy killed.

"Negative on engage Racing Danger One-two, I say again, ARVN (Army of Republic of Vietnam) in your area."

"Request permission to get underway. Over." The Chief tried to convey the danger. "Negative on underway, hold your position," the Charlie boat relayed the message from the Vietnamese Authorities. "Roger." Chief Spencer did not like what he was hearing. The rules of engagement for the river divisions were not fair and the safety of the patrolmen was often controlled by the decisions of the Vietnamese authorities.

Baker was thinking to himself about returning to Illinois someday and getting his old job back with Parnelli Jones, racing on the weekends and traveling the circuit with the guys. If they could see him now, riding as the engineer aboard a heavily-armed Strike Assault boat, what would they think? He recalled the first time he had seen the boats two 427 Mercruiser III gas burning engines.

"The twenty-six-foot aluminum-hull, Styrofoam-filled boats can be sunk only to the gunwale and no farther," his instructor had told the class in 1969 at the Naval Inshore Operations Training Center at Mare Island, Vallejo, California.

"Each boat has two 105-gallon, foam-filled, self-sealing rubber fuel bladders located under the floor plate, below the water line in the crew's cockpit," the instructor quoted, never having seen a STAB himself.

"The Strike Assault boats have three unique characteristics no other boat in the Republic of Vietnam has: fast acceleration, high speed of 50 knots, and very quiet operations at slow speeds due to the sound-proofing of the engine compartments."

Lieutenant Commander John "Kirk" Ferguson United States Navy, Commanding Officer of Strike Assault Squadron 20 looked on as his men viewed the first two STABs that had just arrived.

"They also have ceramic armor and a flak blanket made of kevlar on both port and starboard sides in the crew's' cockpit."

Admiral Zumwalt and his staff had envisioned two high-speed boats with low silhouettes and very quiet operations that could be air lifted in by two Chinook helicopters, lowered down on the still slumbering North Vietnamese campsites along the Mekong tributaries, move in quickly, releasing their M-60s and 40 mm low velocity grenades, and then getting out before the enemy would have a chance to regroup.

"Normal armament consisted of M-60 machine guns and MK 20 automatic grenade launchers on pintle mounts." Commander Kirk Ferguson was to train his sailors with only two STABs. Twenty more were being built at the Grafton Boat Company in Illinois and would catch up to the unit in South Vietnam. Baker laughed the first time he heard the sound of the duel Holley four-barrel carburetors that produced 325 horse power per engine and were identical to the ones he had used in his racing cars back home in Rapid City. When he heard them roar in unison racing across the water, it sounded as if he were back at the drag strip, and he knew that he and all of his shipmates were hooked. When the boats finally arrived in January of 1970, he gathered his tools and box of parts and went to work. He had modified Racing Danger One-two into one of the fastest boats of the squadron.

Baker looked over to his friend Crabtree, the most popular man in the squadron, as Baker soaked his fatigue green uniform down with mosquito repellent. Crabtree smiled back, maintaining noise discipline, as they sat staring into the reeds, waiting. Both men had been with the unit since the formation of the squadron and were well liked by their shipmates. Boats was captain of the boat and had nothing but respect for his men and the job they had performed. It was midnight now and the sounds from the reeds on the north bank were growing louder as the men began to stir.

BOOM! BOOM! BOOM! Suddenly the darkness of night lit up with an orange explosion and flying debris. Chief Spencer leaped, diving in one step from the back of the cockpit onto the bow of the boat, while somehow grabbing the trigger of the M-60 in mid air, swinging the gun 180 degrees, spraying bullets into the night air as he chopped down the craft's antennas.

"GET THE FUCK OUT OF HERE," Spencer yelled.

Boats seemed to come to from a moment of unconsciousness as he picked himself up off the deck and back into the coxswain chair. Reaching forward, he hit the exhaust vent switches, noticing the starboard engine throttle was missing. He hit the ignition button to start the port engine as the Chief somehow freed the rope on the bow while never releasing his finger from the trigger. "GET THE FUCK OUT OF HERE," Chief Spencer screamed as he returned fire like a madman chopping into the reeds as the blood dripped from the wound on his left forearm, down onto the deck. Boats looked over his shoulder as he reversed off the beach to see that Baker, Crabtree and Johns were hit and lying motionless on the deck. The first B-40 rocket had hit the gas tank below the water line. Half a second later, the second rocket had hit the starboard engine, knocking it off its foundation and tearing the starboard throttle column outwards. The third rocket hit the starboard gunwale, and the blast took out Baker, Crabtree and Johns, killing them instantly.

Boats now maneuvered the STAB back off the south bank and into the center of the canal. Then he pushed the port engine throttle forward and the boat cut hard to the starboard, running aground in the very same reeds where they had received the enemy fire. Chief Spencer was burning up the barrel of the M-60 while he swung around in the prone position on the forward deck, as the hot shell casings spit out of the M-60 and down the back of Boats flak jacket, burning the back of his neck.

"GET THE FUCK OUT OF HERE," Chief Spencer yelled over and over again. Boats backed off the north bank and looked up to see the barrel of the chief's M-60 drooping down from the heat of the nonstop flow of bullets leaving its chamber. He then pointed the crippled STAB toward the south bank and throttled forward on the port engine, then all stop as the boat drifted and started shirring right. He gave it a touch of reverse to align the boat back into the center of the canal as he repeated the maneuver again and again. The chief released the trigger as they cleared the ambush site, and with his hands, started removing the shell casings from the back of Boats flak jacket. As the wounded STAB neared Tango One-five-one-six in the pitch black night, they noticed the red light signal for identifying yourself to another friendly force. Boats and the chief felt around in the cockpit of the mangled boat but because of the damage and debris could not find their red light to answer the signal. Suddenly the sound of a .50 jacking a round out of the belt fed ammunition box could be heard. Chief Spencer yelled to the Tango to hold its fire as the sound of a round jacking into the chamber brought Boats to his feet, yelling out words he didn't know he had inside himself. Responding, a loud Black American voice yelled out. "Hold your fire, ain't no fucking gook that knows how to cuss like that," as the disabled Strike Assault boat pulled into view and alongside of the Tango.

The black boat captain, a large E5 boatswain's mate, could see there were men down and that the chief was wounded.

"Get on the horn to command and tell them we need a medevac ASAP," the boat captain shouted to his radioman.

"Romeo, Romeo, this is Tango One-five-one-six. We need medevac to our position. Over." There was a moment of silence as the young radioman listened over the headset. "Roger that Romeo. They're on the way Chief," the young radioman relayed to Chief Spencer as the Tango's corpsman wrapped Spencer's arm.

The alarm sounded shortly after midnight at support base Phouc Xuyen as men jumped from there racks rushing to get their boots on and grab their weapons. Illumination flares left the mortar tub and opened over the north bank of the canal, floating down slowly, lighting up the field so all could see. Chief Murphy and Brown turned the mess deck into a command station as Brown primed the claymore triggers and Murphy questioned his men over the wired phones for any sightings. Sitting next to them was a young radioman listening in to the Romeo boat as it radioed for help.

"Racing Danger double-zero, this is Romeo. Be advised one of your units hit with three KIA and one WIA. Over," the communication boat radioed back to the mother-ship Benewah and Commander Ferguson. "Roger, wait one," the Benewah's radioman went to officers berthing and woke Commander Ferguson.

"Commander Ferguson, wake up, sir, there's been a STAB hit on the canal." The commander sat up, clearing what little sleep he had gotten from his eyes.

"Thank you, son," He slipped on his pants and headed up to the Benewah's radio room.

"Romeo, Romeo, this is Racing Danger double-zero. Understand unit has been hit. What assistance required? Over."

"This is Romeo. Have medevac underway. Request boat to tow damaged unit to home base. Over."

"Roger that. Over," Commander Ferguson signed off.

Men ran half-dressed to their battle stations and crouched down in anticipation of an enemy attack. They aimed weapons in all directions outside the unfinished fence of Phouc Xuyen. The village men herded their families into the bunkers inside their hooches for safety in case gunfire broke out. On the mess deck, Steve and I, along with the radioman, Chief Murphy and Brown, were glued to the radio as we listened attentively to the request to scramble the Seawolves from YRBM 21, who also had sounded battle stations at scramble one alert as they prepared to launch both birds.

The peacefulness of the night had disappeared as all hands were now rushing to get help to the mortally wounded boat on the canal. The sailors, their hearts pounding, crowed around their radios, since it was one of their boats that had been crippled and four of their friends had been hit. Back on the fantail of Tango One-five-one-six, Chief Spencer was retrieving buckets of water from the canal and dumping them down the back of Boats' shirt to cool and relieve his burn - blistered back. The Tango had reversed off the bank and moved to the center of the canal in preparation for Chief Spencer's extraction by the Medevac chopper. Within minutes, the Seawolves had reached their position as one broke off to lay down suppressing fire into the field. The second chopper gently touched down on the small flight deck, hovering above the Tango, not allowing its full weight to bottom out the boat in the shallow canal. The first Seawolf made a beeline for the wilderness as the door gunners hung out the sides, raining down gunfire on the brush along the banks of the irrigation ditches. CHITCHITCHITCHITCHITCHIT! BAMBAMBAMBAM!

All radios from the other guard posts up and down the canal were being surrounded by their crews, listening as the call went out that a STAB had been hit and three of their buddies had been killed. The Seawolf moved into the distance, discharging one last volley of rockets as they pulled off, being relieved on station by an OV-10 Bronco, fixed-wing aircraft from Light Attack Squadron Four (Val-4). The two-seat, propeller-driven Black Ponies, as they were called by the men of the river patrol force for which they provided air cover, had become one of the Navy's most formidable weapons. The bird dove down, unleashing their 5-inch Zuni rockets and mini-guns, as she joined in on the hunt for the retreating enemy. PHOOSH! PHOOST! PHOOST! BRRRRRRRRRRRRRRRRRRRRRRRRRR!

The second Seawolf lifted off the flight deck of the Tango with Chief Spencer on board, heading for the Third Surgical Hospital in Binh Thuy. The Tango's crew tried to coax Boats to lie down in a rack below deck and get some sleep. The first Seawolf moved farther to the east, searching the far-off fields with their machine guns firing in vengeance as the Black Pony swooped down again, releasing rockets on the wilderness.

All along the canal for the rest of the night, the men of the river divisions stared into the fields in front of them hoping to catch a glimpse of the enemy assassins and get even for the loss of their friends. Battle stations was called off as the mess deck of the support base filled with men looking for a cup of coffee and hearing for the first time that a boat on the canal had been hit. The Seawolf and

Black Pony gunships were returning to their bases, disappointed that they were not able to locate the enemy. YRBM 21 stood down as men congregated on the helo deck, anticipating the return of the Seawolves. An ARVN patrol was sent in just before dawn to the site of the ambush. On the north beach, in the reeds they had discovered Communist weapons left behind. They also had counted fifteen blood trails from where the enemy had dragged off their wounded and dead.

In the dim light of morning, Boats splashed water on his face, having not slept, as another Strike Assault boat pulled alongside and prepared to tie up to the disabled One-two boat.

"How you doing, Boats?" asked the Boat Captain, peering into the cockpit at the damage of the One-two boat. Boats grabbed two LAW rockets sitting on the bow of the Tango as he stepped down onto the mangled boat. Baker, Crabtree and Johns had been wrapped in cammi poncho liners by the Tango's crew and were lying across the engine covers on the fantail. One of the crewmen of the assisting STAB noticed there was debris from a rocket imbedded in the back of the boatswain chair, the same chair that Boats had sat in the night before.

"Why don't you come forward and ride with us, Boats?" He turned the crew down, wanting to stay with his shipmates.

"Come on, Boats, ride with us." Again, he turned them down as the STAB untied and pulled away, slowly towing Racing Danger One-two. Boats sat on the back of the cockpit with his legs dangling. In his lap was a LAW rocket with a second one ready to go setting beside him. He tried to raise his eyes up, above the canal, as he thought of his pals' families back home. He looked across into the reeds and farther into the wilderness as he grieved for the pain of a young wife without a husband, and for the tears of the parents who had now lost their sons. He could hear the sound of silent prayers whispering in the early morning light as he pulled away from his friends on the Tango, leaving them behind.

Chief Murphy was yelling out orders at the crack of dawn encouraging his men to start moving. Brown was mixing powdered eggs, a special treat for the men, as he greeted the returning boat divisions with a smile and warm coffee. The men were quiet and subdued; there was no joking or clowning that morning. The ash buckets on the tables were full to overflowing as Brown dumped them in the aluminum trash can, trying to keep up as the sailors calmed their nerves chain-smoking.

I had not slept well and was beginning to smell when I recalled I had not brought a toothbrush or soap. There were no showers; men threw roped buckets out into the canal, and then dumped the water over their heads. Charlie C was nice enough to squeeze some of his toothpaste onto my finger and I swished it around in my mouth.

"You better put some lotion on, Chris. You're red." We all seemed to be looking out for the man next to us that morning.

"Will you rub some on my back for me," I begged.

"I don't know, man, people might talk," he joked, grabbing the bottle of lotion from me.

"Don't worry, Charlie, I'm not gay, I tried it and hated it." We both chuckled seeing each other in a different light.

Each other is all we had out there; we certainly couldn't trust those people out in the village or in the fields. Many of them feared us and supported the enemy. They knew we had been hurt. I would see them differently from that day on.

Boats tensed up as Racing Danger One-two neared the village three miles east of Phouc Xuyen, where they had received fire the night before. He was certain that one of the rockets had originated from one of the small huts, and he prayed that someone would stick his head out so he could blow it off. His blood boiled trying to recall the order in which the events of the night before had occurred. But he knew in his heart it was not to be, as the locals hid from him, seeing the crippled boat with the three cammi-covered figures lying on top.

I slipped on my long-sleeve top and a floppy "boonie cap", trying to cover up my already sun-burned skin. Brown gave us a good meal to start the day off with and we were ready to head back. The wind picked up as the flapping of the Stars and Stripes could be heard behind us in the breeze.

The raw heroism from ordinary men who had stood at their post side-by-side, and the pride that Boats had in his shipmates went unnoticed, as the wounded Strike Assault Boat was towed past Advance Tactical Support Base Phouc Xuyen.

I jumped back on the Mike boat, lifted up the engine room door and climbed down the ladder to check the fluid levels. There was a grated cross-walk between the two three-foot-tall diesel engines to stand on as I made sure everything was good-to-go. I pulled a few cans of C-rats out of my pockets and placed them on the headers to warm up for lunch. After confirming the levels, I signaled to Steve and he fired the diesels up.

"Thanks, guys, for the beer and chow," I yelled out as we turned and throttled back down the canal.

"You're welcome. Ya'll come back now, ya hear," Brown answered as we pulled away from the small outpost. In the distance, approaching us from the rear was a STAB with men kneeling on top. A lone coxswain, sitting up front with six armed men, straddling the gunwale with one leg in and one out, perched as if they were ready to jump off at any minute. The low, sleek, silent, boat passed us, with its antennas tied down so they were undetectable off the bank, and then disappeared into the distance of the long narrow canal. Sampans with motors on poles, carrying bananas and fruit, zoomed by with ease on their way to the marketplace, making us aware ours was one of the slowest boats on the canal. We passed small hamlets, with only the river for transportation. Children gathered along the river bank, waving as we passed, disturbing the still water and flooding their dugout canoes with the wake of our waves.

The two STABs crept up on An Long Village as the locals looked on in silent reverence at the three cammi-wrapped figures. Boats body went limp as they left the canal and he felt the spray off the Mekong against his face. There would be a debriefing awaiting him, and hopefully sleep.

Appearing ahead, YRBM 21 was a welcome sight. After only two days we were ready for a shower and a hot meal. Coming toward us were two PBRs moving at high speed down the Mekong. There crews were sitting on top of the canopy, sunning themselves and waving as they passed. They were beautiful boats to watch as they bounced off the waves with their engines whining in perfect pitch. On the deck of YRBM 21, the winch operator was lifting a PBR out of the water with the boom. He set it down on the second level deck, where a repair team was waiting to work on the hull. As they released the cable, a CH-47 Chinook helicopter lifted off the flight deck. It was a wonder the pilots could land those big birds on that small deck. The naval aviators had become well adapted at landing on ships that were underway at sea. Even with poor visibility they were able to find their mark.

"Boy, those guys are good," I remarked, looking over to Steve. "Where did the Seawolves take off to?"

"They're probably on a run," he answered as he backed down the engines and threw them into reverse, slowing the Mike boat so that she slid gently into the dock. Bailey was there, watching, pleased with the smooth landing of the boat and the return of his crew.

"How'd it go?" he asked as he jumped aboard.

"Good. Chief Murphy fired up the generator last night,"

I answered bending over to tie up.

"Christopher, you're burned. You better get up to sickbay right away." We both looked at me, a red-haired, ruddy boy who had not been in the sun more than a few hours a day his whole life. After one month in Vietnam, I was beyond sunburned, I was pink. It was like a second-degree burn and I should be in bed recovering for the next couple of days.

Navy Chaplain Lieutenant Lester L. Westling Jr. was flown in and presented these stirring words in an unforgettable memorial service for Baker, Crabtree, and Johns on April 4, 1970.

"We are assembled to pay tribute to our comrades who gave their lives in the service of their country and of freedom. Words cannot describe what they have given to the United States of America and to our Navy. They answered the highest call and gave without hesitation. We are here to honor them and to thank God for having had their comradeship, and for the knowledge that they are in the good hands of our divine Master.

It is now our responsibility to redouble our efforts to carry on their tasks and our own in the highest professional manner in tribute to them, proving always that our mission will bring an end to suffering to all in a righteous peace.

These men are our comrades-our friends, a part of each of us has gone with them. They are American sailors who met the test."

Seaman Daniel P. Kurant wrote the following:

WAS A DASTARDLY NIGHT, REMINDED ME OF HOME, WHEN THE WIND PLAYED IN THE TREETOPS, SETTING THEN TO MOAN. THE LIGHTING WAS FLASHING, THE MOSQUITOES WERE PLENTY, THE NIGHT WAS A DARK ONE, AND THE STARLIGHT WAS SCANTY. THE FLASHES INCREASED, AND FLARES LIT THE NIGHT. THEN, SUDDENLY THE RAINS CAME AND THE MOSQUITOES DID NOT BITE. ALONG CAME THE MIDNIGHT, MOMENTS LATER, A RED FLARE, AND SOMETHING ABOUT ITS COLOR SPILLED DEATH IN THE AIR. I WENT TO THE FANTAIL, AS SEAMAN TOOK THE WATCH. NOTHING COULD BE HEARD, LEAST THE FALLING OF BIG DROPS, WHEN SUDDENLY I HEARD, IN A WHISPER FROM THE COCKPIT, "THERE'S A BOAT DOWN THE RIVER, ONE OF OURS, IT'S BEEN HIT!" WE CROWED THE RADIO WITH HEARTS POUNDING IN OUR CHEST. NOT A THING COULD BE HEARD, 'CEPT OUR LABORING FOR BREATH. THEN, A SPLIT SECOND LATER, CAME A VOICE ON THE LINE, "FOUR MEN WE HAVE HIT, ONE DEAD, TWO ARE DYING!" OUR EMOTIONS WENT WILD, CURSES MURMURED IN VAIN, WHEN WE FOUND OUT AT THAT TIME THAT OUR BUDDY WAS SLAIN. THEN "FLASH" ON THE RADIO, NOT ONE DEAD, BUT THREE. THE NAMES OF THESE MEN ARE BAKER, JOHNS, AND CRABTREE. A PRAYER FOR THE FAMILIES, EACH AND EVERYONE, ONE WIFE LOST A HUSBAND; THE OTHER PARENTS LOST THEIR

Ralph Christopher

SONS. WHEN THE SHOCK FINALLY EASED, WHAT STRUCK MOST TO ME WAS THE VOICE OVER THE RADIO SAYING BAKER, JOHNS, AND CRABTREE.

Dear Mom

Sorry it has been so long since I wrote but you know me. Actually I have been pretty busy but that is another story. I have a little information for you today. I am on the Mekong River which is the largest river in Vietnam. If you look on a map it is close to Cambodia between the cities of Tan Chow and Cau Doc, not far from the Grand Canal. That is where I spend a lot of my time. I just got back from a two day river ride and I got a lot of sun. The heat is pretty bad here, I'm pretty sore. The chow on the ship is good but we have to eat sea rats on the river. It is almost as good as dog food if you know what I mean. I have made many new friends one of them being a boy I work with from West Virginia. He is a country boy but a good guy. He said he would be back home for good in about fifty days. Boy I wish I could trade with him.

I put 360.00 dollars in my savings and made an allotment for 20.00 a month to go to you for Jo Ann and Phillip. That leaves me 30.00 dollars a month. I'm going to get my car if it kills me. One month in country today about 300 days left to go. Two Movie Stars came aboard last night and I talked to them for a while. One was a man whose name I can't remember but his face was very familiar. I think he works with Carol Burnett. The woman's name was Susan Oliver.

I am sending you pictures of me and the boats I ride now. Well I'll write more later so all of you take care of yourself and I'll see you soon.

Love Chris,

P.S. I'm trying to grow a mustache.

**Annapolis Hotel, a component of Naval Support Activity
Saigon, Cholon district, Saigon, early 1970**

YRBM 21, Task Force 116, Mekong River, Cambodian border, early 1970

YRBM 21 Crashcrew, "Ready and Able", Robert Fallows rear, Dwight Cabella front, Seawolf gunship, 21's flight deck

Engineman Odie Colon setting the rack on a 6V53 engine

Engine combustion mechanics on YRBM 21, L to R, Staercke,
Rick, Ralph, Walzak and Church, Tango boat in background

Mike boat towing ammi of lumber down the Grand Canal,
An Long village in background, Chief Murphy on left, then
Ellsworth, unknown sailor and Cabella, Ralph on helm

A water cannon "Douche" boat

Strike Assault Boat-STABRON 20

Swift boat leaving 21 for border patrol, Last Chance Saloon

River Division 592 at Ben Luc, relaxing on their PBRs

Seawolf attack gunship, HAL-3

Ralph "Chris"Christopher, Mike boat engine compartment

CHAPTER EIGHT - CAMBODIA

It had been raining lightly on and off on an overcast cloudy April afternoon when the first river division appeared on the horizon. March had come in like a lion but not gone out like a lamb. There was a build-up of boat units and sailors around the repair barges. The USS Benewah had been pulled off station for repairs as hotel services at An Long had been turned over to YRBM 21 and her personnel. USS Satyr (ARL 23), YRBM 16 and YRBM 20 were positioned on the upper Bassac River, also supporting Border Interdiction Operations. There were long lines for the mess deck and showers, with all the racks filled with bright shiny new faces. The boat repair docks were busy with engineers performing maintenance repairs as the boats stacked up around the refueling barge. The various river division members were eye-to-eye as they anticipated something big was about to happen. Scuttlebutt had it that there was going to be a big push into Cambodia, for it was a "New Day" for the administration. Sailors were pumped up with adrenaline and were preparing to go up the rivers that had once been forbidden for them to enter. The Peoples Army had been training and supplying the Cambodian Khmer Rouge rebels and building up ammunition piles along the border. They had pushed into the central regions of Cambodia and were extending their control of the countryside and encircling Cambodia's capital city, Phnom Penh. Prince Norodom Sihanouk had ruled since the departure of the French in the fifties. His government's accommodation policy toward the Viet Communists had fallen to his pro-American Prime Minister, General Lon Nol, who, with the backing of the Cambodian military, had taken power while Prince Sihanouk was away visiting Russia.

It was a new ball game for President Nixon, as he had lifted the embargo on bombing North Vietnam, Cambodia and Laos. The U.S. accelerated turnover plan of Vietnamization had cut U.S. naval forces by twenty-five percent, turning over our war machines and duties to the South Vietnamese military as U.S. forces withdrew and returned home.

But first, there was to be one more big push into the enemy's sanctuaries in the jungles across the Cambodian border. At the Parrot's Beak area of Cambodia, there were Communist sanctuaries that were only fifty miles from the South Vietnamese capital city of Saigon.

A mass slaughter was going on as ethnic South Vietnamese refugees who had been living in Cambodia were being rounded up and retained or killed as they fled for their lives from the newly-powered Cambodian Army. American river divisions on watch on Operations Barrier Reef and Slingshot would be some of the most active for the brown water navy, as North Vietnamese soldiers were spotted leaving Vietnam for Cambodia and what was beginning to be called an Indochina war.

Ten river patrol boats came streaking across the water with the sun over their shoulders, approaching from the Mekong crossover leading west to the Bassac River and South China Sea. Later that day, we spotted six minesweeping boats (MSB), racing each other around the VC controlled island to the south. The next day, out of the French Canal and onto the Mekong River to the north at the city of Tan Chau, came three U.S. Swift boats of the Coastal Surveillance Force that had been transferred to SEALORDS for river warfare. Their grey sleek aluminum hulls cut a pretty picture as they sped toward us through the water. They had made the long trip from support base Ha Tien on the Sea of Thailand by way of the Vinh Te Canal, and would spend the bulk of their time setting a naval blockade along the border. The STAB boats towed over their own maintenance facility from the Benewah and secured it along the stern of YRBM 21, with several other pontoons to provide space for additional sailors and boats. YRBM 21 personnel began assisting the STAB crews in repairs.

The assorted river divisions displayed their homemade brightly-colored division patches on their right arm proudly as they explored YRBM 21 and filled the mess deck looking for chow. Their shoulder patches were made up of designs of dragons, flags, boats and demons. In the colors of red, yellow, blue and black with slogans like River Division 531, DELTA DRAGONS. River Division 592, SAT CONG (Kill Communist). River Division 593, IRON BUTTERFY, who also were known to have played the sixties song In-A-Gadda-Da-Vida, performed by the rock group that shared their name. It was quite a gathering of sailors, as many of them were old salts and shipmates from bygone eras, and then there were many that weren't. The officers and senior enlisted had their work cut-out for them as they tried to maintain discipline with the youngsters.

One boat unit's sailors entered the mess deck clean-shaving, in neatly-pressed green uniforms with bloused pants over spit shine jungle boots, displaying sharply worn Black Berets. Another boat unit's troops entered in Vietnamese tiger-stripe uniforms, wearing shower flip-flops, looking as if they had just returned from a month in the U-Minh Forest without shaving or cutting their hair. The STAB crew members were sitting alongside the Swift boat sailors, who were sitting across from the PBR crews, who in turn were sitting next to the minesweeper crewmen. They all were staring across the mess deck at the Vietnamese boat groups, who were glaring back. The 21's crew tried to stand to the side and stay out of the way, but there were just too many men in too small of a space, and that usually meant trouble. The different boat divisions were all fiercely proud of their respective units and were very competitive. None of them liked to take any guff, and deservedly so. Although all the senior sailors were friendly and well-mannered, some of the younger sailors had strong egos and were cocky to the point of being abrasive. That night, at the Last Chance Saloon, fights began to break out between a few crew members, as the beer mixed with the adrenaline flow of the moment.

"BOATS OF GLASS, BALLS OF BRASS, BLACK BERETS FOREVER," they sang until fists began flying. Men were then separated and escorted out to the docks and warned what their attitudes might lead to. Small pockets of boys circled portable tape decks off in the hidden corners of the barges, listening to the music being played back home in the world, as the smell of marijuana lingered in the air.

"And it's one, two, three, what are we fighting for? Don't ask me, I don't give a damn, the next stop is Vietnam. And it's five, six, seven, open up your pearly gates. Well...there ain't no time, to wonder why, Whoopee... we're all going to die."

The next day two young men came aboard dressed in slacks and white shirts. I thought maybe they were lost until one of the crew told me they were on a mission. At first I was puzzled because they didn't look military. Then they opened their briefcases producing twelve-inch gold bibles. The three-inch-thick King James Bible was loaded with beautiful colored pictures and a place for my family register and military record. I knew my mother would love it, so I signed a chit allowing them to withdraw one hundred dollars from my pay and had it shipped directly to my mother's house. I couldn't get over the fact that the young men from the Church of Christ had traveled halfway around the world to the Cambodian border as I lectured them.

"What are you guys doing here; do you know where you're at?"

I found a leaflet on the pier written in Vietnamese, saying "Chieu Hoi." I asked one of the patrolmen what it meant and he explained it was part of the "Open Arms" program. He said that in the early days, the Viet Cong warned the civilians that PBR sailors would butcher and eat their children, rape their women, and steal their goods. For a while it worked, as the people ran at the sight of approaching patrol boats. The Americans began their own propaganda program by rebuilding structures, digging wells, and treating the sick and wounded. Also by dispensing soap, fishing gear, and school supplies. They did this with loudspeaker programs and distributing leaflets to the Viet Cong promising amnesty and to feed and pay them if they surrendered or Chieu Hoi. It worked so well that in several instances, victims of Viet Cong tax collectors came to the PBRs and guided the patrolmen to the enemy.

"Oh, I see," said the blind man.

The USO Organization sent in a magician from the States to entertain us one night who did a few magic tricks and then hypnotized some of the guys. I'm not sure if he really hypnotized them or if they just played along, but we all drank a few beers and had some laughs.

On March 31, 1970, River Divisions 512, 514 and 592 turned over their PBRs to newly formed Vietnamese River Patrol Groups 54 and 56 and stood down, which was all part of the accelerated turnover program of President Nixon's "New Day." Although the Vietnamese navy had been fighting since 1954, when they took over from the French, they had always been on the losing side until the American river divisions had come aboard in 1966. They were now to begin assuming all river duties as the American river divisions were to turn over their boats and withdraw, leaving advisors behind to support and supervise the freshly graduated Vietnamese brown water navy that had been organized and trained by Vice Admiral Zumwalt. In Zumwalt's own words, recorded in the Navys' *Jackstaff News*, February 11, 1970:

"As we enter the second year of Vietnamization, I would like to review for you the reason behind our accelerated turnover program. This is especially appropriate now that so many new officers and men have joined us in-country. In late 1968, we conceived a plan which would turn over first most of our small combatant craft, and next some blue-water ships, and finally our logistics support responsibilities. We first tripled the in-country Vietnamese navy schools through new construction by December 1969. We commenced recruiting for a doubling of personnel strength from the late -1968 level. We also got a head start on the changing of turnover crews, and were able to turn over twenty-five of our armored river assault craft on 1 February 1969. As the craft turnover program got completely up to speed during the spring, we began refining plans for the Vietnamese Navy Logistic Support Command. In July 1969, we commenced accelerated turnover logistics training for base and craft maintenance personnel. We also commissioned Ben Luc, a co-manned base with two-thirds U.S. navy and one-third Vietnamese navy personnel. At the same time, we looked forward to the day when the Vietnamese navy would take over control of the Barrier Reef Operations. Vietnamese Navy Assault Divisions 70 and 71 were given their own tactical areas of responsibility in Giant Slingshot, and the first of our combined commands was formed on that barrier. We began stressing the development of combined command and control relationships.

"At the start of the year, we shifted our emphasis to logistic support in addition to combat craft turnover. We are searching for additional sites to conduct on-the-job training and maintenance skills and areas, working toward completion of all on-the-job training as early as possible so that we can then employ those maintenance skills."

"Looking ahead, I see the following areas of emphasis in 1970. First, a tremendous effort to train the Vietnamese navy in craft and base maintenance skills. Second, the combining of our operations and bases and the takeover of certain operations and some logistic support by the Vietnamese navy. Third, an even greater emphasis on dependant shelters, food source programs, and rehabilitation of disabled veterans. Forth, a continuing program to strengthen the Vietnamese navy. And finally, the implementation of a program to strengthen 'middle management.'

"Although the Vietnamese navy was able to double in size in one year, it could not produce qualified officers and petty officers at a proportional rate. We have already begun a program to train seven hundred and fifty Vietnamese navy officer candidates at our Officers Candidate School in Newport, Rhode Island. The first Vietnamese navy class will commence in early March. The Vietnamese navy will also utilize the Army of the Republic of Vietnam Officers Candidate School to turn out about one thousand officers during 1970. As another solution, we are co-manning all repair and support bases upon commissioning. As the Vietnamese sailors gain the necessary expertise, we will phase down the U.S. Navy personnel."

Vice Admiral Elmo R. Zumwalt Jr.

The problems of Vietnamization started to affect us soon after the boats began turning over. YRBM 21 was still assigned PBR repair, but was not seeing the Vietnamese patrol boats on a routine basis. The boats that were now under Vietnamese command and without American-trained engineers onboard began to deteriorate. Our repair teams kept busy servicing the many American divisions, but the Viet boat crews were neglecting their service practices and we knew it eventually would catch up to us.

On one occasion, two Vietnamese boat crews were racing on the Grand Canal, which was dangerous during dry season due to the low water level and the draft of the boats. They were trying to imitate the American boat crews that would run up next to the bank for deeper pockets of water to reach higher speeds. They misjudged the water level and jackknifed, flipping on their sides, blocking the canal just past An Long Village. The Americans showed up to pull the wrecked boats off the mud dune with both Vietnamese PBRs suffering hull damage. They had to be towed to YRBM 21. Many said they did it intentionally to keep from going out on ambush. It just didn't seem that the Vietnamese were motivated. This meant that American crews had to give up their day off and go back out. Later that week, another Vietnamese crew pulled the plug on their PBR, half-sinking it while tied to the pier. Also a Vietnamese patrol boat experienced a bilge fire and a Vietnamese crew member was killed, again not-combat-related. This caused much discontent with YRBM 21 personnel and the American divisions who were all fiercely protective of the little boats and the job they had performed. There was a feeling that the Vietnamese navy wasn't going to be able to complete the job that the Americans had started and maintained at a high price over the years.

One evening, twenty minutes before movie call, a disgruntled Vietnamese sailor stormed the mess deck, yelling "grenade in hand" as he held a grenade over his head. Sailors who were scattered around the mess deck stopped and looked up, wondering what the man was upset about. Again he shouted "grenade in hand" as men started fleeing the mess deck out of the side door. Two American sailors circled YRBM 21 and came in behind the Vietnamese sailor without being noticed as he repeated for a third time "grenade in hand."

By this time, only three or four sailors were left with my buddy Sleepy playing cards as the Vietnamese sailor walked to within three or four feet of their table before the two undetected men jumped him from behind. Suddenly the men at the table jumped in as hands restrained arms and legs while they wrestled the man to the deck. They were successful in prying the grenade away as they noticed the pin missing and one of the crew members yelled out, "live grenade" as a warning to the rest of the personnel. The Vietnamese sailor was then wrestled out the hatch and thrown into the Mekong River. Later, he was recovered and turned over to Tieu Ta Sy, the Vietnamese lieutenant commander in charge of operations, who assured Mr. Fry that the sailor would be disciplined. For punishment, Tieu Ta Sy made the man take off his boots and stomped on his feet till they bled. Afterwards, he had the man chained to the focsle and left him there for three days without food or water with a sign hanging around his neck that read, I am a coward.

Warrant Officer Backus witnessed a Vietnamese PBR towing out another Viet PBR with a towline with the forward fiberglass deck coming loose from the bow and both engines inoperative. Later Backus was approached by Tieu Ta Da, the Vietnamese lieutenant commander in charge of all Vietnamese units, who asked him why his boats were having so many problems and not being serviced. Backus informed him that he had not seen one work request, and without one was powerless to do a thing. Tieu Ta Da promptly replaced the river patrol group's officer-in-charge with Dai Qui Bah, a young Viet lieutenant, who returned the PBRs to a system of routine maintenance performed by American engineers, and the boats returned to top running condition.

Most of the South Vietnamese sailors were trained well and the advisors worked with what they had. They weren't the best, but they did their best. You have to remember that many of the young American snipes knew how to tear down V-8 engines in their teens. The Vietnamese were used to being behind a water buffalo, plowing rice fields. They really didn't care about their government; it was what they had to live with to have their freedom. Some were highly cultured and liked light opera and plays. They also got leave/vacation to go home. It was their war and we were helping them fight for their country. They had their superstitions and their own family values and some were very nice and some were terrible when it came to the enemy. A few were corrupt, stealing from the indigenous people and their American counterparts, and this caused anger and distrust.

The French navy left the Vietnamese navy fourteen ships, six River Assault Groups, called Dinassaults, and a small core unit of well-trained Vietnamese naval officers. In 1955, U.S. Naval advisors were assigned to assist in the development of the Vietnamese navy. This effort expanded as the Viet Cong insurgency expanded.

In 1956, the Viet Cong embarked on a full-scale insurgency. To counter the infiltration of arms and men from the north, the South Vietnamese navy re-established the sea anti-infiltration force concept used by the French. By 1959, the Vietnamese navy had a force of twenty-three ships, the largest of which were landings ships, also one-hundred ninety-seven boats with personnel strength at five thousand men. The years 1962 to 1964 were marked by a rapid expansion of the Vietnamese navy. Training facilities, repair bases, and logistics support activities were established; communications equipment and networks were improved; and organizational and administration procedures were strengthened. The number of ships increased to forty-four and the personnel strength to eight-thousand men. By 1969, the number of Vietnamese navy men reached twenty-six-thousand and ships, and boats and junks numbered more than one-thousand. The Vietnamese navy headquarters was adjacent to the Saigon River in downtown Saigon and housed the staff of Commodore Tra-Van-Chon, Chief of Naval Operations. The Vietnamese navy shipyard was the largest industrial complex in the Republic of Vietnam. It was located along the Saigon River also, a mile from the heart of the city. It was the largest shipyard between Hong Kong and Bangkok and covered sixty-six acres.

In 1964, the Vietnamese navy was assigned responsibility for the Rung Sat Special Zone. The assignment was prompted by the fact that the entire length of the strategically important Long Tau River, the major deepwater shipping channel between Saigon and the South China Sea, lay within the Rung Sat Special Zone. The shipping channel wound forty-five miles from Vung Tau anchorage to Saigon. It traveled four rivers - Nga Bay, the Saigon, the Long

Tau and the Nha Be - consisting of about thirty-six-hundred miles of small waterways. The Rung Sat Special Zone was located ten miles southeast of Saigon. A dense, humid mangrove swamp covered eighty-five percent of it; roads were virtually non-existent and the sampan was the major mode of transportation. There were approximately nineteen thousand inhabitants, with no U.S. troops stationed in the swampy countryside from which the Viet Cong launched devastating attacks on shipping. The Vietnamese navy, aided by U.S. marine advisors, river boats and aircraft, waged a tough running battle with the Viet Cong for control of the area.

Beginning in 1966, more than a century after being away from river operations, the U.S. navy started building up a river fleet to combat the Rung Sat assassins. In the early part of the river war, a patrol on the Long Tau was pretty much guaranteed to get shot at; by 1970 it was rare. This didn't mean fighting wasn't going on, only that we were winning. Many Americans were unaware of how well things had been going or the progress being made. By November 1968, the U.S. navy began making plans to turn operations over to the South Vietnamese. In early 1969, the Vietnamese had taken over the first large patrol craft, and by February 1970, the South Vietnamese and Americans were engaged in joint operations, with Vietnamese boats flying the Viet red-and-yellow flag and American boats flying the Stars and Stripes. By April 1970, more then half of the five-hundred boats in the river force had been turned over to the Vietnamese. Their crews consisted of boys around eighteen to nineteen, working under officers around twenty-two to twenty-five. The Vietnamese sailors weren't as aggressive as the Americans. Americans went over for a year, so they had the energy to be aggressive for a short time. The Vietnamese had been living in war since they were born. They had a good nucleus of leadership, and as far as operating the boats and fighting were concerned, they could handle the job. As far as supply and logistics were concerned, Americans would have to stay on for some time, although the progress of turning over the backup facilities was well underway. The base at Ben Luc, the number one support base for all river activities, had co-commanders, an American and a Vietnamese.

Many different river divisions served in the Rung Sat with the South Vietnamese. One such unit was River Division 593, the "Iron Butterfly". They were easily recognized by their yellow-and-black shoulder patches. They were a combat unit in which heroic action was the rule, not the exception. As with many such units, individuals stood out. Names such as Davy, Staples, Larson, Flecher, Morgan, Beachy, Madden, Swain and White were a few of the many who distinguished themselves. Another was Chief Signalman Bob Monzingo of Fort Worth Texas. Not long after 593 was formed, he and his shipmates killed five enemy soldiers in a fire-fight on Long Tau River. The treacherous Rung Sat was 593's official home, and where the division killed more then forty elusive enemy residents. Other 593 campaigns included Operation Giant Slingshot, in which 593 sailors counted ninety-five fire-fights and killed more then seventy Viet Cong in the process. Also, twenty large enemy caches were uncovered. But River Division 593 will always be remembered for their relentless campaign against the enemy along the upper Saigon River, where they accounted for almost two hundred Communists dead.

As with all in-country navy men, the sailors of 593 were planning ahead for the day when their assets, nine battle-proven PBRs, would be turned over to the Vietnamese navy. Iron Butterfly sailors had already trained more than eighty Vietnamese navy men since they received their first class of eleven seamen in March 1969, and at most times had more than twenty serving onboard with the division. The Vietnamese sailors ate, slept, worked and fought alongside their American counterparts, sharing the victories and hardships of men in war, while proudly wearing the famous "Iron Butterfly" shoulder patch. Soon it would be up to them.

Daily duties went on like clockwork as river divisions prepared for what was still only a rumor - a governmental change-of-hands in Cambodia to a pro-American leader who was fighting the Communists. Boats were stacked up around YRBM 21 as the enemy on VC Island began taking notice. This could no longer be called a surprise invasion if it was to happen at all. News was hard to get on the border and they didn't say much of anything on armed forces radio. Sometimes I would learn more about what was going on in letters sent from back home, but they would be a week or so behind.

On a gray, dreary morning, while taking a boatload of 105 howitzer shells up to the Special Forces base at Thuong Thoi, we were surprised to see swollen bodies floating downstream from Cambodia. The sight of those poor people was frightening, with children chained to the adults. What the hell was going on, we wondered. That night, Boatswain Mate Chief Bob Cook on patrol at the border, said he could hear screams coming from the village just inside Cambodia. Scuttlebutt had it that a massacre was taking place. For days after, bodies and animal carcasses came floating by, drifting into the bushes. It was becoming a health hazard, as we drank and showered from the river. A body became hung-up in the ropes between the barges, so "Sleepy" and a few of the guys went down and pulled it out. There was fear that it might have been booby-trapped as they gently laid him in a body bag and zipped it up. Many of the boat units had been ordered to sink the bodies for protective reasons. I don't know what they killed them with, but it left a hole the size of a silver dollar in their backs. That night we all said a special prayer. The smell and sight of their mutilated bodies stayed with me for years.

Still we waited for word from Washington as the whole world watched our little corner of the world without most of us even knowing that they were. The war had spread to Laos and Cambodia, with China and Russia sending in advisers and weapons. American B-52 bombers were flying out of Thailand, Guam and Vietnam to carpet-bomb the Ho Chi Minh Trail along the Cambodian and Laotian borders. Kissinger proclaimed the time was right to clean them out of their sanctuaries, with Cambodia building an army to combat the Viet Cong and drive them out of their country. A battle plan was drawn up by Admiral John D. McCain, Jr., for the attack on Parrot's Beak and Fishhook, believed to be the command center for the Communist war in the south.

The men were becoming impatient as they joked about the incursion and nicknamed it "Nixon's Invasion." No one seem to know what was going on as the South Vietnamese and Americans stood purged to pounce on Cambodia on a moment's notice. We watched as the Communists seized the border town of Snuol, Cambodia, twenty miles from the tip of the Fishhook. Still, the refugees up-river suffered and the bodies continued floating across as we stood by helpless. But not the SEALs. They would say they were having fun, along with other advance scouts who were probing into Cambodia. Rear Admiral H.S. Matthews Jr., Deputy Commander U.S. Naval Forces Vietnam sent his personal Intel Officer and Public Affairs Officer down in an army helicopter to explore and survey the area. Lieutenant Alan P. DeRoco, Commanding Officer of River Division 593, went along to eye ball the feeder canals and small tributaries flowing into the Mekong River near the areas into which he would soon be leading the Iron Butterfly boats. The radio relayed a message that an element of Vietnamese had captured documents, and the Intel Officer directed the pilot to proceed to the location and pick them up. Since he was senior, the pilot concurred and flew deeper into enemy-held territory.

Suddenly, they took ground fire, as smoke trailed out of the engine. "Mayday, mayday, we're going down." The pilot fought for control and attempted to auto-rotate the helo down to a dry rice paddy. Everyone braced for a collision as the bird's nose pulled up hard and the struts hit the paddy dike. They had escaped the crash, but the tail rotor hit the ground, snapping the tail blades, shaking and vibrating the bird like a "chicken with its head cut off." Some yelled "Get Out!" while others yelled "Stay In!" The large center blade whipped through the air above their heads as men went both directions. Eventfully, the engine and blades stopped turning, and it became deadly quiet while they sat listening for the movement of enemy soldiers. Suddenly, a grizzly old marine advisor with a group of Vietnamese Ruff Puffs (Popular Forces) popped out of the jungle tree line and approached, offering additional firepower against whatever was to come their way. Since most of the naval officers had only their pistols, they were never so glad to see the marines. The marine informed the party that they had been observing small bands of Communists operating throughout the area. The army had picked up the co-pilot's distress call, and soon a second helo set down to shuttle the men to safety as the marine and his Ruff Puffs disappeared back into the jungle. Later, a CH-54 sky crane helicopter was sent in to recover the crippled bird.

Lieutenant DeRoco got an ass-chewing administered by Rear Admiral Matthews when he returned for having taken the public affairs officer along. In turn, DeRoco went looking for the intel officer who had disappeared and was nowhere to be found. Soon, the whole incident was buried and Lieutenant DeRoco was neck-deep in plans for the final invasion as everyone forgot about the incident and went back to preparing for the big day.

Then it came. Nixon authorized the South Vietnamese invasion of the Parrot's Beak area. Two thousand ARVN troops hit the enemy's sanctuaries, killing one-hundred forty-four of the Communist as the battle of Prey Veng pitted Cambodian and South Vietnamese soldiers with American air support against an entrenched Communist force. The American ground forces were not to be used, as it was to be a South Vietnamese victory to build up their confidence in the Vietnamization program, allowing them to take control of the war.

Three pristine Cambodian gunboats crossed the border and came alongside YRBM 21 as we invited them on to the mess deck and exchanged military souvenirs. It was difficult to communicate with them since only one of them spoke a little English, and we spoke none of their ancient language of Khmer. Luckily, the Cambodians spoke French as a second language, so Ralph and the other Viet trainees translated for us. After a couple of hours, the officers came down from the wardroom and there was no doubt we would be working together, as the Cambodian crews went back for third helpings.

Monsoon had arrived and the rains were beginning to pour. If you worked outside, you got wet. Then the sun would come out, drying you off naturally. An hour later, it rained again and you went back to soggy. From then on you never really got dry. You just caught a cold and got sick and were expected to continue working away in the rain. "Somebody pass me the soap, please."

On a drizzly April afternoon, the tugboat USS Winnemucca appeared, approaching us from the lower Mekong and towing a pontoon full of lumber and corrugated steel. She pulled alongside aft as we secured the pontoon of building materials and prepared a

Mike-6 to take another trip down the canal to support base Phouc Xuyen.

The next morning, Bailey pulled Cabella and me aside and told us to take charge of the trip back down the Grand Canal. This time we would be towing the materials needed to finish the building of the base. The pontoon was going to find it a little tight going down the canal. Especially the entrance and passing under the bridge. If we weren't careful, we could run aground or beach in the mud, leaving ourselves vulnerable. Bailey ordered more armed sailors to ride along and informed us we would have Chief Murphy onboard and an Alpha boat for escort. We packed up and pushed off, with yours truly at the helm. Cabella didn't want the responsibility of making a mistake and insisted that I had become a better helmsman. I didn't believe him, but I wasn't worried about making a mistake. Besides, what were they going to do, send me to Vietnam?

I swung wide and came up on the entrance of the canal from downstream so I could control the weight of the massive amount of material on the pontoon against the current of the Mekong River. With one wrong turn I would wipe out the junks inside the mouth of the canal, leaving the families who lived on them homeless and upsetting the village.

The lumber was precut; all that had to be done was assemble it. This was about the thirtieth navy support base to be built, so they pretty much had it down. Most likely it was a disassembled base that was no longer needed, so the Seabees tore it down and sent it to us. Some of the lumber was the size of railroad ties, and other cuts were two-by-twelve planks or two-by-fours. Most of it had been treated with a brown sticky resin like telephone poles, so painting was not necessary. The steel was bundled together in four-by-twelve-foot cuts and had teeth on the sides, ready to assemble into a helo pad like a puzzle. On the aft of the long pontoon were two small utility boats with outboard motors so the support sailors could have their own transportation for getting out.

We squeezed under the small bicycle bridge, leaving a couple of feet to spare. Hitting it could have brought the whole thing down on us, causing a tremendous uproar in An Long. After pulling out into the open canal, I turned the wheel over to Cabella and crossed over the ropes onto the pontoon, checking to see that all was secured. Approaching us from behind was the Alpha boat, cutting well over ten knots.

"I thought she was assigned to escort us," I said as she skimmed past us, spraying us with water, while one of her crew members on the fantail dropped his trousers.

The fifty-foot attack support, or Alpha boat as she was called on the rivers, had many functions in river warfare. She often was used in spearheading infantry assaults on bunkers along the beaches, as well as in towing chain drags for minesweeping on the smaller canals. She stood night guard-post and performed daytime patrols and special operation duties alongside the Monitors. She was a pretty lady moving in the water with her pointed steel bow and long slender body. Except for the cannons and machine guns, she looked a little like an old river keel boat with one long, concealed cabin to protect her crew and the various assault troops she discharged in battle. Of the heavy boats, she was the quickest and always a welcome sight, even if the crew were showing their asses.

It was a long slow tow and we ran aground only once. I jumped off on the beach and pushed the pontoon free, pulling myself back aboard with a rope covered in mud.

"Chris, get your butt over here and cut that shit out," Cabella scolded for my taking stupid chances.

Looking back, it wasn't very smart. That's probably why they liked me so much. Vietnam was not for the faint of heart. I waved to our friends in the little mud-and-straw fort. Two of the child warriors had bagged a twelve-foot Komodo dragon, a distant relative to prehistoric dinosaurs, and were carrying its carcass into the compound hanging from a pole. We took turns sitting on the ropes running from the boat to the barge, with our legs dangling in the canal. There were several Chieu Hoi leaflets in the water that had been dropped by the Psy Ops planes. The spray of the water off the boat was the only relief from the hot sun glaring down on us.

We arrived at noon, just in time to stop in to see Brown working on the mess deck as Chief Murphy joined him. There was lots of white bread sandwiches stacked four or five high on one of the tables, with cans of C-rations scattered in a box.

"Hey Brown!"

"Sure good to see you boys," Brown said as he waved back.

Looking around, I could see that the Seabees were coming along well on the construction. They would pretty much be able to complete the job with the additional materials we had towed in. The young sailors of the base were working with the Seabees, performing the manual labor, while they sweated in the light rain.

I grabbed a sandwich and wolfed it down while scrounging through the open case of C-rats to see if anything good was left. All of a sudden, we heard the sound of small air boats racing through the tall elephant grass. Sounded to me like a pack of angry giant bumble bees. Ten small swamp boats jumped out of the tall bamboo one by one onto the canal and sped toward us. There was a driver sitting on the aft of the boat with two long throttles, one in each hand, with a large caged fan pushing the boat from behind. On the front was a single pole-mounted .30 cal, machine gun with a gunner standing in the open. There was no protection for either man.

The strangely-dressed men tied-up alongside of the support base and walked onto the mess deck accompanied by Australian and U.S. Army advisors. A few of them had cut off the enemy's ears and wore them around their necks. The two advisors explained to Chief Murphy and Brown that their unit was made up of Chinese Nung mercenaries working out of Ap Bac. They patrolled the Plain of Reeds and hated the Communists. Some said the mercenaries were paid by the local province chief for each ear they produced. Others said the Viet Cong believed they couldn't get to heaven if they couldn't hear Buddha, and the sight of the ears put the fear of God into them. Whatever the case, they scared the crap out of me and I wanted nothing to do with them. Brown, on the other hand, extended his southern hospitality to all as he invited them to sandwiches and coffee. The little pack of men wiped out the sandwiches and Brown started slicing and spreading to make more. The advisors grabbed a cup of coffee and sat down to chew the fat as they thanked the Chief and Brown.

"Thanks for the cup of joe, mate."

"Ya'll are more than welcome." Brown's smile lit up the room.

I turned to watch the harmony between the Chinese Mike Force, who had crowded around the table until they were almost sitting in each other's laps. Damn this is a strange war I thought, as the airboat men devoured the food as if it were a feast.

Cabella and I decided to cut the pontoon free and speed back down the canal to try to make it back to the 21 before nightfall. We thought that with an empty boat it should be no problem. Brown gave me a box that said SP Pack on top to take along. We gathered the crew and waved goodbye as we pushed off and went to full-speed with the engines performing splendidly.

Charlie C and I thought it might be a good time for a little siesta, so we stripped down to our underwear and lay down on a couple of old mattresses we'd found down below in the hole. I opened the SP box to find all kinds of goodies. There were little Marlboro boxes with five cigarettes to a pack. Chocolate candy bars, razor blades, needle and thread, long-range patrol packets of dried food. Everything but socks and underwear and mine were almost gone. Charlie C cut on AFVN on his am/fm radio and we went to work on our tans in preparation for when we would get back to the world and meet "round-eyed" women.

"Good afternoon. This is Army Specialist Jackson Q. Crawford with checkpoint news.

Five North Vietnamese Regulars, part of a enemy force that fired on Fourth Division helicopters Wednesday afternoon, were killed when gun-ships and scout ships opened up on the area.

Warrant Officer Jack R. Morris of Granite City, Illinois, was conducting visual reconnaissance with Troop D, First Squadron, Tenth Cavalry, seventeen miles northeast of Pleiku when three enemy soldiers from the rocky area below fired on the aerial scouts. The cavalry's gun-ships rolled in, expending rocket and mini-gun fire killing three NVA.

Later in the afternoon, a half-mile northwest, First Lieutenant Jerry P. Escher of Davenport, Iowa, led gun-ships against an unknown-size enemy force expending ground-to-air fire. Gunships rolled in, killing two more NVA.

A Fourth Division ranger team killed two more enemy soldiers nineteen miles southeast of Pleiku.

Wednesday afternoon, the Rangers came in contact with an estimated North Vietnamese squad approximately fifty yards from their position. Gunships were called on station, expending in the area. The team was extracted and a reconnaissance of the area turned up the bodies of two NVA.

Another division ranger team found the body of a dead NVA, estimated to have been dead for six month, fifteen miles west of An Kay. They also found an AK- 47 rifle, three clips and a canteen.

Fourth Division infantrymen uncovered an enemy arms cache twenty miles southwest of An Kay shortly after noon Wednesday. First Brigade infantrymen and airmen flying in support of First Brigade operations discovered a large enemy hut, bunker, and cave complex Wednesday in VC Valley, twenty miles southwest of An Kay. Night observation helicopters and Cobra gun-ships of Troop A, 7 Squadron, 17 Cav made the initial sighting while conducting bomb damage assessment from B52 bombings Tuesday. The units moved into the area and found fifty bunkers in the side of a rocky ravine, plus four hooches and several small caves. Infantrymen recovered two SKS rifles, an AK-47 rifle with 300 rounds of ammo, twenty enemy uniforms, a fifty-pound rice cache and two compasses. Enemy complex estimated recently used by a squad-size enemy force.

This is Army Specialist Jackson Q. Crawford, and this is checkpoint news.

The Disc jockey slipped on the long version of Creedence Clearwater's hit, "Suzie Q," I thought it odd that the announcer had not mentioned one American casualty in his report.

"Damn, we're picking up Pleiku in the central highlands," I commented to Charlie C as the realization came over me.

In the middle of nowhere, I felt the sandwich and coffee passing through me as I grabbed a roll of toilet paper and headed back to the fantail of the boat to take care of business. No one was around at the time so I grabbed hold of a rope secured to the aft horn and hung my butt off the boat with my shorts around my ankles. It was a little awkward and took a little longer than I had planned, as we passed a small hamlet with a group of kids laughing and waving at me. It was a bit humbling, but what could I do. I laughed and waved back while wiping my butt as the spray from the churning water douched me off.

Three quarters of the way back down the canal the sun started to set and it became chilly. All of a sudden, it started sleeting golf-ball-size drops of ice as we ran for the cover of the coxswain's roof. The sleet stung as it hit me on my back and made a loud percussive sound bouncing off the deck and rolling over the side. Then it stopped suddenly as it had begun. We were actually able to gather it in our hands and pitch it at each other as I slipped on the icy deck, almost busting my ass. I believe it dropped into the fifties, which seemed freezing to me as I shivered and wrapped myself in a cammi poncho liner. I looked up to observe the orange glowing ball of the sun, burn its way into the horizon of the Mekong Delta off in the distance. Soon it would be night, and night belonged to Charlie. We turned the boat starboard out of the canal as another body floating down the Mekong River bounced alongside, bringing us back to the reality of the time and place in which we were living.

Dear Rachel,

Hear I am again tired and homesick as usual. I hope you are in a little better mood. Seems like I have been gone a long time and have such a long time to go. I have been sick for the last few days. Only thing about being sick in the Navy is you have to have a temperature of 101 before they will let you go to bed. Mind wasn't that high.

I have been working pretty hard lately but not to dangerous. They had a party the other night. When it just got rolling the fights started, I stayed out of them. We got a new Captain and he seems like a cool guy. He is pretty young.

We had a hypnotist come aboard that was pretty good. He did a few magical tricks and hypnotized a few people. It takes your mind off everything in a way.

They had three boats run aground since we turned the boats over to the Vietnamese. They don't take care of anything. They had one boat catch fire and a VN sailor was killed.

I bought myself another tape for my tape recorder. It helps to listen to a little music now and then. You told me in your letter I had received another Bond. How many do I have now? What do you figure the total amount comes to?

I received a letter from Crystal and Sherri and I finely got one from Bruce Shorter also. It is pretty good to here from all of them. Everybody is either talking about where they are going on R and R or going on R and R. I told them I was to short, I'll have R and R at home.

I would like to be home for the summer. It has been a long time. I hope everyone is feeling well. Tell Jo Ann and Phillip I send my love. I'm going to stop hear and go to bed. I'll write more later.

Love Chris

P.S. Tell mom to send me all my old pictures.

After the fall of Prince Sihanouk's government, foreign correspondents flocked toward the Vietnam border to report on the story. Ignoring warnings, many journeyed into Cambodia southeast of Phnom Penh and were intercepted by men carrying Chinese-made weapons. Twenty-seven journalists did not return from Cambodia. One of them was Sean Flynn, the son of famous swashbuckling actor, Errol Flynn.

CHAPTER NINE
NIXON'S INVASION

By the end of April President Nixon had addressed the nation from the Oval Office at the White House in front of a large map of Cambodia. He explained how the enemy had concentrated its main forces in sanctuaries along the border in order to launch massive attacks on American and South Vietnamese forces. He informed the American people that the Cambodian people had sent out a call to the United States for assistance, and that he and his advisors had concluded that the actions of the Communists in the preceding weeks endangered the lives of Americans who were serving there and would constitute an unacceptable risk to those who would still be there after the withdrawal of another 150,000 troops.

"To protect our men ... and to guarantee the continued success of the withdrawal and Vietnamization programs, I have concluded that the time has come for action."

The following day, public protests disrupted colleges throughout the country and angered many in Congress, who felt that Nixon was illegally widening the war.

First, President Nixon issued orders to the South Vietnamese 25th Armored Cavalry, 5th Infantry and 2nd Ranger Battalions to bite off the Parrot's Beak and to sweep and clear Highway 1 and the Mekong River.

Then he released the 11th Armored Cavalry Regiment and 1st Air Cavalry Division, along with the 1st ARVN Armored Cavalry

Regiment and the 3rd ARVN Airborne Brigade to the Fishhook region, north of Parrot's Beak, where they attacked the city. A huge tunnel and base complex cut into the dense jungle housing the 7th North Vietnamese Division, Viet Cong and Khmer Communists soldiers.

And then May came. Just when I thought it couldn't get any worse, it did. All hell broke loose as letters from home were describing how they were enjoying the beautiful spring weather with the dogwoods and azaleas blossoming. But for us on the border of Cambodia, it was Bloody May and the world was watching, as it provoked massive public outcry.

From day to day, the times-they were a-changin', as we waited for orders from Washington. Nixon and Kissinger agreed to commit American forces even after three National Security Council staff members and key aides to Kissinger resigned in protest of the invasion. Secretary of Defense Melvin Laird and Secretary of State William Rogers continually argued against involvement by U.S. troops and were excluded from the decision-making. The order to prepare for an incursion was welcomed in Saigon by MACV (Military Assistance Command, Vietnam), by the American Embassy, and by the South Vietnamese government. General Abrams and U.S. Ambassador Ellsworth Bunker were enthusiastic and thought it was long overdue.

On May 1st, just before dawn, preparatory strikes by artillery and air began as two columns of tanks and armored personnel carriers of the 11th Cavalry, joined by an armada of helicopters carrying troop from the 1st Air Cavalry, rumbled into Cambodia.

On May 2nd, there was an unverified swimmer attack on YRBM 21, situated on the Mekong River, supporting Border Interdiction Operations.

On May 3rd, the Communists captured the strategic ferry in Neak Luong Cambodia, cutting off Highway 1 from Saigon to Phnom Penh.

On May 4th, one-hundred Ohio State national guardsmen opened fire on a crowd of bottle-throwing college kids who were protesting the Cambodian invasion at Kent State University. Ten students were wounded and four were killed. American newspaper headlines read "FOUR DEAD IN OHIO."

On May 5th, South Vietnam's President Thieu arranged with Cambodia's General Lon Nol to repatriate tens of thousands of South Vietnamese refugees as both North and South Vietnam mourned the slaughter of innocent Vietnamese. The Cambodians continued rounding up the refugees and placing them in detention camps.

On May 6th, Vietnamese River Patrol Groups 56, with River Patrol Group 53 and 54, entered Cambodia from Tay Ninh Province and encountered the 9th North Vietnamese Division in a three-day brown water brawl.

On May 7th, police wounded with buckshot four students protesting at the University of Buffalo. Twenty-six schools around America witnessed clashes between students and the police. At twenty-one of them, a state of emergency was declared, and thirty ROTC buildings were burned or bombed.

On May 8th, more than 100,000 Americans marched on Washington in protest of the invasion, while Communist units shelled sixty-four South Vietnamese and American installations near the provincial capitals of Tam Ky and Hoi An.

On May 9th, as result of a U.S. presidential executive order, a rescue flotilla of more than one-hundred vessels with more than three thousand sailors and South Vietnamese Marines sailed up the Mekong River to Phnom Penh, joining the invasion. Late that evening, President Nixon confronted a group of protesters at the Lincoln Memorial in Washington D.C.

On May 11th, South Vietnamese vessels relieved Phnom Penh and began evacuating Vietnamese refugees back to South Vietnam for repatriation.

On May 14th, following several days of protest over the Vietnam War, racism, and local issues, police fired into a women's dormitory, killing two students and wounding twelve during a protest at Jackson State College in Mississippi. The police claimed they fired in response to a sniper.

On May 20th, 100,000 construction workers, tradesmen, and office workers marched through Manhattan, chanting "All the way U.S.A.," and "America, love it or leave it," waving thousands of

American Flags in support of the President and the troops fighting in Cambodia.

Actress Jane Fonda and activist Tom Hayden arrived in North Vietnam and visited the prisoner-of-war camp dubbed the Hanoi Hilton. While there, "Hanoi Jane" denounced the war and accused the Americans of being baby-killers and war criminals. Then she toured a North Vietnamese anti-aircraft gun emplacement and was photographed in the gunner's seat, surrounded by smiling North Vietnamese soldiers.

One bright and sunny morning, the lookouts noticed a green vessel steaming up-river and approaching us. We all let out a cheer, welcoming back USS Benewah. It had seemed like months since she left, when in truth it had been less than thirty days, as the grand lady passed us, heading up river to take her post on the border.

Bailey approached me with that look in his eyes.

"Okay, what is it this time?" I asked reluctantly.

"I need a snipe for a STAB night patrol," Bailey said, shrugging his shoulders and frowning at me.

"What am I, the only engineman you got, or do I have stupid written all over my face?" I wanted to jump at the chance, but didn't want to seem too eager.

"All my men are either short or just got here. Besides you know you love this shit." Damn, why was he always right. I shook my head, knowing he had me again. Where was that guy who told me never to volunteer?

At dusk I headed out to the starboard dock, where a lone sailor was feeding a belt of ammo into an M-60 machine gun while trying to maintain his balance in a small green boat.

"Hi, I'm Chris. I was told to report to you," I said not knowing what his response would be.

"Hey, I'm Stan," he replied, continuing to prepare the guns.

"Why they got you out here?" I asked jumping aboard, knowing this was a little out of the norm?

"I'm not sure, I think I fucked up."

Stan stood six feet tall with sandy blond hair blowing in the breeze. He was a little older and heavier than I, but not by much. He was wearing his jungle greens, and his flak jacket had no rank or insignia. He handed me a flak jacket and told me to put it on. I was also fully dressed in my greens and jungle boots as I dragged along my M-16 rifle and slipped on the jacket without argument. I wasn't about to question his authority; I would be his crew for the night.

He pulled back the engine covers, exposing two 427-cubic-inch gasoline engines with dual Holley-four barrel carburetors.

"Holy shit!" I said looking down at the beauties.

"I didn't know we had anything like this." I started to flash back to Dunn's Drive-in in Henrico County, with my buddy Roger Cassidy and our girls, cruising in a Ford on a Saturday night.

"Yep, and she can get up and fly." He pulled out the dipstick and checked the level.

He started up the engines and pulled out to a fueling station on the aft, where we topped off the tanks as the smell of gasoline filled the air.

"Damn, that smells good," I said, sticking my nose in the air like an old hound dog in spring time.

We untied and pushed off with Stan at the controls and me holding on to the gunwale walls. Sure enough, he was right. The little boat got up out of the water and flew. I laughed as the G-force and wind blew me back and my cheeks flapped in the breeze as we snorted pass VC Island in the center of the river. YRBM 21 made a pretty large silhouette in the moon behind us as I grabbed hold of the M-60. We turned, making a run within twenty feet of the beach. I thought to myself that this was a little risky as I looked over to see Stan having a wonderful time, smiling from ear to ear. I could see why they had picked him. He had no fear and seemed to be trying to draw fire from the shore as I kept my mouth shut and hung on for the ride of my life. They were remarkable boats as we raced in and out and up and down around the barges, looking for swimmers or anything unusual floating in the water.

Eventually, we slowed down and putted around up-river as Stan turned the helm over to me and cracked open a can of C-rats.

"I was a member of the Hell's Angels in the San Diego chapter, with hair down to my ass, when I got in trouble with the law and had to go up in front of an old judge who gave me two choices." I listened attentively.

"He said, Son, you go sign the papers and I won't send you to the State Penitentiary," Stan spoke as he devoured the can.

"I didn't have much choice in the matter, anyway, so I joined the navy and volunteered for small boats. I figured it would be the closest I could get to my Harley Davidson, and besides, if I got to go, I might as well go with the best." He pitched the can over the side and hung his Johnson out to take a whiz.

I liked Stan a lot and his story reminded me a little of my own. We were two lost youths in the middle of an upside-down war, not really knowing why we had volunteered to be there.

"I love the fucking world and the world loves fucking me." Stan squatted down in the boat like a gook and cupped his hands over a cigarette as he took a long draw and exhaled the smoke out his nostrils with a distant stare. I didn't know who was crazier, him, or me for wanting to be there with him. He took back over the controls, and standing up, threw the throttles forward, racing down river. The bow slapped the water, bouncing the boat in the air at a 90 degree angle. I hung on as I listened to the sound of the carburetors sucking in air. Something was wrong. "The tide's changed."

Just then we spotted a log speeding up-river heading straight for YRBM 21 as Stan cut starboard and positioned the boat to intercept, throttling down. He jumped over and handed me the wheel as he jacked a round in the chamber and fired a burst into the log. The log blew sky high, BOOM! The rounds had triggered an explosion and the log came back down in pieces, knocking both of us off our feet.

"Holy shit, what the fuck was that," Stan looked over to me as I rubbed my head, not really understanding what had just happened.

"I'd better report this." He reached for the radio as I turned the boat to inspect the debris.

"Racing Danger double-zero, this is Racing Danger Zero-nine. Over." "Go ahead, nine."

"Be advised, we just blew a log sky high with a machine gun. Over." He turned to me as I started to come back to my senses.

"Roger that, will inform." The radioman on the other end didn't seem to know what to make of it, either.

Then the alarm for battle stations went off on YRBM 21 and the crews arose to man the rail.

Stan and I switched positions as we continued till night started to fade into a gray dawn. The junction of the canal and river was filled with fog as fishing boats became visible. We returned to YRBM 21, where we reported what we had witnessed in the early morning hours.

Nothing seemed to come of the event as we went back out the next night, looking for trouble again.

A few days later, I was sitting in the galley, eating lunch, when a PBR sailor came by and grabbed my half-full carton of milk and walked off without saying a word to me. I got up and walked over to where he and his friends were sitting and asked for it back. He looked up at me and looked back. Then he rose to his feet and shoved the carton into my chest, causing the milk to explode over us both. Without thinking I went into auto-pilot and came around with a right cross, picking him up off the floor and sending him to the deck. The yell "FIGHT" went out as YRBM 21 and river boat personnel rushed in. Senior petty officers came over to reprimand us as the PBR sailor appeared embarrassed to have been knocked off his feet by a support puke and swore revenge.

"I'll see you later, buddy," he promised as he left the deck with his friends.

Later that afternoon the sailor and several of his buddies came gunning for me as I stood up to them by myself, not having much of a chance. Suddenly, my friend Stan came running down the gangway to the dock where they had me surrounded and in a fearsome battle cry screamed for them to back off or he was going to kick the shit out of them. As he stood beside me the boat crew backed off and returned to their craft and left the area. I didn't know Stan very well and I didn't know why he came to my aid, but for the next couple of weeks till he transferred, he was my pal and nobody messed with me.

It was 0600 hours on a cool May 5th morning when Vietnamese River Patrol Group 56 units received orders and were called in from their double shift stations along the Vam Co Tay. They departed support base Tuyen Nhon at approximately 1100 after rearming and refueling and set sail for support base Go Dau Ha, traveling around the Parrot's Beak of Cambodia.

Operation Giant Slingshot was initiated on December 6, 1968 as a major interdiction on two rivers, the Vam Co Tay, and the Vam Co Dong. There were six Naval Advance Tactical Support Bases built on the two rivers that had become valuable assets to both the U.S. and Vietnamese river craft patrolling the areas. Moc Hoa was the farthest out on the northern tip of the Vam Co Tay, with Tuyen Nhon to the south near the entrance of the Grand Canal. Starting at the most southern base on the Vam Co Dong was the river supply depot of Ben Luc, followed by the isolated Tra Cu. Next outpost was the strategically located Go Dau Ha, near the bridge crossing Highway 1. Then last but not least was Ben Keo, which was the last to be built in June 1969 in Tay Ninh Province, where she maintained her lonely vigil above the most northern tip of Cambodia's Angel wing area. All the bases were manned and operated by Naval Support sailors who had volunteered to work alongside the river divisions assigned to patrol the various zones. The U.S. Navy Seabees were brought in to manage the construction and maintenance of the small bases.

On January 29th, 1969, four boats from River Division 532 were sent to Tra Cu to start relieving another river division. It was getting late in the day and on the trip up the Vam Co Dong they were ambushed at a place called the Horse Shoe. Except for some minor boat damage, they made it okay. Tra Cu had the look of a place you would only see in a movie. No real person could make a base camp like that. It was as if you were looking at a place that you knew was going to be the last assignment for a lot of good men. After settling in for the night they realized that the C-rations they had, was their only food and they only had a small amount of fuel to share. No one was able to sleep that night. The sounds were new. The voices of Cambodian mercenaries were reminders that they were in a camp with several different fighting groups who did not get along.

January 30th, was spent on the river getting acquainted with the hot spots and the different locations of the few villages along or near the twisting Vam Co Dong.

January 31st, then it came. It was a slow night at first. Nothing was going on. Then when they were about two miles north of Tra Cu, three RPG rockets slammed into PBR-139 amidships near the water line. Then AK-47s and 51 calibers opened up on them. The lead boat had also been taken under fire and was hit by a rocket propelled grenade. Then from behind came a thunderous blast just below the aft .50 caliber. They had taken a recoilless rifle round in the stern and were finished. EN3 Robert L. Blais of Revere, Massachusetts was killed. He never had a chance. Married and the proud father of a three year old daughter, he was taken from this world in a bright light. Boat Captain, BM1 Wild Bill Akin, was hit in the back by shrapnel and was calling for help. But their radios were gone because a RPG had exploded in the radio shack.

When the first RPG hit under GMG3 Paul Wayne Cagle's feet below the M-60 he was manning, he was blown straight into the air with a terrific ringing in both ears. Everything went into slow motion. Green tracers were going by as he thought of reaching out to touch them. He had no idea how far he had been blown into the air, but he could see the recoilless rifle round streaking towards the stern of PBR-139 and going off. When he came down he landed on top of the canopy and loss consciousness for a second. When Paul regained his senses, he was in a fire as the PBR began sinking stern first and he rolled off the canopy onto the engines which were also burning. Meantime, SN Carl A. Gerkin was blasting away on the forward 50s, even as the boat was sinking. As the PBR sank, the fire was extinguished. Paul was trapped as the water's forced him under the canopy and the PBR went to the bottom of the dark, flowing waters of the Vam Co Dong. He could hear things falling away from 139 and resigned himself to die. Finally 139 touched bottom and the water's force released him. He got out of his flack jacket and started for the top, but first he had to determine which way was up. He covered his mouth with his hand and blew a few bubbles and felt which way they traveled and that was the way he went. When it seemed he could go no longer, he broke from the water gasping the humid, stall air and filled his lungs with as much as possible in rapid short gasps. It was very dark, and all firing had ceased. Then there was a sudden noise in the water behind him. About ten feet away was the bow of PBR-139. He had been blown on another PBR that sank and that one had floated too. Thank God for the men who had thought of that idea, Paul thought. Then the cover boat came along and gathered them up, including EN3 Blais. Then and only then did

Paul realize that he had been wounded in his left arm, leg and back. He was dusted off to Cu Chi Army hospital.

After being out of action for weeks, Paul was wounded again on March 7th and then again on March 27th. He was told not to go out on night ambush by his CO, Lieutenant Commander "Big George" Steffencavage, as Paul already had three Purple Hearts and was due for rotation in ten days. Paul pleaded with Big George to let him complete his tour of duty on the River of Death. He could not sit safely on YRBM 18 while 532 had men in harm's way. Big George talked to Paul for a long time before agreeing to let him go back. The first night back was March 27th. On that night Paul was shot on the right side of his head. This ended all his dreams of a Navy career. He was medically retired from the Navy at Bethesda Naval Hospital on October 10th, 1969. He tried to stay in the Navy, but was turned down because he could not perform his duties. So he returned home to Florence, South Carolina, but it did not take him long to realize that he was not the same man that had left four years earlier.

Paul Cagle was finally awarded three Purple Hearts for wounds received on January 31st, 1969, March 7th, 1969, and March 27th, 1969, on Monday, February 23rd, 1998, from U.S. Representative Mark Standford, who later became Governor of South Carolina.

"PRAISE THE LORD AND PASS THE AMMUNITION"

GMG3 Paul Wayne Cagle
River Section/Division 532
American by Birth
Vietnam Veteran by Choice

Operation Giant Slingshot was officially turned over to the South Vietnamese on May 6, 1970.

Vietnamese Patrol Group-56 came into being in March 1970 when American River Division 592 turned their Mark I PBRs over to the Vietnamese navy on board USS Benewah. The Vietnamese sailors had been relieving the American sailors for months; as one American's tour ended, two Vietnamese would step on board the patrol boat in his place and begin their training.

March 31, 1970, was a sad day for the American river divisions as they stood stiffly at attention while the boat captains marched aboard their patrol boats and lowered the colors that had flown on their flagstaffs into battle so many times.

Days later, graduation papers were handed out to the new Vietnamese crews onboard YRBM 21, presented by Lieutenant Commander Poe and Lieutenant Arjie as part of Operation PBRs, a program designed by Vice Admiral Zumwalt to bring the Vietnamese sailors up to speed. Traveling with each boat would be one U.S. senior petty officer, chosen from the crew members of the defunct American division to stay on as advisors to the newly formed Vietnamese patrol groups.

The twenty PBRs of RPG-56, assisted by units from RPG-54, were manned by Vietnamese sailors with one usually in charge of the rest. The boats were under the Vietnamese command of Lieutenant Commander Nhon, a soft-spoken leader from the village of Chau Doc. He was assisted by senior U.S. advisor, Lieutenant Arjie.

Group-56 sailed southeast, and then turned north, taking a short-cut through the middle of the wetlands of Long Ann Province, utilizing the shallow waters of the Thu Thra Canal. Cutting back north on the Vam Co Dong, they stopped at the desolate Tra Cu to refuel before pushing on. Patrolling cautiously, they entered the section of river known as "Blood Alley," where many a good sailor had been lost. Continuing on, they watched their backs all the way up to Go Dau Ha on Highway 1, where they stopped to catch a meal. While there, they observed a homemade sign over a hooch that read.

WELCOME TO GO DAU HA
WITH RIVER BLUE AND TREE LINE GREEN
AND MORE DAMN VC THAN YOU EVER SEEN
LEARN THE RIVER AND LEARN IT WELL
YOU'RE TAKING OUR PLACE IN THIS PART OF HELL.

They were then ordered to continue on as they jumped back on the river, steaming under the bridge of Highway 1 and disappearing into the moonlight, passing the different river divisions on their assigned guard posts along the river. Arriving at Ben Keo at 0300 on May 6th, they tied up and bedded down, sleeping on their patrol boats.

Rising at dawn, the advisors of Patrol Group-56 were summoned at 0800 to receive a short briefing as to where 56 and Vietnamese Patrol Group-54 were assigned positions on an unfamiliar river that forked off the western tip of the Vam Co Dong left into Cambodia. It would be a combined mission, with the U.S. Army 25th Infantry Division sweeping northwest toward the PBRs' positions on the Rach Cai Cay River. They had been given fourteen maps, which was enough for approximately three quarters of their boats. They also had been denied permission to refuel at support base Ben Keo. They were ordered north, pass Black Virgin Mountain to the village of Ben Soi to await a refueling barge. Upon arriving, they positioned one boat to keep the pontoon bridge open until noon, when the fuel barge arrived with only one small hand pump. During this time, the senior advisor denied several requests from the army to move.

After expending five hours topping off all the boats, they departed Ben Soi and journeyed northwest, passing Patrol Group-53, who was returning south loaded with rice, weapons, NVA uniforms, pigs, chickens and any other cache they could commandeer without tipping their boats. The first boats of Group-56 arrived at 1900 in the area of a confluence where the Vam Co Dong split into two smaller rivers. The Rach Cai Cay and the Rach Cai Cay Bac were fast-moving streams both of which entered Cambodia. After regrouping at the confluence, Lieutenant Arjie began experiencing communication problems between the boat's radios and Ben Keo. At this point, the group began receiving sporadic small-arms fire. One of the boats observed a Hoi Chan enemy defector and pulled onto the beach to pick him up. The Hoi Chan stated that there were many enemy soldiers in the area located one-hundred yards back off the bank. After distributing night guard posts, the PBRs got underway, leading the formation left into the Rach Cai Cay. They again began receiving sporadic small-arms fire from the tree line.

Soon after entering the river, it narrowed, averaging 40 to 70 yards wide. It was transparently clear as it flowed past them. Eerily, all units stood fast to their weapons, as they noticed human skulls mounted on stakes as warnings of death. Both banks were heavily fortified, containing numerous bunkers which had been spaced roughly twenty yards apart. It appeared that they had been designed for defense against air attack, as the NVA had dug-in and pointed their entrances toward the river. Most were covered by thick vegetation, and both banks were hidden from above by heavily-foliated trees and triple-canopy overgrowth. The south bank appeared to be one continuous bunker for the next three miles. Bunkers on both banks became more individualized and began spreading out until the units began observing jungle hooches and farms through the undergrowth. The whole area was well developed, with tended gardens, rice stashes, sampans, motors and livestock.

The sunlight had begun to dim at 1930 hours when the boats at the back of the column came under fire from a .51 caliber Chinese machine gun, which the PBRs suppressed within five minutes. Simultaneously, other points received B-40 rockets as Nhon and Arjie's boat came under automatic weapons fire at the middle of the column. Up and down the progression of PBRs, the units drew fire as the sailors fought their way in. An explosion in the trees sent shrapnel flying wounding the Hoi Chan in the back, hitting Arjie in his leg. At this time Nhon received orders to return to Ben Soi with the wounded Hoi Chan, but Arjie was unable to make radio contact with anyone other than his own units. One boat accessed communication with a Command Communication, Charlie boat at Ben Soi and relayed Arjie's protests against leaving the area. Nhon also protested through his radio. Suddenly, enemy contact quieted as the U.S. advisors again lost communications with each other. Lieutenant Arjie pulled out of range.

125

The advisors were using PRC-25 radios with limited range, as both of the stronger VRC-46 radios were being used on Viet pushes to communicate to Vietnamese command. Two units of Group-53 worked their way up-river and picked up the Hoi Chan, returning him down-river for questioning. It was completely dark when Arjie recommended that he and Nhon set up night guard post in the immediate area due to their having lost their cover boat. The night ambush site was set. Lieutenant Arjie had no more communications with any advisors or command for the rest of the night. Prior to 2300, units reported killing three people on the beach and five in a sampan. After that, units monitored heavy movement on both beaches, but were unable to call in air strikes due to communication problems.

At 0705, May 7, 1970, a unit intercepted five people crossing the river in a sampan north to south. Two were killed, two escaped, and one was captured. Communications were still on the blink as advisors were unable to report action to U.S. Command, and Arjie had no communications with his units.

At 0715, Arjie and Nhon's boat got underway and proceeded west, while all boats maintained their positions with a two-mile gap in the center of the formation. Units to the west were moving around, checking the beach. At 0720, units to the west reported finding a large ammo cache. At the same time, other units reported receiving automatic weapons fire as the prisoner, fearing for his life, confessed that the 9th NVA Division were to attack the boats in twenty minutes.

Automatic weapons fire began to intensify as Arjie, paying heed to the prisoner's words, recommended that all boats get underway. Nhon concurred, and the units began to reverse off the beach and proceed out of the area. Suddenly, the units came under moderate to intense automatic weapons and rocket fire, as an all-out exchange erupted. Because of damage sustained by the lead boats, the speed of the column was slowed to around 2000 rpms as the sound of fiberglass ripping and bullets ricocheting off the metal armament rang out. All units continued pouring fire into the enemy's positions, not allowing him to coordinate a successful attack, while inflicting heavy damage on his bunkers as they continued to clear the area. The greatest amount of enemy fire was going over the boats, and most of the rockets hit in the trees, as they were not fired from the bunkers. The enemy seemed to lack coordination and was firing blindly through the undergrowth. The smell and sight of gunpowder, smoke, and green and red tracers filled the air, forming a fog over the battle as thousands of rounds were exchanged from both sides. The horrendous sound of bullets zipping and rockets exploding against metal and earth partially hid the moans and cries as men's bodies were torn into by hot flying metal, debris and bullets. The events combatants feared most had fallen over the two opposing divisions like a shroud as both sides fought desperately to end the other's existence.

Lieutenant Commander Nhon yelled continuously over the radio, reminding his units to control their return fire on the twisting and horseshoe curves of the winding river so as not to hit one another's units with friendly fire. He knew this was a favorite tactic of the enemy, to place guns in a manner that would draw fire from two or more boats on opposite sides of a dense peninsula, resulting in their rounds continuing past the enemy and hitting each other. He also checked to see his units continued moving out of the area without slowing the long column, causing a pile-up of death and destruction.

Units from Patrol Group-53 reentered the Rach Cai Cay to pick up the prisoner and were waved to reverse direction by Nhon and Arjie. One of the boats lost steering control, causing two boats from Group-56 to collide, as the rockets and .51 caliber guns blew holes through the boats from one end to the other, penetrating the engines and disabling the steering units.

Units continued the terrifying exodus out of the Rach Cai Cay as they towed the crippled boats of the division back down the Vam Co Dong after failing in an attempt to set up a dust-off at the confluence due to intense enemy fire. At that time it was learned that PBR 671 was three or four miles behind the main group and limping out at 1500 rpms because of pump casualties. Both PBR 671 and its cover boat, PBR 104, had received several direct hits with B-40 rockets and continuous fire from .51 caliber and automatic weapons and were heavily damaged. PBR 671 had received a rocket up forward, demolishing the gun tub and killing the Vietnamese gunner. It also had taken a hit amidships and had lost the helm. The crew was now steering the boat by transferring their weight on the aft, from side to side. PBR 671's advisor, Radioman First Class Farrior's lung had been punctured and had collapsed as he continued directing fire. The battling crew had radioed ahead for aid several times. PBR 104, with its two American advisors, Chief Mineman Robert (Willie) Wilson and Boatswain Mate First Cornelius, had passed PBR 671 in an effort to get its seriously wounded to the dust-off site. Boatswain Mate Cornelius had received a spent round through his mouth that did not make contact with either his teeth or his tongue. Chief Wilson was at the helm, yelling out to his men to keep up their fire, with fiberglass debris protruding out of his back. Due to communication problems with the command boat and the amount of enemy contact being experienced, PBR 671 had to fight its way out by itself. By now, just about every man on both boats had been hit as bunker after bunker sat up, waiting for the last boats to pass. Seawolf gunships arrived and flew overhead as their door gunners lay waste to the pursuing enemy. The two birds continued diving low over the river, avoiding the canopy and drawing fire - one chopper on the tail of the other, covering for the crippled 671 boat which was now down to one working engine. Air cover had arrived forty-five minutes after the initial contact, although repeated efforts had been made on the radios to reach Command at Ben Keo. Lieutenant Arjie was informed by Chief Wilson that PBR 104 was last in line, and that he had several wounded men, for whom he requested assistance. In all the confusion and gun fire, PBR 104 apparently had not realized that they had passed PBR 671. The Command PBR, which had been waiting at the confluence for all boats to get out, turned down the Vam Co Dong at Arjie's request to aid PBR 104. After proceeding five hundred yards, Arjie was informed by Nhon that PBR 671 was still in the Rach Cai Cay behind them. The Command boat then turned and went back down the Vam Co Dong to aid PBR 671, but due to damage was only able to meet the boat as it emerged from the confluence with its guns white hot from firing. The Command PBR then secured a line and escorted PBR 671 down to the dust-off site as men concentrated on stopping the flow of blood and saving their friends' lives.

Seawolves and Army Cobra gunships with painted shark's teeth placed air strikes along the river banks all the while receiving enemy fire. The dust-off choppers from the 12th EVAC also drew sporadic sniper fire while coming in for the first pick-up of wounded. "Romeo, Romeo, where do you want us?" The sound of rounds hitting the helo could be heard in the back ground. BANG, KLINK, KLINK!

"Popping smoke. Over," the guns of the Command boat echoed over the headset. BAMBAMBAMBAMBAMBAMBAM!

"Roger that, we're inbound." The wind created from the chopper's blade suppressed the tall grass as the pilot pulled the nose up at the last minute, dropping the bird into a clearing. A mass of PBRs had run aground as the sailors carried their wounded shipmates off on litters and set them on the muddy banks. Medics moved among the wounded and relayed them to the choppers when they became available. Soon after the remaining casualties were dusted off, Patrol Group-53 relieved the mortally wounded 56 and 54 so they could return to Ben Soi to refuel, rearm and survey damage. The lightly-armored PBRs and their crews had taken the battle to the enemy on his own ground, and in narrow shallow waters had administered a devastating blow to the North Vietnamese Division. In the process, fifteen boats sustained heavy battle damage. One Vietnamese Navy man was killed-in-action. Fifteen Vietnamese navy men and nine U.S. navy advisors were wounded-in-action.

The radio became alive as boats reported receiving AK-47 fire from a bunker on the Vam Co Dong, and Seawolves covering began to set up for an air strike. However, since Patrol Group-53 was preparing to enter the Rach Cai Cay, Lieutenant Arjie requested that the Seawolves save their loads to give full coverage for the re-entrance. The boats suppressed all fire in forty-five seconds.

Upon arriving at Ben Soi, Arjie reported to Ben Keo on a secure voice radio, giving a detailed description of the area and reporting the casualties. He informed Ben Keo that there were five boats of Group-56, with two engines and radios. He recommended that the boats not be sent back in, and if it was necessary to return, that continuous air cover is supplied for communications and contact missions.

Lieutenant Commander Nhon had received orders to operate from the Command Communication Charlie boat, which had gotten through the bridge at Ben Soi. Senior advisor Arjie and Commander Nhon transferred tactical command over to the heavily-armed-and-armored Monitor, then proceeded north, accompanied by three PBRs from Patrol Group-56 and four from Group-54. At about 1500, Nhon had received orders to place fifteen units inside the Rach Cai Cay. Believing that his report on the situation had not reached higher command, Arjie requested that the orders be confirmed by Commander Sigmond. Confirmation was received and two more PBRs of Group-56, which were able to run on two engines, and one PBR, with only one engine, got underway. Two of the boats had one operating radio, and one had no operating radio, as more than half of the radios in the division had been damaged. Ben Keo was informed that this was the maximum number of boats that they could get underway. At dusk, Patrol Group-56 and Group-54 units took positions extending inside the Rach Cai Cay, and from the confluence down the Vam Co Dong. About 2300 hours, the boats began monitoring movement on the far end of the Rach Cai Cay, and a unit from Group-56 on the Vam Co Dong also monitored heavy movement on the west bank across from his guard post. Black Ponies and Seawolf gunships were called in, and air strikes were directed in each of these areas, with no enemy return fire as the night lit up with white flames and the orange-red glow of rockets striking enemy positions. About this time, the Charlie boat took four mortar rounds near its position, but because it had shifted its guard post after dark, all rounds had fallen off target. Movement continued all around the units on the Rach Cai Cay. However, due to the proximity of the movements to the boats and the nature of the area, the units were ordered to hold their positions, which made air strikes too hazardous. After 2400, eight PBRs, which had been repaired from battle damage by crews of engineers scrambling nonstop, salvaging parts off the 671 boat and other damaged PBRs, returned and set up ambush positions, extending the line on the Rach Cai Cay River. These boats were ordered underway from Ben Soi to fulfill the need for fifteen boats. They were manned by bandaged sailors who volunteered after being released from the field hospital at Cu Chi Army base. All boats were in position at approximately 0300, May 8, 1970.

Again all units radioed, making contact at first light and returning fire as they reversed off the beach and again were forced out of the area. One of the boats from Patrol Group-53 took a B-40 rocket through the bow, passing in one side and out the other, resulting in no serious personnel or materiel casualties. These units cleared the area and waited for air coverage. Patrol Group-56 and 54 units took B-40 rockets and AK-47 fire from the bunkers near their positions. They moved to the confluence near the Charlie boat to await air coverage. As the Seawolves appeared overhead, the patrol units at the confluence began drawing sniper and automatic weapon fire from the north bank. Arjie directed a Seawolf air strike into the area of the enemy fire and recommended that Group-56 and 54 units get underway and move back while the Charlie boat remained behind to direct air strikes. This decision was made due largely to the fact that the Seawolves had been taking automatic weapon and B-40 rocket fire from several fortified fighting positions and were unable to suppress fire. Enemy fire was uncoordinated and ineffective throughout the morning. Although intense at times, it had inflicted only slight personnel casualties. Cobras were in the air and placed strikes in the area of the confluence. Patrol Group-56 units to the south were ambushed from fortified fighting positions on both banks of the Vam Co Dong. A small Viet Cong force utilizing B-40 rockets and automatic weapons had joined the fight. This force may have been set up to ambush medevac attempts, as it was in the area of the previous day's dust-offs. The Seawolves were directed to move into the area and to expend their ordnance as they complied. During their first run, they were fired at by B-40 rockets, AK-47s and .51 calibers. Tactical air support was immediately called in and placed two air strikes in the area of the VC and another in the area of Patrol Group-53's contacts with the NVA. After all air strikes were completed, Group-53 units withdrew to the Charlie boat, while Groups-56 and 54 units returned to Ben Soi to rearm, refuel and gather water and supplies.

At 1700 all units were back at the Charlie boat for a briefing. It was decided that the Charlie boat would lead the way back down the Rach Cai Cay River in order to boost morale and to ensure radio communications. Seawolves were requested for air coverage, and at 1800 Groups-56 and 54 units entered the Rach Cai Cay. All units dispatched men ashore for visual reconnaissance from their guard post sites and checked bunkers before dusk. Charlie boat checked its communications with the base at Ben Keo, and when found to be satisfactory, set a guard post. Soon thereafter, one boat observed a man leaving a bunker and took him under fire. Seawolves overhead put a strike in this area with negative results. At 2200 all Group-56 units monitored talking and what sounded like ox carts moving along the north bank. Seawolves went overhead, but they were diverted south to assist Group-53, who had intercepted three sampans crossing west to east. After putting in an air strike for Group-53 on the Vam Co Dong, Seawolves returned to the Rach Cai Cay to expend the rest of their ammunition in support of Group-56 who continued to hear movement. On the Seawolves first run, they took ground fire as tracers lit up the night. At this point a Nighthawk from the 187th Assault Helicopter Company and a U.S. Army heavy-fire team was brought in and on station. But before they placed a strike, Charlie boat came into contact with the enemy and ox carts, receiving automatic weapons fire and two B-40 rockets from them. This fire was suppressed with small arms and two LAW rockets. While the Cobras were vectored for their strike, the enemy moved for cover in their bunkers and utilized the darkness of night to move in close to the patrol boats. It is likely they suffered only slight casualties. The air strikes lasted until 0200, May 8th.

The final air strikes were directed to within fifty yards of the boats. Black Pony strikes were cancelled because of the extreme closeness of friendly units to the targets. After 0230, communications ceased between Charlie boat and Ben Keo, and no more air support could be called in, although movement continued for another half hour. At 0300, artillery began firing and incoming rounds splashed all around the units on the Rach Cai Cay. Again, because of faulty communications it was impossible to find out who was firing, or what their intentions were. The closest rounds were reported landing between five to seven-hundred yards from the boats, as the sound of screeching thunder overhead and the explosions of earth and wood into the air sent both sides digging for cover.

At first light all units prepped the area with M-79 grenade launchers and M-60 machine gun fire. Men were placed on each beach as a security force. This seemed to be successful, as the boats received no more fire during the next four hours. At 1000 hours, May 8th, the Patrol boats left the Rach Cai Cay and proceeded to Ben Soi, and later to support base Ben Keo, ending the three-day brawl.

HE RUNS THE RIVER NIGHT AND DAY
UPON HIS HEAD A BLACK BERET
COMBING WATERS FILLED WITH DEATH
KNOWING FEAR WITH EVERY BREATH
FIGHTING FOR A CAUSE THAT'S RIGHT
A CHANCE OF NOT LIVING THROUGHOUT THE
NIGHT, SAILORS OF A DIFFERENT BREED
TRAINED TO FIGHT BORN TO LEAD
FIGHTING BOATS WITH HULLS OF GREEN
THE VERY BEST YOU'VE EVER SEEN
WE STANDS' UP STRAIGHT WITH HEAD HELD HIGH
WILL ALWAYS LOOK YOU IN THE EYE
SO MY FRIENDS WHEN I'VE GONE TO REST
LAY A BLACK BERET UPON MY CHEST

Chief Robert "Willie" Wilson
River Division 592/ RPG-56

CHAPTER TEN
BY DAWNS EARLY LIGHT

In the early morning hours of May 9th, the PBRs of River Division 593, along with the STABs of Squadron 20, were on the docks, preparing to get underway. There was a calm among the sailors dressed in their green battle attire, donning flak jackets and helmets as they smoked one more cigarette and prepared their weapons. Lieutenant Commander Ferguson jumped aboard the lead STAB, joining the Mark II PBRs of Lieutenant DeRoco of the Iron Butterfly. Along with three Swift boats, they pushed off and led the way up the Mekong spearheading into Cambodia.

They were followed by the heavies of River Assault Squadron 13 and 15, along with six fifty-seven-foot, wooden-hull minesweeping boats, whose job was to find and destroy enemy mines. The U.S. minesweepers left YRBM 21, towing their trailing cutters on chain drags behind them to clear the way for the flotilla that was to follow.

The non magnetic minesweeper boats were diesel-powered, but equipped with two turbine engines to produce enough electricity to cause a magnet pulsating field, discharging magnetic-acoustic mines in the water. The cutters on chains concentrated on severing the detonation wires leading from the enemy on the bank to the command–detonated mines planted on the river's bottom.

Seawolves circled overhead, flying close to the deck and providing fire support and reconnaissance, scouting for enemy gun emplacements. In the days that were to follow, they also would provide support for other friendly ground forces, carrying out rocket and strafing strikes, rescuing downed pilots and others in distress, and providing cover for medical evacuations.

The flotilla of vessels was composed of Vietnamese and American craft. Their mission was to clear the Mekong of Communist troops and to retake the strategic ferry crossing at Neak Luong, reopening Highway 1 between Saigon and Phnom Penh. In addition, Vietnamese tank landing ships (LST) were to evacuate the refugees from Phnom Penh in a humanitarian effort and return them to Vietnamese soil for repatriation.

We were informed by returning Seawolves that they had made contact farther up river. At various points, Vietnamese marines had landed in combined assaults with a brigade of Cambodian soldiers. The allied forces had swept the town of Neak Luong, chasing off the Communist troops.

Several days were spent at the ferry crossing. Enough time for Captain Joseph Roy Faulk, Commander River Patrol Flotilla Five, to don his SCUBA gear. He dove alongside navy divers working in their John Brown rigs with mask, fins and black air hoses. Vision was poor at best in the murky Mekong River as the divers worked from utility landing crafts. A week earlier, vehicle/personnel ferries had been sunken by the Communists, who had planned to return them to use another day. It seems they did not blow or damage the hulls, only opened water-intake values, scuttling the ferries to the bottom. Divers positioned air bags in strategic locations and raised them back to the surface. Although still in relatively good shape, the electrical wiring and motors were damaged and had to be repaired. The LST USS Hunterdon County moved up to Neak Luong, providing protection and support for the divers and Vietnamese marines, who attacked and kept the Communists on the run. Later, USS Askari would tow the ferries to Dong Tam for repair. Reporters from *Life Magazine* were ashore, and for a short while, newsman Dan Rather, rode with River Division 593.

Lieutenant Al DeRoco, a second generation sailor whose father, Vernon, had been awarded the Distinguished Flying Cross while serving in WW II, supervised his men with a keen eye. He was heavily influenced by his dad, who was Admiral Halsey's personal photographer at one point. The days spent at Neak Loung allowed Lieutenant DeRoco time to reflect on his Dad and the difficult war he himself was now fighting.

Al DeRoco's father – Vern, as his friends called him - transferred off the carrier USS Lexington just before she was sunk in the Battle of the Coral Sea and island jumped through the Pacific as a photo reconnaissance specialist before being transferred to seaplanes flying out of Alaska, where his plane was shot down by the Japanese in the battle of the Aleutians. Vern was reported dead after they found his dog tags, but managed to hop on a plane and beat the Chaplain to his front door step, saving his wife the grief.

Al DeRoco was very close to his career officer father and traveled to distant lands, graduating from high school in Taiwan. He understood the mindset of the Asians and had studied naval tactics as a young man. He had been trained in operations and communication, but had served as weapons officer aboard the destroyer USS Warrington. When asked to serve in Vietnam, he hadn't made excuses or found ways to escape duty like many of his fellow officers. Instead, he requested that if he was to go, that he be given a job that would have meaning and purpose.

Al had learned three things from his mentor father that helped shape his career.

First, take care of your men and your men will take care of you. Second, don't worry about your fitness report, just do your job and your report will reflect your efforts. And third, follow your last order first. Vern's understanding of the politics of the navy and his great sense of humor was an inspiration to his twenty-seven-year old son.

After River Warfare training, Al came aboard River Division 593 in September of 1969, and although slated to take command, had agreed to serve as XO under Lieutenant Laurence A. Bissonnette, a leader who was respected by the sailors of the already-famous Iron Butterfly.

On the evening of September 15, 1969, while transiting the Thi Tinh River North of Phu Cuong with eight river patrol boats, a sampan was sighted evading by going into a small canal. With two PBRs, Bissonnette pursued the evading sampan. Suddenly, the enemy took the PBRs under fire. Bissonnette was struck by an AK-47 round on the left side of his body above his hip. Disregarding his wounds, he directed the return of a steady volume of accurate weapon fire until the enemy attack was suppressed. He then directed the administration of first aid to the other five 593 personnel that were wounded, and arranged for a medical evacuation helicopter, while establishing a defensive position against reattack, and utilizing his remaining six PBRs to carry out their primary mission of extracting Bravo Company, 1st/505th, 82nd Airborne. Upon completion of his assigned mission, he then allowed medical attention for his wounds, which were located below his rib cage and luckily had not penetrated his stomach wall. Larry Bissonnette was medevaced to the 25th evacuation hospital at Cu Chi and later to the hospital at Vung Tau. Lieutenant Ralph MacCumber from River Squadron 59 was temporarily transferred to River Division 593 and worked alongside newly-arrived Lieutenant DeRoco. River Division 593 was then transferred to Nha Be. After three weeks, Bissonnette rejoined 593. Although Larry was taking his daily and weekly pills, he contracted Falciperum malaria and was admitted to the Saigon hospital. He was told a person would either die from the disease or recover with no recurrences. River Division 593 was transferred back to Phu Cong on November 1, 1969. Lieutenant Bissonnette finally rejoined 593 and was relieved by Lieutenant DeRoco in December. Returning home, Larry Bissonnette spent Christmas Eve with his family in Reseda, California, before embarking on a speaking tour of the Pacific Northwest, where he stopped to visit with Vern DeRoco.

At approximately 0800 hours on November 13, 1969, while on a routine boat patrol, Vietnamese Seaman Nhan Dung was thrown from his boat during a high-speed maneuver. After several hours of searching with boats and helos, boat search efforts were halted due to severe currents and undertow. Helos continued to search until dark, but to no avail. Seaman Dung's body was recovered several days later downstream by one of 593's American sailors who unselfishly jumped in and pulled the decaying body out. Some days later at Phu Coung, DeRoco was visited by a contingent of Viet women; among them was a very distraught woman who was eventually identified as Seaman Dung's mother. One of the women attempted to interpret the mother's wailing words of agony, but it was very confusing. At one point, Dung's mother threw herself at DeRoco's feet in a begging motion and out of compassion Al bent down to help her. All the other women rushed over and pulled her away as they began scolding Al for interrupting what must have been a normal grieving gesture. Not truly understanding their customs and wanting to console the woman, Al DeRoco was left standing, holding the bag. This must be the worst part of being in command, the disturbed DeRoco thought. The feeling of responsibility when you lose a man – time to write Dad a letter.

Lieutenant DeRoco took command on December 17, 1969, and continued to lead 593 units into the dangerous waters of the upper Saigon River. Working closely with the 2nd of the 29th Infantry, the Army's Black Lions, out of firebase Kein, and the navy support base Phou Chong, he had proved to be an effective leader. Between the two bases was a series of bends and twists in the river that took the shape of a giant mushroom from the air. The Viet Cong had built an extensive tunnel system consisting of R-and-R facilities and a hospital located at Cu Chi that at one point ran under the Saigon River. The two opposing divisions had been battling for the region for years, and the Americans were beating the enemy soundly and denying them the river.

Christmas Eve 1969 was just like any other day for the sailors of River Division 593 as they sat quietly in their night ambush positions, thinking of loved ones and home far away. There was a chill in the air as a faint sound could be heard in the distance. As it neared the men stirred and prepared for what was to come their way. Ears perked up to attention and emotional levels raised as the sound of the Christmas classic "Silent Night" eerily filled the air. DeRoco turned slowly to witness his young aft-gunner crying, as they all strained to hold back the sea of tears. Suddenly, a helicopter appeared in the sky and flew overhead with its loud speaker projecting to all. Necks stretched upwards and bodies froze till the chopper slowly disappeared. Then the men wiped their faces and smiles were shared between friends as the Iron Butterfly said their prayers and went back to the job at hand.

Flying overhead had been a Seawolf Huey carrying Navy Chaplain Lieutenant Lester L. Westling Jr., with a homemade tape of Christmas carols sent to him from his wife Marjorie in the States.

Lieutenant DeRoco spent many hours surveying the river banks from the air and at low tide had found footprints of the enemy movement. After bribing the army artillery boys and discussing tactics, he had devised a plan and appointed his units their positions as he initiated his trap. It didn't take long before the enemy appeared, as the night lit up with tracers and flares. At the end of the battle the enemy bodies lay still, as the sailors of 593 stormed ashore and returned with captured VC nurses from the tunnels within. In Lieutenant DeRoco's first months of taking command, the division had racked up one of the highest kill ratios in Vietnam, but it was about to come at a high cost.

In March the division lost another man, this time an America. Gunner's Mate Seaman Frank Jacaruso was a popular young man whom all the sailors had come to love and trust. On a night ambush, three of the boats came under fire and Frank was on the front .50s when multiple rockets hit. He never stood a chance as they were attacked by a combined sapper and rocket company. DeRoco received a radioed transmission from a U.S. Air Force squadron returning from a mission loaded with napalm and asked if he could use any assistance. "Hell yes," DeRoco responded as he tied a rescue strobe light to a boat pole and directed the bombardiers to dump their load into a free-fire zone two miles up a feeder canal from their position. The fireworks were impressive, but the units knew it was too late and they were just beating their chest in anger.

Following a service for Frank, DeRoco took on the difficult task of writing Frank's parents, telling them that their son had not died in vain. This was especially hard due to all the antiwar sentiment and seeing Jane Fonda sitting in an antiaircraft gun turret, pretending to shoot down U.S. airmen. It was difficult to find the words to express what Frank's loss had meant to his shipmates. DeRoco tried to convey what conditions they had been fighting under and how Frank had always led the way. But he knew it would be little comfort for the family of such a fine man. Frank had answered every call to arms, even though the night was black and thick with fear. He never wavered and was always there. All of us would miss Frank and his warm and friendly ways. We would never forget him and what he gave. The next night the Iron Butterfly returned up river with sorrow in their hearts and vengeance in their thoughts.

The following are poems written by shipmates of Frank Jacaruso.

WHAT IS A HERO?

HIS UNIFORM MAY BE A DIRTY T-SHIRT; HIS FACE MAY BE CAKED WITH BLOOD AND SWEAT. HIS HEART MAY BE POUNDING WITH FEAR AND HE MAY HAVE TO WHISTLE OR SING TO KEEP UP HIS COURAGE. HE MAY BE A BLUE JACKET OR AN ADMIRAL, A PILOT OR A RADAR MAN, BUT THERE'S ALWAYS A JOB TO BE DONE AND HE'LL DO IT, BECAUSE HE'S IN THE NAVY AND ITS WARTIME AND SOMEONE HAS TO. AND EVEN THOUGH HE'S SCARED, HE WOULDN'T HAVE ANYONE ELSE DO IT FOR HIM. THAT'S A HERO.

IN MEMORY OF FRANK JACARUSO

IT WAS A DARK DAY WITH ALPHA PATROL WHEN THIS GOOD MAN DID PAY FULL TOLL. WE PAY REVERENCE TO THIS BRAVE MAN, WHO GAVE HIS LIFE FOR FREEDOM'S STAND. THERE CANNOT BE ENOUGH SAID HERE TO JUSTIFY THE PRICE HE HAS PAID IN THE NAME OF IRON BUTTERFLY. KNOWING FULL WELL THAT VENGEANCE WILL KEEP, REGRETFULLY AGAIN THE IRON BUTTERFLY DOES WEEP. THE DAYS THAT COME WILL SURELY PROVE THAT IT DOES NOT PAY THE ENEMY TO REMOVE FROM OUR MIDST THIS BRAVE MAN SO FAIR TO HEAVEN ON HIGH, AS WE SAY THIS PRAYER. THE RIGHTS OF OTHERS, THOUGH THEY MISTREAT, WE DEFEND. YES, JUSTIFY THE LIVES GIVEN OF OUR MEN. ONWARD WE GO AND FIGHT WE MUST, FOR WE KNOW HE WAS RIGHT, IN GOD WE TRUST.

On May 11[th,] two of the South Vietnamese landing ships, the Vung Tau and her sister the Cam Ranh, each with the capacity to hold 1,700 refugees, arrived in Phnom Penh with the remaining Vietnamese flotilla and began evacuating the more than 50,000 refugees crammed in regroupment camps. Those who didn't want to repatriate were forcibly expelled by the Cambodians. All up and down the Mekong and Bassac River the refugees waited on the banks, wailing in sorrow, clinging to what few belongings they could carry as they were forced to leave their villages and positions behind. Boats were stopping to pick them up and transport them back down the river to the southeast bank of the Grand Canal across from An Long village, where the Red Cross and South Vietnamese Army were hurriedly setting up a relief camp complete with a dozen huge circus-size green army tents.

I was working on the dock for Chief Catorie when I looked up to see a strange sight. We all froze as a large tank landing ship passed us flying a CBS News Flag from its mast.

"Hey, I wonder if Walter Cronkite is aboard," someone said as we started waving and jumping in the air.

"What the hell they doing here?" Chief Catorie groaned. "Probably on the way to Phnom Penh, Chief," I said.

The large grey Vietnamese landing ship passed us, cutting white contrails as she rocked YRBM 21 with her waves and leaving us in the foam of her dead trailing water. Later, I was called over to the chief's quarters. I knocked and requested to enter. Chief Catorie was preparing some sort of Cajon meal. The smell filled the room and all the other chiefs were at the table licking their chops.

"Christopher, the Red Cross has requested some provisions. Get your crew together and take them to the landing craft. Meet up with the storekeepers on the aft."

"You got it, Chief." I gathered up my men and went to prep the boat. The storekeepers had laid the food out on pallets as a boatswain from the deck force picked them up with the winch and boom and set them down on the sunken deck of the Mike boat like a baby. We left soon after, heading downstream a couple miles on the left to the refugee camp. Floating out of the Grand Canal was a headless body to greet us.

"Damn," this must be the Viet Congs way of telling us they were still here, terrorizing these poor people, or was this one of the people killed by the Cambodians whose body had floated down river. It had been a long month and still the carnage continued.

In a few minutes we were running up onto the muddy bank of the Red Cross camp. There was a constant movement of humanity as the supplies were offloaded by hand. Hundreds of refugees passed the food off man-to-man while the Vietnamese soldiers stood guard with their rifles slung over their shoulders. The sun shone brightly as the little tattered and torn ragamuffin refugees carried blankets full of belongings that they had been allowed to take, while mothers grabbed their young daughters and held them close. The old men looked angry and confused; they had lost all they had worked for over the many years. The young people seemed to come together and work as a team in an orderly fashion. There was no way of telling who were the good guys and who were the bad, they all looked the same. The only ones who might have known the difference were the refugees themselves, and they were too terrified to say anything. They feared the VC would retaliate and release their anger not only on the individual but his entire family. The Viet Cong used these tactics effectively as we backed off and tended to our own business. I tried to see some beauty in this disaster, but could not as I looked out into a sea of sad faces. I didn't want any part of it as I reminded the men of our motto, never get off the boat.

Later, upriver, on the mother ship, USS Benewah, a closed meeting with crew members of Strike Assault Squadron 20 and an insertion team was taking place.

The USS Benewah (APB-35) was an old World War II self-propelled barracks vessel, painted jungle green and updated for Vietnam. At the time, she was positioned off Thoung Thoi in support of a Green Beret A-team stationed at the Army Special Forces base. The command control flagship for the brown water fleet provided air conditioned quarters for five-hundred men and was the first of her class up the rivers.

In the private meeting, STAB crews and South Vietnam's SEAL-like troops, LDNNs, "Warriors from beneath the sea," and other indigenous scouts were being given a classified briefing, one that would take them behind enemy lines. President Nixon and Rear Admiral Matthews needed intelligence in order to clean out pockets of Communists who had found refuge in Cambodia. On point, in charge of the mission, was a tough, seasoned, U.S. Navy SEAL by the name of Chief James "Patches" Watson. He would be Admiral Matthews's eyes and ears, and the silent-running, low-silhouette STABs, were the fastest in the green fleet. Calmly, the insertion team left the briefing and walked down the suspended gangway onto the barge mooring the boats. They went unseen as the men with green faces armed themselves and pushed off into the dark, windy night.

In Racing Danger Zero-one was a feisty Texan gunner's mate by the name of Dempsey Bumpass. Zero-one would lead the way as LDNN Group Alpha, settled in and the STABs turned up-river without being noticed. They were on a classified mission, so radio silence would be observed. Stealth and intelligence was the theme of the day; to get in and out without being detected was ideal. On board Racing Danger Zero-one next to Dempsey stood Chief Watson, wearing Levi jeans and a black pajama top, armed to the teeth. On Patches' arm was a skin graft from an old wound received earlier in the war. Watson was a plank owner of SEAL Team Two and had returned for his third tour of Vietnam. He answered only to Rear Admiral Matthews. Admiral Matthews only concern was in holding him back.

Racing Danger Zero-one took the lead as they pondered their first worry, which was running the blockade set by the U.S. Navy Swift boats on patrol at the Cambodian border. The STABs were rigged for silent running, allowing them to reach high speeds without being heard. The whining of the engines was dampened by the sound of the rushing currents of the Mekong River and the howling wind, allowing them to sneak past the Swifts, blending into the night. About six miles inside Cambodia, Chief Watson motioned where intelligence had said there was a trail. It was to be a VC body snatch. The target was a Viet Cong finance chief returning from South Vietnam with money he had collected. A friendly agent had brought Chief Watson information earlier in the week and Watson and the agent had performed an air recon by chopper to familiarize themselves with the terrain and where they would most likely find the VC finance chief. Cutting the engines back, the first STAB slid onto the shoreline, deploying half the men, while the second boat stood off the beach, supplying cover. As the first group disappeared into the dark, the second STAB slid onto the beach and the second group quietly scrambled off while the first boat circled, providing cover.

After the landing party disappeared, the STABs dispatched men onto the beach to set trip flares for a warning to protect their position. Crouching quietly, listening to the sounds of the jungle, the crews blended in and settled into watching and waiting for the Chief and his men to return. Chief Watson and Alpha Group hiked in and set up an ambush at a small road. Later, two men on bicycles sped pass the alert and watchful ambush too quickly to be taken under fire, so the insertion team returned, signaling the boats to land and extract them. The STABs loaded the men back aboard and pulled off without being detected as they traveled south to the border, passing the blockade into the clear. The insertion team returned the next night and rigged a wire across the road. A man came along the road on a bicycle and ran into the wire. He was captured but released when it was found that he had no documents or weapons. The insertion team, their ambush site compromised then extracted.

For the next couple of months, the brave Chief Watson and his men spent most of their time camped out at the Army Special Forces base at Thuong Thoi, along with a Green Beret A-team. They successfully returned to Cambodia many more times, normally being inserted by choppers. On one of their many raids they captured a Chinese general and his staff and returned to Vietnam with them. They were believed to be the only Chinese to be captured during the War. Scuttlebutt had it that after being turned over to Saigon, they were traded back to China for the release of two agents who had been captured in Korea.

The following letter was written on May 26, 1970, by Lieutenant Alan P. DeRoco and addressed to his father, retired Lieutenant Commander Vernon J. DeRoco.

Dear Dad,

Haven't got but a few moments but needed to get a few lines off to you and assure some of your questions. Things are pretty busy here and I sometimes feel as if I'm traveling in 360 degrees all at one time.

My division was the second wave of amphibious craft up the Mekong River into Cambodia during the Navy's big push into this "hollowed" VC sanctuary. Our job was to set up a blocking force on the river after the Vietnamese marines landed. There wasn't very much opposition to the entire operation. Charlie got wind some hours earlier and beat feet. He just dropped everything and ran. It was beautiful! We've done more in the past two weeks to the enemy's position than we've done all year. When he did stop to fight, or where some of his groups were caught by surprise, these scrappy little Vietnamese marines started kicking ass and taking names. They're a fine bunch of little fighters. Their USMC counterparts left them at the President's 21.7 - mile limit into Cambodia and they continued on. Right now we're engaged in mopping up our area along the Mekong River and back into the jungles about 4 miles. This is the first fully-planned operation by the Vietnamese Navy and their amphibious force of marines and most everyone is pleased. Of the 120 small river craft involved only 20 are USN and all of these have Vietnamese onboard. We're playing down our role and more or less standing back watching the Vietnamese have at it.

My job here has been to act as surface ops officer for the staff under RADM Matthews. He's the Deputy to Zumwalt, or now to VADM King, who just replaced Zumwalt and who is our new CNO. (That's an interesting story!) Along with my division, I've been assigned some PCF's and Strike Assault Boats (35 KTS plus!) to keep the lower Mekong (from the border north to about 17 miles into Cambodia) free of VC. There's not too many around and they don't come down to the river because about every half-mile sits one of my little green monsters. We're providing security for the "heavies" sitting just on either side of the border, several LST's, repair ships, etc. I've also been given the job of coordinating the salvage of several Cambodian ferry boats which the VC sank along the river bank. These ferries were the main transportation across the Mekong and linked the main road between Phnom Penh and Saigon. The Admiral's hot to get these back to the Cambodian's as a political gesture. We've got every U.S. salvage craft in South Vietnam up here in Cambodia working on this thing.

I REMEMBER THE ALL DAY ALL NIGHT RAIDS INTO CAMBODIA.

ADJ3 John Perry
Seawolves HA(L)-3, Det-9

Chief Robert Wilson in formation with River Division 592

**Lieutenant Commander John Poe with Vietnamese River
Patrol Group 56 on ammi of YRBM 21, Operation PBRs**

Crew of PBR 104, River Patrol Group 56

Red Cross camp, Viet refugees, An Long village, Grand Canal

Lieutenant Bissonnette, River Division 593, Iron Butterfly

Lieutenant DeRoco briefing River Division 593

**River Division 593, Iron Butterfly, on their PBRs
preparing for Waterborne Guard Post**

PBR on step

**Monitor, Alpha and Tango boats of River Assault Division
15, Task Force 117, preparing for Cambodia**

Seawolf gunship diving on the Vinh Te Canal, Cambodia in background

Hamlet, keep an eye out Pena

Gunner's Mate Frank Jacaruso, with two Vietnamese sailors

CHAPTER ELEVEN
HEARTS AND MINDS

On May 31st, a local farmer at Thanh Loi Village on the Grand Canal informed South Vietnamese Army Forces that within two days, five Viet Cong planned to cross the canal adjoining his land. The Viet peasants, who occasionally cooperated with allied forces, were by far the best source of information regarding Viet Cong activities. VC guerrillas who traveled in small groups at night were often visible only to the indigenous population, who they relied on for supplies and geographical information. Units of Squadron 20 assisted, by an Army Hunter Killer Team, set an ambush at Thanh Loi on the evening of June 1st.

At 2200 hours, Racing Dangers One-five and Zero-eight sighted two persons fording the canal and opened fire with M-60 machine guns and M-79 grenade launchers. After the assailants lost sight of their prey, three U.S. sailors and one Vietnamese translator from Racing Danger One-five landed to investigate, while Zero-eight provided illumination and cover. The landing party discovered two men hiding in a ditch, one of whom tossed a grenade at the group, wounding the translator. Fire erupted as the landing party and Zero-eight saturated the area with bullets. Meanwhile, Racing Danger One-five got underway and evacuated the wounded Vietnamese to support base Phouc Xuyen. Seawolves from Detachment Seven, aided by an army Cobra team, placed air strikes along the bank of the canal and reported two Viet Cong fighters killed in the action. A

U.S. Navy investigation of the area the following morning resulted in the capture of one of these so-called dead Viet Cong. During interrogation by the National Police at Phouc Xuyen, the thirty-one-year-old suspect admitted to being a Communist from Hanoi who had lived in the village for six years. He had two other Viet Cong working for him and reported to a Viet Cong captain as to the hull numbers and types of boats on the canal each night. The captain had been the other man who was wounded in the previous night's conflict. The Phouc Xuyen police reported the rather incredible fact that the man's wife and child were unaware that he was a Viet Cong spy.

The National Police discovered two Viet Cong located in hooches on the south bank of the Grand Canal, whose job was to monitor and relay information concerning all U.S. traffic along the canals to their cohorts, who were waiting for a safe moment to cross the canal. Lieutenant Commander Ferguson, who had become the Barrier Reef commander, had instituted a two-fold plan to stop the crossings. Strike Assault boats began random day patrols, and troops were occasionally inserted between areas covered by nightly ambushes. Despite these efforts, Viet Cong intimidation continued at a high pace along the border areas. Intelligence reports indicated that the VC guerrillas had ordered inhabitants in the Phouc Xuyen vicinity to do away with their dogs, as they often barked and compromised their positions. An old man living on the plains reported that the Viet Cong had ordered him not to stray more than fifty yards from his hooch, as the entire area had been booby-trapped.

The National Police also reported that the Viet Cong were forcing the local population to inform on the locations of U.S. crafts. In one case they had murdered a local man for giving government officers information about Communist troop movements. The civilian population often suffered as a result of the destruction surrounding them and the methodical terrorism used against a people caught in the middle.

Elsewhere during the month of June, United States Navy assets and advisors continued to take part in the Cambodian Invasion. A heavy portion of the burden of the operation was borne by the Vietnamese.

On June 1st, at 0200 hours, U.S. Tango boat 50 while on routine night patrol about five miles south of Neak Luong was taken under fire by small arms and B-40 rockets. Tangos 50 and 47 returned the fire and cleared the area. One U.S. sailor was wounded as a result of the action.

On June 2nd, at 0345 hours, PBRs 61 and 14 with Lieutenant Junior Grade Picket in charge used drifting tactics on the Vinh Te Canal and surprised two enemy fighters in the water and one on the bank, taking them under fire with M-60 and .50 calibers, and using concussion grenades. A team from the 162 Aviation Company was in the area and placed a strike. The boats recovered three packs and one body, and a sweep at first light confirmed two NVA soldiers killed in the action. A 61 mm mortar was also captured, and documents identified the unit as a mortar team from the 95th Regent, 325th Division NVA.

On June 4th, USS Askari departed Neak Luong towing the ferries which had been salvaged in May to Dong Tam.

On June 5th, the USS Jennings County (LST 846) reported a temporary grounding. The Jennings County was transiting the Banc Soirap enroute from Vung Tau to the My Tho River. It was first thought that the ship had grounded on an uncharted sand bar. A later report indicated that a sunken wreck had possibly been struck. An underwater hull inspection after the ship entered dry-dock in Saigon, revealed that nine of the ship's bottom tanks had been ruptured as a result of the incident.

The first combined operations of the month commenced June 6th, at 0530 hours, approximately fourteen miles south of Nha Be. No contact with the enemy was made. One regional soldier was injured during an insertion and one Vietnamese civilian was wounded by a ricochet. Sixteen bunkers were destroyed as well as 45 Chicom grenades, assorted cooking utensils, assorted clothing, and four rocket launchers.

Also on June 6th, at 0700, Seawolves from HAL-3 Detachment Nine on patrol received heavy automatic weapons fire from a point twelve miles north of the Cambodian border. They returned the fire and called in Black Ponies for assistance. They made two hot turn arounds off USS Hunterdon County (LST 838) and continued to place strikes until Black Ponies arrived. The Seawolves made one last strike after the Black Ponies had finished making their air strikes. Initial results were reported as three structures destroyed and two damaged. At 1830 hours on the same day Seawolves again took fire from the same area. Black Ponies were again called in, but they were unable to suppress the fire. The next day, the 520th Tactical Air Squadron placed heavy air strikes in the area.

On June 7th, PBR 706 of RPG 59, on guard post on the Kin Moi Hai canal, southeast of Moc Hoa, reported Engineman Third Leonard Warnick as falling overboard after breaking ambush to flee enemy fire. After a search, he was listed as MIA. His body was recovered days later by Viet Special Forces, shot in the back of his head. Also, a brief mortar attack was staged on Moc Hoa the night of June 7th, to no consequence.

On June 8th, at 1000 hours, the Hunterdon County moved from its position in Cambodia to a point just south of the border. One U.S. Tango boat was left in Cambodia for communication purposes.

PBRs 36 and 38 were thirty miles northwest of Phu Cuong on the Saigon River on the evening of June 8th, when a crew member sighted two personnel approaching. PBR 38 was on the east bank when one of the men hurled a grenade at the boat, but it failed to detonate. The boats fired .50 calibers at these men and two others they sighted and killed all four. No U.S. or Vietnamese personnel were injured. Two days later two other PBRs on the upper Saigon River scored a larger kill. From guard posts 20 miles northwest of Phu Cuong they observed approximately twelve men on the east bank and in the water, attempting to cross the canal. They were using inflated plastic bags and rubber rafts to float boxes and equipment. The PBRs attacked the group and killed twelve. They salvaged several documents which indicated the men were members of the 101st North Vietnamese Army.

On the same evening, PBR 30 was sunk when it struck an underwater piling 25 miles northwest of Phu Cuong while proceeding to a guard post. The accompanying PBR quickly picked up the crew, all of whom were unharmed, and set a security watch in the area. Salvage operations were begun the following morning by two medium landing crafts and two vehicle, personnel, landing crafts of River Assault Group 24.

On June 8th, 15 miles northwest of support base Moc Hoa. PBRs 87 and 148, with QMC Buffington and TM1 Burtes in charge, opened fire on two of four VC on the north bank, approaching the boats at a distance of 25 yards. The boats then broke guard post and made three firing runs, receiving no return volleys. Air cover and illumination assistance from Brinh Thanh artillery were requested. The first round fell at 2045 hours. Then Seawolves placed a strike at 2055 hours. At 2116 the Black Ponies made a pass, and at 2130 an intelligence report was received of a possible battalion-sized crossing in the contact area. A ground sweep the next morning revealed freshly-used trails and, of course, the usual definitive body count. Two VC killed, probable.

A more substantial confrontation took place the same night at 2118 hours, 10 miles from Ben Luc, when PBRs 7552 and 7550, with Ensign Ty and advisor EM1 Herera in charge, sighted a sampan emerging from a canal on the east bank with three occupants. The boats took the sampan under fire, killing one man and inducing the other two to surrender. Two AK-47s were seized. A subsequent search of the area revealed no personnel.

There were six enemy attacks on shipping transiting the Long Tau shipping channel in the Rung Sat for the month of June. The merchant ship Finnamore Valley was hit by three B-40 rockets while transiting north on the Long Tau. Two rockets penetrated on the port side into the engine room and one rocket exploded on deck injuring one crewman slightly. Minesweepers from River Assault Group 91 immediately returned the fire. A Seawolf fire team was called in for a strike. Within fifteen minutes after the attack, two Regional Force companies were inserted into the ambush area and conducted a sweep. The results of the sweeps were negative.

Slightly over an hour later, the merchant ship Raphael Semmes also transiting north came under a rocket attack. This attack occurred approximately five miles distant from the position where the Finnamore Valley was attacked. Three rockets were fired but none struck the ship and there were no casualties. PBRs on patrol sighted the firing position and reconned the bank by fire receiving sporadic return fire. Two Regional Force companies conducting day sweeps on opposite banks swept toward the firing area. One company detained one suspect while the other company located and detained four suspects. Results of the operation were three sampans, eight bunkers, an assortment of clothing, 100 pounds of rice, and two sleeping platforms destroyed.

Approximately four hours later, the French merchant ship Godavery, while transiting south came under attack by one B-40 rocket but was not hit. PBRs and Regional Force troops were unable to confirm this incident of shipping harassment. This attack occurred at a position approximately one mile distant from the attack on the Finnamore Valley earlier in the day.

On the morning of June 10th, Vietnamese Alpha patrol boats conducting a bunker-blowing patrol, nine miles from Tra Cu received small arms fire from the east bank and immediately commenced firing runs on the area. The crew conducted sweeps at 1300, discovering one VC killed, capturing one NVA soldier, an AK-47, twenty B-40 rockets, and many launchers.

At 2235 hours on the evening of June 10th, PBR 764 in an ambush guard post on the Vinh Te Canal, received a grenade from a nippa palm grove and small arms fire from adjoining positions. For some unknown reason, the enemy then fired a red flare which provided sufficient light for the boat officer, GMGC Porter, to find the grenade and throw it overboard before it exploded. PBRs 764 and 109 made firing runs on the area, but they received no return fire and found no indication of an enemy crossing. One U.S. sailor was slightly wounded.

Seawolves accounted for the largest number of enemy killed in a single June action. On June 11th, before dawn, Seawolves 62 and 63 scrambled to assist ARVN and U. S. troops in contact with a battalion-size enemy element eight miles north of Thoi Binh in the Ca Mau Peninsula. They placed two air strikes in the area during a 90-minute period and received sporadic AK-47 fire. The allied ground elements counted the bodies of 15 dead Viet Cong.

Throughout the month operations in the Ca Mau continued to be the most active in the entire SEALORDS area. There were 15 friendly-initiated firefights, 11 enemy-initiated actions, and 30 unilateral firings by allied forces. U. S. and Vietnamese Navy forces killed 63 of the enemy and captured eight, while suffering only six wounded themselves.

A new and different sort of combat activity also arose during the month as two unexplained explosions resounded at Ben Luc, at 2353 hours, June 11th. A search of the base and the perimeter produced negative results, and it was surmised that the explosions were grenades detonated by someone inside the base. One U.S. sailor, DC1 Haislip; was wounded and dusted off to Tan An. A similar explosion occurred on June 15th, this time wounding five U.S. sailors, and one Vietnamese: YN1 Felkins, RM1 Reynolds, AN Higgins, EN1 Sexton, SK1 Windel, and Vietnamese CPO Ghenh. The explosion was a fragmentation grenade. Investigation by Office of Naval Intelligence the next day, revealed no racial or U.S./Vietnamese Navy conflicts, so it was concluded that a VC had infiltrated disguised as a Viet sailor, with three suspects detained for further questioning. Base security was strengthened accordingly and an earlier curfew established.

On the afternoon of June 13th, four PBRs of River Patrol Group 55 received heavy automatic weapons fire, a B-40 rocket, and mortar fire from a village three miles into Cambodia on the upper Bassac River. Seawolves were scrambled and observed numerous personnel fleeing from hooches but could not fire because of the density of the civilian population. The Seawolves did receive permission to fire into the structures from which enemy fire had emanated. Seawolves medevaced two wounded sailors, 1 U.S. and 1 Vietnamese, to Binh Thuy. One Vietnamese sailor was killed-in-action.

Also on June 13th, the USS Hunterdon County grounded near the mouth of the Bassac River. That night, on the rising tide, the Hunterdon County was able to get underway on her own power. After careful sounding of the ships tanks throughout the night, the ship was able to report that no apparent damage had been sustained.

On June 14th, a major reorganization took place due to the dwindling U.S. role in the Cambodian operation. River Division 593 was withdrawn from Cambodia and reassigned to Operation Tran Hung Dao on the Vinh Te Canal while Squadron Twenty STABs were reassigned to Operation Barrier Reef on the Grand Canal.

On June 15th, four PBRs of River Patrol Group 55 were attacked while on patrol on the upper Bassac River three miles into Cambodia. The units returned fire, and Seawolves scrambled to assist and accounted for two secondary explosions. After enemy fire was suppressed, the PBR crews made a sweep and found three blood trails and seven destroyed bunkers. They captured thirteen suspected Viet Cong and delivered them to Vietnamese Authorities in Chau Doc.

On June 16th, at 2210 hours, River Assault Division 43 units with Patrol Officer Thanh in charge sighted a sampan crossing the Vam Co Dong from east to west and took it under fire. All four passengers were thrown into the water, followed by concussion grenades from the River Assault units. Two AK-47 rifles were recovered from the sampan, and the four previous occupants were considered probably killed in the action.

The River Assault Groups of the Vietnamese Navy carried out normal river interdiction and amphibious operations during the month. Elements of River Assault Group 26 and River Assault Groups 23 and 31 took part in operations in Cambodia. The base of River Assault Group 21 and 33 at Dong Tam suffered a misfortune. The base came under a mortar attack and approximately 10 rounds of 120 mm mortar fire impacted in the area. Nine U.S. sailors and one Vietnamese were wounded by shrapnel from the mortars. The ammo dump took a direct hit and was destroyed by fire with most of the ordnance therein being destroyed by cooking off. As the month ended plans were underway to build a new ammo dump for the base.

River Assault Group 91 continued minesweeping patrols on the navigable rivers east and southeast of Saigon. On June 15th, while on a routine minesweep patrol about twenty miles southeast of Saigon, minesweeping boat, HQ 157, was taken under fire by small arms. A second boat, HQ 158, was sweeping the opposite side of the river when the ambush occurred and immediately came to assistance of HQ 157. They returned the enemy fire for approximately five minutes. Then a landing craft carrying ARVN troops came up the river. The troops were landed to fight the enemy and the minesweepers continued on their patrol. Minesweeping boat, HQ 154, received small arms fire while on patrol on the Dong Nai about ten miles east of Saigon. The fire was not returned and the minesweeper cleared the area.

Elements of Operation Tran Hung Dao I operated inside Cambodia and along the border throughout the month. They were involved in nine firefights, five friendly and four enemy initiated, and reported killing six of the enemy. There were no friendly killed in the actions, but six allies were wounded.

The participants in Tran Hung Doa II continued their activity at a moderate tempo in June, producing six enemy definitely killed, twenty-four probable enemy killed, and only two of their number decimated in a total of 19 enemy-and 25 friendly-initiated firefights.

As the U.S. Navy's involvement in Cambodia continued, Operation Trang Hung Doa V experienced the same level of activity as in the past few months. On the upper Saigon River there were only three firefights during the month. U.S. Navy personnel, by the end of June serving only in an advisory capacity, accounted for the ten VC killed.

On June 18th, 0800 hours, Regional Force operations continued 6 miles southeast of Nha Be Navy base. Once again, the enemy was able to avoid the area of troop sweeps. A total of ten VC were sighted, six of whom were killed by air units supporting the operations. There were no friendly casualties.

The United States' most effective counter-guerrilla forces, the U.S. Navy SEALs, were quite successful during June operations. Especially against the Ca Mau Viet Cong who aggressively operated from their sanctuaries in the U Minh Forest.

On June 17th, Lieutenant Boink led a squad of SEALs from Detachment ALPHA with their Vietnamese counterparts and inserted in sampans. The SEALs established a guard post along a trail and encountered two men. The men began to run, and the SEALs killed one and captured the other. These men were later identified as the VC province chairman of finance and economy and his assistant. An estimated eight Viet Cong then attacked the SEALs who called in Seawolves to cover their escape. One Vietnamese agent was wounded as they boarded the sampan and a Seawolf hovered to evacuate him in the midst of the firefight. The Seawolves continued air strikes until the SEALs successfully extracted.

Lieutenant Boink's platoon successfully captured three other members of the Ca Mau Viet Cong infra-structure a few days later. Acting on Hoi Chanh intelligence, the SEALs departed Ca Mau and landed 8 miles northeast on the Quan Lo River. Two men crawled into a nearby hooch pointed out by the Hoi Chanh and encountered two male and one female VC. The female struggled briefly with one SEAL, and one of the men tried to stab Lieutenant Boink with a bayonet. The SEALs quickly withdrew with their prisoners and returned to Ca Mau. The captives were identified as the village propaganda chairman, a bodyguard of Ca Mau City committee chairman, and a member of the VC female proselytizing cadre.

On the evening of June 19th, about five miles northeast of Sa Dec, twelve SEALs and one Kit Carson scout were inserted by medium SEAL support craft to conduct a target operation on a VC firing position discovered on an earlier SEAL patrol. While approaching the firing positions two VC warning signs were seen and then three males were sighted fleeing into the tree line. A few minutes later the point element spotted two males walking along a dike carrying AK-47s, a B-40 rocket and a launcher. They took the men under fire and the men dropped the rocket and launcher and ran. The rocket and launcher were captured. As the team approached the firing position, which had been the mission's objective, a SEAL stepped on a booby trap and suffered multiple fragment wounds in his legs and feet. The support craft was called in for extraction as members of the team placed charges in and blew up the bunker in which the VC firing position had been. When the bunker had been destroyed the team extracted and returned to Sa Dec.

June 20th, the merchant ship Albany became the object of two rocket attacks during a single transit of Long Tau shipping channel. At 1015 hours, when the Albany was fifteen miles southeast of Nha Be, five B-40 rockets were fired at the ship. None of the rockets hit and no casualties were sustained. A Provincial Force company on a security sweep saw the rockets fired and marked the enemy position. At 1018 hours, an ARVN artillery battery commenced firing into the area. Provincial Reconnaissance Units were inserted by Slicks into the area but found only launching stakes which they destroyed.

Meanwhile, the Albany proceeding toward Saigon, received a second barrage of B-40 rockets. Her position now was only five miles southeast of Nha Be. Two rockets were fired, but once again, the Albany suffered no hits and no casualties. Personnel on board Alpha Assault boats, which had gotten underway to provide additional security, saw the rockets fired and marked the position. Black Ponies were called in and placed a strike on the suspected position. The Alpha boats embarked troops and inserted them into the area. During a sweep, the troops located and destroyed the rocket firing stakes.

Later the same day, the British merchant tanker SS Hemisinus reported coming under attack from three rockets fired from the east bank of the Long Tau shipping channel approximately four miles southeast of Nha Be. The ship reported that no hits were scored and that the nearest round had landed about 100 yards astern. Seawolves were vectored to the scene but were unable to place strikes due to operations of the 18th ARVN Division in the general area. The ARVN troops were alerted to the harassment area and patrolled the area. Due to the unusual number of harassments on this day, extra security precautions were taken prior to the transits south through the shipping channel of special interest ships USNS Bland and SS Robin Hood.

On June 21st, at 1325 hours, a Vietnamese Tango boat received a sniper round in Cambodia which killed one Vietnamese sailor. At 1520 hours, units of River Assault Divisions 74 and 75 and River Assault Groups 23 and 31 proceeded to the area and took twenty Viet Cong in houses and bunkers under fire. Seawolves scrambled and placed multiple rocket and machine gun strikes at the direction of U.S. Navy advisors aboard River Assault Division 74 and 75 boats. Nine houses and one sampan were destroyed and one Viet Cong fighter was killed by air units.

There was another SEAL effort to locate a Viet Cong supply station on June 23rd. Lieutenant Short led a six man platoon two miles north from Rach Soi to an area pointed out by a Vietnamese informer. The unit patrolled 150 yards crossing the Rach Vay Canal, and entered a suspected hooch. The SEALs detained the five occupants and fired at one man who escaped from an adjacent hooch. The Americans' security guard reported suspected enemy activity in the jungle surrounding the hooches, and the SEALs quickly retreated to the extraction point. They held one man who admitted to frequently supplying the local VC with rice and food. He was turned over to the Roch Gia Naval Liaison Intelligence Officer.

In the afternoon of June 26th, Tangos 5162 and 5167, units of River Assault Division 45, were proceeding south on the Rach Cai Khap Canal when they came under small arms fire. The Tangos returned suppression fire. Black Ponies 10 and 13, in the air on a routine patrol over Sea Float, placed strikes on the ambush site.

The same evening, Swift boats 3 and 9 were transiting east on the Cua Lon River enroute from An Thoi to Cat Lo when they ran into a B-40 ambush. Three rockets were fired at the boats but all fell short. The Swifts returned fire. Swift 3 beached opposite the ambush area and blanketed the area with 81 mm mortar fire. Swift 9 made one firing run through the area, then beached, and added to the 81 mm mortar barrage. The Swifts retracted and continued on their assigned mission. Upon inspection, the total damage was one bullet hole in the main cabin of Swift 9.

Activity in the Fourth Coastal Zone was at a fairly high level during June, especially in the area of Sea Float. The enemy carried out ten ambush operations against the Sea Float forces. SEAL operations in the area accounted for the majority of the casualties inflicted on the enemy during the month. Four platoons of SEALs conducted 60 distinct operations to search out the enemy forces. Biet Hai troops (Viet Rangers) conducted another 26 operations on their own. The enemy lost 25 killed and 24 captured. Friendly casualties were seven Sea Float personnel killed in a helicopter crash and seven U.S. sailors, two U.S. civilians, and 12 Vietnamese sailors wounded. Extended Market Time activities were continued along the Cambodian coast. Under an agreement reached with the Cambodian authorities, Vietnamese vessels patrolled in Cambodian waters as far as Phu Du Island. Coastal traffic in this area was very light. At the end of the month all U.S. advisors were removed from Vietnamese vessels patrolling in Cambodian waters.

June 26th, 0600 hours, four miles east-southeast of Nha Be, regional force operations resumed. Later in the day, activity was shifted to an area eight miles due east of Nha Be. Further operations were then shifted to an area 14 miles south of Nha Be and ended on June 29th. There were no friendly casualties while friendly air and ground units accounted for 11 enemy fighters killed. Four of the enemy fighters were killed while transiting in a sampan at night. The sampan was searched prior to being destroyed. A document captured in this action indicated that one of those killed was a squad leader with many decorations for firing at merchant ships on the Long Tau River. Casualties for the month in the Rung Sat Special Zone were three killed and three wounded. Two of the wounded were U.S. Navy personnel. Enemy casualties were 31 killed, three captured, and one Hoi Chanh deserter.

In the afternoon of June 29th, a group of sailors were throwing a football around on one of the pontoon causeways trailing aft of our sister ship the YRBM 20, when Seaman Leroy B. Mudd dove into the Bassac River near Chau Doc City to recover an errant football he had thrown, and was immediately swept away. A thorough search for his body by all small boats in the area and Seawolves was futile. He was very athletic young man, who was an excellent swimmer and knew all the warnings not to jump in. He was never seen alive again. The incredible turbulence of the river, rolling and boiling with such force from the oncoming torrent which started in China was enough to suck this Class A swimmer under the silty water and drown him. We had lost another good man to the river in what was considered not-combat-related. The treacherous currents of South Vietnam's small rivers and streams claimed the lives of several U.S. Navy men in the month of June. In addition, two Seabees lost their lives in the month. SWCN Gary L. Mercer was found dead at the worksite in Chu Lai and EOCN John A. Gioia was killed in the line of duty at Hai Van Pass when his pneumatic-tired roller rolled off a cliff. A third Seabee, CE3 Terry L Kennedy, received serious frag wounds to the chest during a mortar attack on Dong Tam.

Also in the area of operations of Barrier Reef in June, there were eight firefights in which allied forces accounted for twenty-seven enemy killed and one captured. No Americans or Vietnamese were killed, but eight U.S. and three Vietnamese sailors were wounded. Seven U.S. Navy men were wounded-in-action when a satchel charge was tossed into Tango boat 50 while it was on night guard post. A STAB made firing runs along the bank, while the wounded were quickly cared for by a Navy corpsman who had disembarked and rushed to the scene.

PBR 145 of River Division 532 on a guard post ten miles south of support base Moc Hoa sighted a moving light on the north bank, fired a short burst, and then moved to a new guard post. Thirty minutes later, the boat stopped a lighted sampan moving west along the canal with a young girl aboard who was in serious condition from a bullet wound in the hip. The boat crew took the girl aboard and she was medevaced to Tan An, where she was identified as a Viet Cong spy whose job was to signal the positions of U.S. river boats to Viet Cong units in the area.

During June, Rear Admiral H. S. Matthews, Deputy Commander Naval Forces of Vietnam continued to concern himself primarily with the Cambodian operation as naval action in Vietnam itself continued along the same sporadic course of the past several months. The only organizational change was the disestablishment of River Assault Squadron 13 and River Assault Divisions 131 and 132. The remaining assets and personnel from these units were assigned to River Assault Squadron 15.

First, Admiral Matthews expressed concern for the growing number of sniper attacks in June. In addition, he pointed to evidence that the Viet Cong and North Vietnamese were reorganizing and infiltrating with the civilians into villages along the Mekong and her tributaries in an effort to regain dominance in the area. The admiral warned against a tendency for U. S. boat crews, relaxed after the initial lull in Cambodian operations, to anchor too close to shore without proper lookouts, to wander ashore in unauthorized groups, and to swim within sniper range. The battle against boredom is one of the greatest struggles in which a river sailor must engage. The long hours, emotional strain, and oppressive heat normally work with the Communist in weakening the Americans' guard.

One gray, cloudy day, Mr. Fry informed us that we had a new agenda. He called it the Winning of Hearts and Minds Program. We were to make friends with the indigenous people so as to win more of them over to our side. In view of the way the enemy was treating them, it sounded like it should be no problem, if only the Viet Cong had not already terrorized the people and filled them with fear of Viet Cong retaliation. Mr. Fry had arranged for us to play a football game with the local team at An Long Village. He needed volunteers, so he came to us young sailors, who usually hung together on our off hours on the docks. I was hesitant at first; we weren't really in that great a shape. Most of us had been out of school for a few years and smoked heavily. We also had been enjoying the beer privileges at the Last Chance Saloon, even though we were all under-age by U.S. standards. But what the heck, I was the leading yardage gainer on my high school football team. There were enough of us to take these little guys on.

"Sure, Mr. Fry, we'll kill 'em."

"No, don't do that," Mr. Fry cautioned. He was very popular with the village chief and the powers that be. In fact, we all had come to like Mr. Fry and the village chief, but we were still making plans to kill them. On the morning of the game we suited up pretty much as usual. I was wearing cut-off jeans and jungle boots with white socks up to my shins. Some of the guys had tennis shoes and some wore long pants. About thirty of YRBM 21's personnel signed up to come along. They grabbed cases of beer and food on the dock and passed it over to the Mike boat. It was another overcast day with a huge black cloud blowing away in the northern sky. You could still smell the rain that had recently passed, and the metal on the boat was cool and slippery. We pushed off and turned downriver, admiring the five heavy assault boats dug into the bank below the village. Ten feet up the muddy bank were dancing girls in their tribal dress, moving to the sounds of melodic music from the village square. We watched them as we passed, wondering what types of musical instruments the band was playing.

"Boy, I bet even the Beatles don't know this stuff," I commented.

I steered the boat into the canal and came up on the village from the side. I had two chief petty officers aboard as I cut her in easy and ran up against a small plank pier and backed down without knocking it over. A long, wobbly plank system connected the pier to the shore.

I watched Chief Catoria's two-hundred-plus pounds bounce across. I could just make out the top of a little brown bottle peeking out of his back pocket. Just as we climbed up the hill into the village, we passed three Viet Cong prisoners, squatting down and blind-folded, their hands tied behind their backs. Several provincial soldiers stood guard with their rifles.

I ran out, jumping mud puddles as one of the guys threw me the long ball with the pigskin we brought along. A Seawolf stirred the air as she slowly lowered and lightly touched down. All the river division leaders jumped out with Mr. Fry in the lead, as they walked over to a small, roofed seating area to join the village authorities. We walked onto a wet field with hundreds of fans from the village cheering. At the other end of the field was a well-organized Vietnamese team, wearing yellow shirts and red pants with running shoes. They were kicking a white soccer ball around and I froze, realizing what was about to happen next. "Uh-oh... we're in trouble."

None of us knew anything about soccer as we stared at each other and then downfield at the approaching team.

"Come on you guys," I implored. "One of you has got to know something about this game. Okay," I said to Ellsworth, "you defend the goal and the rest of us will take the field." The referee blew his whistle and informed us that we had too many players. We kicked off in the center of the field and they immediately took control of the ball. Their team was passing off well as we chased the ball around from player to player. I tried not to run into the little guys. Most of them came up to just my chin and I didn't want to lay anyone out or piss off the village which outnumbered us about a hundred to one.

After a lucky break and getting control of the ball, I had no idea what to do with it. My high school days flashed before me; I wanted to pick the ball up and bury my head, running for the goal. They surrounded me and I ended up kicking it away, then sprinting downfield with my opponents on my heels. Reaching the ball about the same time as their goalie, I kicked high in the air, missing the bouncing ball and nearly falling on my ass. Suddenly, a laugh and applause went up in the spectator section. I turned, being surprised, and was caught off-guard by the moment. When I think about it, I guess the sight of a skinny red-head kid running across a wet field in his muddy jungle boots was a little funny. I started to relax and enjoy the game as I looked over to see a South Vietnamese general smiling with Mr. Fry and the village chief sitting alongside. It was obvious that we were not going to beat those guys, as they passed and scored easily, looking like pros. So we simply continued running up and down the field, entertaining the village and drawing laughs and cheers. I would never have guessed my red hair and bronzy freckled skin would be so amusing to those little dark people.

Coming off the field after being beaten three to nothing, we were gracious and congratulated the victors. Again, I was overtaken by the onslaught of children who wanted to be close to me. It was absolute chaos as their parents brought them over to view the strange-looking white man with orange hair and polka dot skin. The only other person to get such a welcome was the young black cook who we had to talk into coming along.

We approached Mr. Fry sitting at a long wooden table, smiling ear-to-ear, with a can of beer in each hand. He was accompanied by the commanding officer of River Division 511 and Vietnamese river group commanders who had chopsticks in hand. There were heaping platters of steamed rice, noodle-filled soup and chopped-up barbecued chicken, chopped into small pieces, bones and all. The Vietnamese dipped each bite of food into nuoc mam before eating it. Fry was wearing a tee shirt with no blouse and looked just like the locals, I mean I couldn't tell them apart. There was a long, iron cattle trough full of Pabst Blue Ribbon beer and Vietnamese sodas floating in icy water. There also was an ample supply of Ba Mui Ba beer, which was a Vietnamese favorite; maybe it was the only brand available in those war-torn years. It was mellow-flavored and must not have had much alcoholic content because there never seemed to be a kick to it. It was usually served over large chunks of ice in giant-size plastic glasses. Ice was a real treat out in the middle of the hot, humid Mekong Delta. Of course, we had ice machines on our U.S. Navy ships and repair barges which supported the small boat operations. But other than for the occasional Vietnamese towns in the Delta where some might be made, there was little or no ice to be had. The Vietnamese made their ice with river water, which served as the natural sewage system for all animals and humans from the high Himalayan Mountains all the way to the South China Sea! Knowing this, The Americans tried to stay clear of the ice with the frozen little microbes inside and preferred chilled bottles or cans. All the men at the table had either one or the other in their hands and smiles on their faces. The only thing that separated Mr. Fry from the villagers was that we knew he was a Lieutenant in the U.S. Navy. Other than that, he blended in perfectly. I couldn't get over it. Same slender build, same skin color, same black hair as the South Vietnamese.

We all grabbed a can of beer and passed by another table of exotic fruits and unfamiliar fried foods covered with local seasonings which were very hot and spicy. Flies and insects swarmed overhead as I reminded myself that I already had had one bad experience, which resulted in dysentery for a week. I passed, saving myself the misery and waiting for dinner that night back on the 21. A few of us began playing a friendly game of American football with the kids, who by now were walking around with cans of beers in their hands and cigarettes hanging out of their months. I tried to tell them it would kill them, but stopped myself, realizing that most of them probably wouldn't live long, anyway.

There were literally hundreds of children in the village. Some joined in or waved at us; others just stood there with big, sad eyes riveted on us as we passed by. How many of these hundreds of children possessed brilliant minds, how many could have become leaders of their country, how many had the potential to become scientists, surgeons, historians and philosophers? There must have been dozens, but none of them would ever escape the poverty and squalor in which they lived. There was an old black limousine from the 1940s in pristine condition, sitting under a shed next to a hut. It looked as if it hadn't been moved since the French had left in the fifties.

The indigenous people of the area were of the Hoa Hao religious sect. They numbered more than forty-thousand and lived in small villages and hamlets throughout the Plain of Reeds. Their leader, Huyn Phu So, was killed in the 1950s by the Vietminh, so the Hoa Haos hated the Viet Cong. They also distrusted the South Vietnamese government in Saigon. Thanks to the good work of a previous naval commander, Civil Action Programs, and a continuing good relationship with Mr. Fry, they had developed a strong alliance with U.S. Naval Forces. The chief of An Long Village somewhat adopted Mr. Fry and invited him to dinner nearly every week. Once, after capturing several VC, they had a big celebration inviting Mr. Fry over as the honorary guest. They passed him a tray of spicy cooked meat as Mr. Fry began to wonder if they had slaughtered one of their buffalo. Mr. Fry thought it unusual to be served steak as he grabbed one small ceremonial piece and quickly washed it down with a beer. Afterward, Mr. Fry questioned Minh, his interpreter and the professor of the village school, as to what kind of meat it was. Minh explained it was the heart and liver of the VC and by eating it he would become strong. After dinner the chief presented Mr. Fry with a Chicom rifle and Mr. Fry accepted the honor.

Eldon J. Fry was nominated to the Naval Academy and graduated president of his class in 1967. He was born in Honolulu to a Japanese mother and English-Irish, navy chief father, who had been stationed at Pearl during World War II in Intelligence. His first duty was as assistant gunnery officer of USS Fletcher DD-445 until volunteering and being assigned to South Vietnam in 1969. When he first arrived, he was told to report to NSA My Tho, but due to the fact the base was being rebuilt after having been overrun, he was assigned to Nha Be. After serving six months as maintenance officer for II, III and IV Corps, Mr. Fry was reassigned to Ben Luc as XO. He was later appointed in-charge of all support for the five navy support bases of Operation Slingshot. On his second tour he was promoted to Officer-in-Charge aboard YRBM 21, where he served until April 1971.

Before leaving to visit his sick father in April 1971, Mr. Fry was warned by his friend the chief to move YRBM 21 south to Tan Chau after an informant reported that NVA soldiers were infiltrating and planning to rocket YRBM 21. Fry notified his replacement before departing and encouraged him to take the warning seriously. The chief also informed Mr. Fry that if the North won the war, the Hoa Haos would continue fighting on. When Mr. Fry returned to Vietnam to complete his third tour, he was informed that YRBM 21 had not moved and had been hit by 57mm recoilless and B-40 rockets. The first round blew the front off a PBR moored in front of a shed, in-line with the wardroom. The second double-headed rocket, glanced off the tin roof of the shed and then into the wardroom, penetrating the pantry in officer's country, wounding both stewards. The third round hit one of the Seawolves sitting on the helo deck in the lower divider between the two lower front windshields. The forth round went wild due to the fact YRBM 21 was returning heavy fire and one of the Mike boats was charging the beach. Mr. Fry never returned to YRBM 21. He was reassigned and left the Navy in 1973.

After a while people began drifting off and one of our sailors popped a smoke grenade, which was our cue to leave. We headed toward the boat when a kid picked up the smoke grenade and started to play, running along the top of the high bank. We looked up as the Seawolf chopper blew the smoke into swirls, lifting up and dumping to the left as it swooped away with Mr. Fry and the officers on board. As I got back to the Mike boat I noticed the cover for the lower deck of the boat was off and there was a congregation of sailors and village girls on deck. Then a sailor's head popped out of the hole and he climbed up and out. Then another sailor handed over cash to a Viet provincial soldier and disappeared below deck.

"Uh-oh, what are you guys doing?"

"Hey Chris, get in there." The drunken sailor said, grabbing me to keep from falling overboard. "No thanks, I'll pass." I flashed back in my mind to the Philippine Islands when I was seventeen years old.

On my first liberty call in the PI, I was caught completely off-guard. I had been to Japan and Taiwan, completed In-Port replenishments at Vung Tau, Cam Ranh Bay and Da Nang, stopped to replenish Swift boats at An Thoi Islands and to sit out Typhoon Carla anchored off the coast of Hong Kong, but nothing in my life had prepared me for Olongapo City. By this time I had become a little smarter and had decided to go on the beach with a couple of old salts. I think they found it amusing, taking the kid ashore. Both Spaniel and Pedro were Second Class Boiler-men on their second hitches. Spaniel and I had become good friends. He had taken me under his wing. He was a funny little guy from the Boston area with tattoos all over his body. He had an eagle across his back and ships and ladies up and down his arms and chest. I once witnessed him betting a sailor in a bar that he had a cock that hung below his knees. Sure enough he pulled up his bell bottoms and there was a tattoo of a roster, hanging from a rope on his calf. We enjoyed a free round.

Leaving Subic Bay Navy Base, we crossed a bridge over a yellow-brown, smelly stream named Shit River. At the bottom was a bunch of kids, encouraging sailors to throw shiny dimes and quarters as they dove for the pocket change. Pennies were not acceptable and they would not waste their time diving for them. The water was so dirty from sewage you would have thought there was no way those kids would dive into it. But sure enough, one of the little guys would return to the surface with the shiny coin and hold it over his head so all could see.

Moving across, I was stunned at the number of bars on both sides of the street, all with small hotels next door. There also was an abundance of tattoo parlors as I pulled my friend Spaniel away. You could hear the sounds of the live musical bands reaching the streets, trying to lure you in. I stopped to listen to a Doors song "Come On Baby, Light My Fire" and a kid runs up and yells "Shine, mister" while throwing a handful of wax on my already-spit-shined shoes. That cost me a couple of pesos to get him to clean them off. While the kid was polishing, I noticed a guy barbecuing chicken and some kind of meat on sticks on the dirty busy corner. Just then he looks up at me and holds one of the sticks up in the air and says "Monkey Meat." Holy cow. I shook my head and politely declined, thinking that the guys weren't going to believe this one. Finally, we ducked into a bar full of lovely young Filipino women. There was a four-piece band called the Sun Spots, dressed in white suits and looking and sounding just like Frankie Valli and the Four Seasons. I sat there and listened to them perform "Rag Doll" and I couldn't tell the difference. We drank and danced for hours and I had a pretty little sweet thing hanging all over me as I imagined I had died and gone to heaven. One of my buddies thought it was time to move on as I protested. After they talked me into it and I promised the young lady I would return, we got up and went outside into the busy, lit street. Now I was hungry and the guy was still there with the monkey meat and it smelled good. Next thing you know, I was eating it. My buddy pulled me into the back of a Jeepney taxi as we headed deeper into town. The brightly colored Jeepneys were left behind when General MacArthur had to retreat in World War II and the Filipino taxi drivers had kept them running.

We continued traveling over a small bridge until we came upon a grass hut. We paid the driver and were welcomed inside. There was quite a bit of difference between bars as we sat at a small bamboo table on the dirt floor, listening to the jukebox playing Motown hits. The waitress approached us for our order. Both my buddies asked for San Miguel. I said I'd have a beer and everyone started laughing. What the hell, I didn't know San Miguel was a beer. The next thing I knew, a young girl jumped up on the table and lifted her shirt as she danced to the music. My eyes popped when she thrust her hips toward me and I noticed she wasn't wearing any panties.

"I'm out of here," I said, jumping up and ran like a scare rabbit. My friends couldn't understand it, but I had never seen anything like that before. It took them half a block to catch up to me. We spent the rest of the night watching Spaniel get a tattoo of a house fly on his penis. When the artist asked if he wanted it colored in, Spaniel said no with tears in his eyes. From that day on Spaniel swore it turned into an eagle late at night.

On another night, my whole ship showed up to the Super club where the floor show was a young lady performing tricks with cigarettes and bananas without benefit of her hands or feet. Halfway through the show, one of our officers decided to take the stage and show the young lady what he could do with his mouth. Since the officer was a married man with children and a devoted Christian, it was some time before he was able to hold his head up in ship's company. The next day liberty call was cancelled for the remainder of our stay due to the fact that more than half of our two-hundred-and-seventy crew had come down with VD, and Captain Burkart was afraid it would affect battle efficiency and our ability to handle the workload when we returned to Yankee Station in the Tonkin Gulf to replenish the carriers and their escorts. I'll never forget the hospital corpsman informing me that because of my young age they would have to notify my mother.

"Please don't do that," I begged him, tears in my eyes, and they reeled me in, stuffed, and mounted me.

VEGAGRAM, November 1967
UNCLASSIFIED NEWS FOR ALL VEGAFAMILIES
A LETTER FROM THE CAPTAIN:

Vega has just completed one of our most unusual "swings" on the line and has just returned to Subic Bay, Philippines, for reprovisioning and repair. I say "unusual" for several reasons. Already during the cruise we have replenished more than 75 ships while underway. We started this swing by steaming directly to An Thoi Islands in the Gulf of Siam, where the Navy has stationed a group of small Swift boats. From An Thoi, we followed the coast of the Republic of Vietnam, replenishing small Navy units and the Coast Guard vessels of "Market Time" operations, and entered Vung Tau for some In-Port replenishing. Vung Tau can easily be recognized by the line of merchant ships extending seaward from the mouth of the Saigon River. These ships were awaiting their turn to be escorted up the narrow and winding river to be unloaded at the Saigon docks. Further up the coast, we again entered the harbor at Cam Ranh Bay.

The next day, Vega was moored at a pier at Da Nang. This in itself is unusual in that we have always anchored out in the Da Nang harbor because space there is limited to the merchant liners. Vega was an exception because we had such a large amount of stores to unload that it would be impractical to attempt to use small boats to unload us from anchorage. Our schedule dictated that all 1500 tons of groceries would have to be unloaded in a twenty-four-hour period. Because special Navy cargo teams from Da Nang were assigned to unload the Vega, we sent the crew off on a "beach party."

By early afternoon, however, it became apparent that the Navy cargo teams could not meet the deadlines necessary to allow the Vega to return to sea and fulfill her replenishing commitments. Vega crewmen were hastily recalled from their party and organized into work teams so that the ship might be off-loaded in time. One estimate of completion was midnight of the next day. Vega sailors, working around the clock, completed the job at five o'clock the next morning – seven hours under the most optimistic estimated time of completion.

This action certainly reaffirmed the feeling of pride I shared with many other Vega sailors, and prompted a message from Rear Admiral Osborn to Commander Service Group Three, Vega's senior in the chain of command. Rear Admiral Osborn who commands the Naval Support Activity at Da Nang stated, "Vega offload in Da Nang in 19 hours, indeed splendid testimony to 'can do' spirit and readiness of Vega officers and men. Naval Supply Activity appreciated opportunity to assist and work with this fine team. Well done to all hands."

As it turned out, our next customer, the hospital ship USS Sanctuary, decided to enter Da Nang harbor to replenish from the Vega. Now, instead of going to sea, all we were required to do was to move from the pier. It was another "Vega first" as we transferred vegetables, fresh fruit, frozen provisions, stateside ice cream and one blue bathtub. The Sanctuary nurses so appreciated their luxury at sea that they sent a thank you note.

Finally, we entered the Tonkin Gulf off the coast of North Vietnam once more to pass supplies to the carriers. This swing on line included an unusual and unexpected type of replenishment for Vega, when we transferred stores to the submarine USS Pickerel, which had been on patrol for more than a month without fresh provisions.

I have particularly enjoyed talking to all the new young sailors who are only a few years older than my son. They are pleasant and personable and I'm calling them the "new breed". Anyone who thinks the 18-19-year-old generation is going downhill would be very pleasantly surprised to see these young men. It is a pleasure to have them on board. For you mothers and fathers who read this, your son feels fine and looks wonderful – even with shorter hair in some cases. If you are the wife of one of our old-timers, or one of the newly-arrived petty officers, we are certainly appreciative of and need your husband's experience. We have about 270 men on board, and 217 are on their first cruise in the Navy. The Vega's chiefs are the finest with whom I have had the pleasure to serve.

Our next swing on the line is our last; then we set a course for home. On the way, we expect to visit such interesting ports as Sasebo and Yokosuka, Japan, as well as Pearl Harbor. The one port we are all looking forward to is, of course, homeport. I hope to see you all there.

Sincerely
John C. Burkark

The smoke started to drift down as it woke me up and I came back to the present, losing my patience. "Come on, you guys, its time to get out of here." The last sailor escorted the young lady in a red silk top and black pajama bottom off the boat.

After counting heads, I reversed off the bank, waved goodbye and became aware of how drunk we were. Including me, who was at the helm. Some guys stripped down to their underwear while others were sprawled on the deck, moaning. We must have been a funny sight as I returned the rowdy bunch back to the 21, stumbling and laughing.

That night I vegged out in my rack and took a little time to rest and recoup from the game and beer. We had rigged poncho liners like curtains around our racks for privacy, which was hard to find. I had ordered a Sony tape deck and spliced my headphones into the ear jack and it worked. With a small light and the tapes my Aunt Rachel sent me from her record club, I could block out the war for short periods of time. I wore out my Steve Miller sailor tape lessoning to "Living in the USA" as I lay in my rack, writing letters and reading hot rod magazines dreaming, about the Ford Boss Mustang I was going to buy when I got back to the world. I also studied a catalog from the ship's store and special-ordered more than five hundred dollars worth of stereo equipment. I ordered a reel-to-reel Akai tape deck, a Pioneer receiver, turntable, power amp and speakers, and a TV, watch and clothes, which were all being sent directly from Japan to my mother's house. I spent a lot of money on batteries reading and listening to my music. It was my salvation. Every now and then one of the guys would come along and stick his head in and try to talk me into coming out for a card game or something. But I would pass explaining I needed a little down time to recharge my battery. Most nights I feel asleep lessoning to "Sea of Joy" by Blind Faith. Later that night, one of my bosses came and roused me, telling me to dress and go to the armory and draw a weapon.

"What's going on," I asked.

"We received a radio message that one of the women along the river is having a baby and needs the Doc."

Lieutenant Phillip C. Carling was the ship's doctor, and next to Mr. Fry, the second most popular man on shore with the indigenous people. He allowed the locals to come aboard and performed routine visits to the villages and hamlets of the area. He was very compassionate and treated the sick and poor, ensuring their kids were strong and healthy. It was the best tool we had for the winning of hearts and minds. The local population was much more VC than we thought, but they would have objected very strongly to the 21 being attacked. Their families depended on the 21 as their hospital the same as everyone else. Often Doc Carling and Mr. Fry would take gifts and stay for dinner or a beer with the local chiefs or chief of police. The people had come to trust us and were reaching out for help. The young woman had no chance to live except for the 21. Her water had already broken and she was insufficiently dilated. Doc Carling was the only Doctor anywhere close and YRBM 21 was the only hospital.

It was a beautiful moonlit night when Ellsworth, Walzak and I prepped the Mike boat and pulled alongside so that Doc Carling, Bac, Doc's interpreter/assistant, and Mr. Fry could jump aboard. We were told to head upriver to a small hamlet near Tan Chau. We pulled alongside a large formation of concrete steps that came down into the river. As usual, there was a group of children to greet us as Ellsworth jumped over and secured the rope to a pole. One hundred feet from the river was a large house big enough to accommodate the entire hamlet of Vietnamese families. The house was painted white and yellow, with a high roof and a long porch with a grand staircase descending to the ground. Two of the local provincial soldiers with weapons slung over their shoulders were there to meet Doc Carling. The children called the Doctor "Bac Si" because of the little black bag of medical supplies he carried on his visits.

"Bac Si! Bac Si!" the children chanted with smiles on their faces. "Okay, okay," said Doc as they entered the hamlet. We never patted the kids on the head, this was an insult. They walked up the stairs and disappeared through the double doorway as the three of us stayed behind with the boat, watching over our shoulders for anything strange.

"Keep an eye out, you guys, don't fall asleep on me," I said, playing sergeant as I usually did.

I stayed on the boat near the .50s with Walzak while Ellsworth sat on the steps with the kids, playing hand games and laughing. Next thing I knew, Mr. Fry, Bac, and Doc, came out with two soldiers, carrying the young girl on a litter, heading toward us. They transferred the girl to the boat and we pushed off, waving to the kids as we turned and throttled back toward the 21 in the cool river breeze. To our left in the distance we could see the nonstop trail of red tracers of Puff the Magic Dragon's six barrel gattling guns raining down on the Ho Chi Minh Trail. The converted AC-47 gunship, code named Spooky, circled, releasing 6000 rounds per minute from each of her three mini-guns. Every fifth round was a tracer as she lit up the night with a sea of red. She made it difficult for the enemy to advance and kept us grunts on the ground warm and safe in our racks at night.

Arriving back at the dock, they carried the girl up the gangway to sickbay as we secured the boat. I returned to my rack to resume catching up on my sleep. The next morning I arose to the news that the Doc had delivered a baby boy and the young girl was okay. It felt great to do something positive in the middle of that screwed-up war, as we all had occasion to celebrate life and not mourn death. Later, Doc Carling was transferred to YRBM 16. He was not happy about it at all.

Bac came aboard YRBM 21 at the age of sixteen and knew working for the Americans was dangerous. She had lived her whole life in war, and like everyone else, hated it. When the American GIs came, the villagers hated the war even more. The Viet Cong had taught everyone that Americans were heartless killers, but she knew better. She had worked around GIs at a Viet Special Forces' camp. In the Viet Cong's eyes, her new job as housemaid for the EOD divers made her a war criminal and subject to execution. Then again, the VC saw everyone who did anything they didn't like as war criminals. The Hoa Haos had already killed members of her family, so she though the money would help keep the rest alive, or at least a little longer.

One day, she was asked to assist Doc on a visit to the village. She had always dreamed of being a nurse, so the invitation to accompany Doc was a dream come true. The nearest Vietnamese doctor was hours away and the village needed help. It made the long hours she had spent studying English, seem worthwhile. They used the shade of the trees along the river bank as a make-shift clinic, giving medications, cleaning infections, and bandaging wounds and cuts. Bac made friends quickly and translated their words to Doc Carling.

Every Tuesday, the team returned and the barefooted children ran to them, no longer afraid. Their eyes glued on the GI's pockets that they knew would be caring candy and gum. As usual, the older kids pushed the young ones out of the way. When all the candy was gone one particularly sad-eyed little boy who got nothing started to cry. All the EOD team had left was a cigarette lighter, so they gave it to him, and the boy laughed in delight.

When Christmas arrived, Dan and Rick from the EOD team, collected money from everyone on the 21, bought gifts, and spent all night wrapping them. When Bac came down for work, they surprised her with a tailored uniform, complete with belt, black beret, and shiny boots. She was overjoyed, having always wanted to be a combat nurse, but being a third grade dropout, she thought her dream would never come true. They packed all the presents on a boat, Chief Rick dressed in a Santa suit, and off they went to Coa Lanh Hospital, waving Merry Christmas along the river.

After arriving, they started handing out presents to the Vietnamese, who had never seen anything like Santa before. The children's eyes glistened as their shaking little hands quickly ripped off colorful wrapping paper and stuck candy in their mouths. They watched tiny sick children play with toys, as eyes recently full of fear turned happy. The team had their reward, as hot happy tears ran down their cheeks. At that moment Bac no longer felt just a housemaid. She had become a member of the kindest, most extraordinary, carrying team in the world, and she knew the American Santa, would always live in her heart. That day, Bac discovered there was something worth dying for other than her family, not that dying was a big deal to her. She had always hated the VC and had seen all too often what heartless killers they were, not to say the Saigon government was much better. But she had seen that the American mission in Vietnam was a mission of caring and trying to make the Vietnamese lives and country a little better, and that was worth dying for. Dying had always been a possibility that she had never been allowed to forget. Many times she had sat by the river watching the bodies float down stream, looking for family members and friends. It was then she had learned that there was something worse, having one missing and never found.

Bac began instructing Machinist Mate Second Sam Eaton in the Vietnamese language, and in exchange he helped her with English. Both Sam and Bac left YRBM 21 after the turnover to the Vietnamese with Sam receiving orders to Japan. Sam returned many times and they were married in Saigon on August 22nd, 1973. They both evacuated Vietnam April 5th, 1975, during the fall of Saigon.

HE WHO SEES THROUGH LIFE AND DEATH WILL MEET MOST WITH SUCCESS.

A few days after the baby was born, there was a Seawolf scramble early in the day. I thought nothing of it, since they launched so often. I made a run downstream to one of the little outposts. When we returned, one of the Seawolves had landed on the 21. The crash crew was hurriedly reloading the rockets and refueling the bird. Whenever we refueled helicopters we had to pump a sample of aviation fuel into a glass jar and hold it up so the pilot could see there was no water or sand in it. After a while, we had broken all but one jar, and we protected it like a baby. After filling the Huey's tank, she took off and headed back across the border; then the second Seawolf returned and landed for a hot reload. One of the rockets prematurely fired shooting across the helo deck and skimming over the river before sinking. Woe that was close. After lifting off, we could just make out the tails of the birds as they dove down on the jungle near the shoreline. We never found out who they were fighting, as there was little communication that day. But we knew they were putting the hurt on someone, as they fought all day and into the night, making more than a dozen hot reloads back to YRBM 21. Thanks to God and the Seawolves and their crews, with their rockets and guns aboard YRBM 21, the enemy dared not show their ugly faces. Without the Seawolves, we would all have been in a world of shit.

USS Iredell County (LST 839) came alongside one day and replenished our supplies as the Iredell County did periodically. After untying and breaking away, one of her sentries fired at an object in the water and triggered an explosion. Another VC attack foiled by a sentry who was alert and on the ball.

Then there was the time someone double-ordered Zuni rockets for the Seawolves and they all showed up at once. We had them stored in crates stacked on the deck from one end of YRBM 21 to the other. It was a little scary and became an unnecessary hazard, so we began loading them on the Mike boats and delivered them to all the support bases that had helo pads and rearming stations. It took a few days, but we finally got rid of enough of them so they weren't exposed out on the decks of YRBM 21.

Sunday was a special day on YRBM 21, for the Filipino stewards would come down to the ammi pontoon housing the Last Chance Saloon and barbecue steaks on the dock for the crew. There would be beer and sodas in a tub of ice and baked potatoes on the side. It was quite a picnic, and a nice break from the norm. One Sunday, several strangers joined us. None of us recognized them, but that night when they came down the gangplank with painted faces and boarded PBRs headed into Cambodia, we had a good idea.

CHAPTER TWELVE
JUST ANOTHER DAY IN PARIDISE

One day, Chief Catorie instructed me to ride along on a trip to support bases Tuyen Nhon and Moc Hoa to replenish their supplies. We often made runs up to the support bases, for which we were responsible for keeping stocked with food and ammo. It was one of the most desolate areas to which we had to travel. I packed up and jumped on the Mike boat with Steve and Pena from New York. A couple of gunner's mates came along and brought extra fire power. We were to run the entire gauntlet of the Grand Canal. We traveled all day, waving at Phouc Xuyen as we churned by. Just beyond the base was pretty rough country. The reeds became thick and visibility was zero, so the gunners stayed close to their weapons. We all breathed slowly as we passed what seemed to be an embattled bunker system. Nearing the end of the Canal, we landed at Tuyen Nhon in time to catch the end of the chow line. The base was full of Vietnamese patrol group sailors and mercenaries, who hated each other. There I saw one of the monster hovercrafts I had heard so much about.

The green hovercraft streaked across the plains and came howling pass us like we were standing still, slinging mud and misty water every direction, as if in a wind storm. The indigenous people and their water buffalos ran when they heard the roar of her blades and caught sight of the "Dragon". She slowed down and then sailed up a ramp into the base, set down on a graded deck, and came to rest.

The air cushioned vehicle was developed by Bell Aerosystems in the late 1950s. The ability to move quickly over land and water using a cushion of air left other vehicles and watercraft behind, and caught the attention of the Army and Navy.

Bell first developed the U.S. Navy's Patrol Air Cushion Vehicle (PACV) based on a modified British design. The Navy's PACV first arrived in Vietnam as a unit in 1966.The Army worked with Bell to develop its own version of the ACV in February 1968. It was wider, longer and carried more weapons than the Navy PACV. It also had stronger side decks and the front door of the cabin was widened to accommodate soldiers with gear. It had a turbine-powered, turboshaft GE engine, a Hamilton 3-bladed, variable pitch, fully reversible propeller, and a centrifugal, 7 foot diameter, 12-bladed blower fan. They were over 38 feet long and 24 feet wide. Their height was 16 feet, and their speed over land was 40 mph and 70 mph over water. It had a crew of two, an operator and a radarman, and were in assault configuration with a full weapons load, M-60 and 50 calibers. There were 3 ACVs under the control of the 3rd Brigade, 9th Infantry Division initially stationed at Dong Tam, and later relocated to Ben Luc. They spent allot of time pulling guard on the Plain of Reeds along side the U.S. Navy and the mercenaries. One ACV was destroyed in January 1970, and another destroyed in August 1970 by an unexploded B-52 bomb that had been planted by the Viet Cong.

The village of Ap Bac was about ten miles south of Tuyen Nhon, where a north-south canal intersected. A major ARVN/Viet Cong battle was near there in the mid-sixties, and the ARVN decided that the area was too hot for major ops, so they built some small outposts about half-way between Tuyen Nhon and Ap Bac. Civilian Irregular Defense Groups, sort of like militia, were based out of these camps. The South Vietnamese did not like them at all, and the VC and NVA feared them. The Chinese Nung airboat men, and Hoa Hao reconnaissance units, were some of the lesser sects in Vietnam and Cambodia and were recruited mainly as mercenaries. The river divisions had the mercenaries do body search and counts in the thick reeds after firefights. The airboats and hovercraft were the only craft that could penetrate the thickets of reeds and bushes, and the Hoa

Hao units went in on foot. Later, the mercenaries would invite the river division sailors to dinner. Because of the rumor that the Hoa Hao practiced cannibalism; no one ever accepted the invitation.

After dinner we off-loaded the boat and then headed to the club house for a beer. The room was filled with South Vietnamese and mercenaries sneering at each other. Soon after, an altercation occurred between the two groups and they all filed out, going to fetch their weapons. Anticipating trouble, we rounded up all our personnel and left the firebase. We hauled ass up the Vam Co Tay River, as the light of the tropical sunset faded and the fear of being caught on the river at night sat in. Eventually, the dim light of support base Moc Hoa appeared, guiding us to safety. We knew it was a bad idea, but we felt safer on the river at night than with those people at Tuyen Nhon. Most of us didn't sleep much that night. We took shifts on watch, hugging our guns and fighting off the mosquitoes. I couldn't see a thing, and every twitch on the beach made me jump. I sat up listening to the creatures of the marshes and watching the sentries manning the perimeter of the firebase.

The next morning we got an ass-chewing from the chief at Moc Hoa. Seems the chief at Tuyen Nhon had gone back aboard our Mike boat and stolen all the frozen steaks while we were enjoying our beer. The chief at Moc Hoa got on the horn to Mr. Fry and expressed his anger.

"Now Mr. Fry, you know we didn't mind eating a few livers, but this has gotten out of hand."

"Yes Chief, I'm sorry. I'll see that it never happens again." Fry cursed the chief at Tuyen Nhon for putting him in that position.

On the way back we stopped at Phouc Xuyen for a short visit and were happy to see the base was just about completed, with the water rising. Seven wood and sand look-out towers had been built, lining the perimeter of the base with wire and claymores. A four-foot, raised, wooden plank walkway connected the towers as the waters in the canal were beginning to overflow onto the base. In the center of the compound was a raised helo pad and ammunition bunker. I didn't see any drums for refueling the choppers, but there were definitely rockets for rearming. Next to the helo pad was an 81 mm mortar tube positioned next to a bunker close to the junction of the mess hall and enlisted-man berthing barge. The mortar tube was aimed over the roof of the hooch to the opposite bank. Tower number five on the corner of the base had a .50 cal with a large starlight scope mounted on top. There were M-79 grenade launchers, hand-pop flares and rifles everywhere. The Seabees were behind in their work and needed to move on to their next assignment, so Chief Murphy and his boys were helping with the remaining construction. What with the all-night watches, the men were putting in long hours and surviving on C-rats before sleeping a few hours. Then they would get up and work on the base, before going back on watch and beginning the whole routine all over.

The kids from Phouc Xuyen village would come down during the day when the sailors were working outside the perimeter. The men gave the kids beer and cigarettes for helping. One evening about dusk, they caught one of these kids walking through the free-fire zone. They went out and apprehended him, even though he smiled and waved as if he was just a friend passing through. Turns out, he was pulling a small wagon which had not been visible due to the tall grass. The wagon was full of contraband he'd stolen while helping on a work-detail outside the perimeter.

At night, in the dark, there always were surprises as they ate cans of beef stew that had lumps of lard that resembled pieces of potatoes, until they chewed, discovered what it was, and spit them out. The men bartered among themselves for the peanut butter with crackers or the pound cake. Most wore P-38 can openers around their necks for convenience, with their dog tags taped up so they wouldn't clank around and disrupt noise discipline. Many of the support sailors had volunteered to go out on ambush with the river divisions. The men had lost track of what day it was, since there was no down time and all days seemed to be the same at the summer resort. Whether it was Christmas, Easter or the Forth of July, it didn't matter. The village women came to the base each day and for a little money would wash their laundry in the canal. On the large pontoon barge where the enlisted slept, there was a head and shower hanging off the side over the canal leaving less than two hundred feet to the opposite bank. Someone had rigged a pump from the canal to the shower, so you got only as clean as the canal water was that day. The barge farthest away had the generator and pumps, next was the chow hall, then the berthing hooches. Each barge was ninety feet long and thirty feet wide. The whole base could fit inside half a football field, with space to spare.

After months of intense heat and very little sleep, seven days a week, one of the sailors on a communication boat docked next to the provincial base on the canal, went berserk and jacked a round in his .50 cal and pinned down the soldiers inside the base. Men scattered and took cover, unable to close in and subdue the madman. There was an alarm to launch the Seawolves from YRBM 21 to go out and take the man out. Luckily for everyone, by the time the choppers arrived, the man had run out of ammo and been captured without harming anyone. They jumped him, hogtied him, and placed him on the bird. He again started freaking out when the helo lifted off. The door gunner calmed the man down somewhat by comforting him and positioning his head near the door so he could feel the breeze. The next day, the man came to his senses and was diagnosed with extreme battle fatigue. Secretly, he confessed to the door gunner that someone had sent him some bad LSD in the mail. Admiral King caught wind of the affair and flew out to check on the base. Shortly after arriving, he fined just about everybody a reduction in pay due to the fact that they all needed haircuts. I guess he didn't care that there wasn't a barber nearby, or that the men hadn't had a hot meal in weeks. Again, the Seawolves to the rescue as they flew the barber from YRBM 21 out for the day.

On the other hand, on a different occasion, a young Hispanic sailor who was kind of rough around the edges, reported to support base Phouc Xuyen for temporary duty and while unpacking exposed a bag of pot. Phouc Xuyen was used by several of the NSA detachments as a place to send their hard-cases, so they had several difficult people. Ken Scott and Randy Strickland, who was over six feet tall, saw the pot, grabbed, and dumped it over the side. The sailor became furious and made all kinds of threats, but did not follow up and left the base soon after. Although there were a few hardship cases at the base, most of the sailors were aware of where they were and what they needed to do to stay alert and survive. Later, a case of frozen lobsters found its way to the base but nobody knew where it came from. They ate lobster morning, noon, and night, for two days. You couldn't help but feel compassion for those few sailors stranded out there with army gear holding down the front line of defense alongside the river patrolmen. I left Phouc Xuyen that morning, not knowing I would never see the base again. When I arrived back at YRBM 21, the yeoman approached, informing me that he needed an engineer volunteer to transfer out to one of the support bases. He told me there was a three-day in-country R-and-R attached, but warned me that it wasn't going to be any picnic. After observing the men at Phouc Xuyen, I wanted to go. So I packed my gear, said my goodbyes and left on a chopper for Saigon.

At the end of June the withdrawal of all U. S. personnel and assets from Cambodia territory was carried out. At 1055 hours on June 29th, a U. S. Navy Swift boat, PCF 74, while on its way out of Cambodia, received B-40 rocket and sniper fire about nine miles south of Neak Luong. The Swift boat did not return the fire but cleared the area. One U.S. sailor was slightly wounded. All U.S. Navy and U.S. Marine Corp personnel had withdrawn from Cambodia by 1430 hours, June 29th, 1970.

On June 30th, the U.S. Senate voted 58-37 to adopt the Cooper-Church amendment to limit Presidential power in Cambodia. The amendment barred funds to retain U.S. troops in Cambodia after July 1st, or to supply military advisers or mercenaries, or to conduct any combat activity in the air above Cambodia in direct support of Cambodian forces without Congressional approval.

During the two-month Cambodian operation, allied forces disrupted supply lines, capturing 23,000 weapons and 14 million pounds of rice. North Vietnamese and Viet Cong forces lost an estimated 11,000 men, the U.S. lost 338, and the South Vietnamese lost 638. Allied wounded-in-action was 4,500 men. An estimated 50,000 to 70,000 Vietnamese refugees were evacuated and repatriated to South Vietnam. 50,000 were left behind in detention camps.

The following is a series of voice letters recorded by Seaman Ken Scott, describing life at Phouc Xuyen to his friend in California. The letters were recorded on a Sony tape deck purchased on YRBM 21 and Ken sounded like he was fifteen years old. In the back ground, you can hear the Ray Charles classic, "I Can't Stop Loving You."

"I'm getting pretty short up here at Phouc Xuyen. By the time you get this tape in fact, I should have already been to Saigon and called you up. I can't wait for that. I guess you might be interested in sort of a rundown as to my time spent up here at Phouc Xuyen. I'll give you a little elaboration on some of the highlights, there haven't been many. Basically this is a dull place. I guess the first big thing was getting that mosquito bite and going down to the YRBM 16. Did I say mosquito bite? I don't really know what kind of bite it was. My parents suggested a leach and it probably could have been that. Anyway, I did get bit by something. It started some place down the back of my heel on my right foot and worked its way up my leg to my groin. You probably know this pretty well from the letters I sent. I went down to YRBM 21 and had them look at it and they couldn't help me. There wasn't a doctor on the 21; however there was a doctor on YRBM 16. So I took a small boat up to the 16, which was a pretty interesting trip. I went up with a couple fellows from the EOD team. EOD stands for Explosive, Ordnance, Disposal. They blow up bad ammunition and any bobby traps and satchel charges that they find or is reported to them. At any rate, we started out on the 21, which is about eight miles from Cambodia on the Mekong, and we went up in this small open boat with an outboard motor. We went up the west bank of the Mekong to the 16 which is in rifle-shot of the border. It was a pretty interesting trip, I got to see quit a few small villages, a lot of sampans, fish traps along the bank, it was all very educational. While I was on the 16, I had a lot of fun talking to Ace. You remember Ace from Travis Air Force Base. He's stationed permanently on the 16 as a gunner's mate. He seems to enjoy himself pretty well. He's got a real nice set up, he doesn't work real hard and he has pretty decent living quarters. The whole ship is air conditioned on the inside. Anyway, after three days on the 16, it looked like I might have some trouble getting back. There were no boats going back that day and I was a little upset because I wanted to get back. So I went up on the helicopter deck of the 16 and there was a LOACH, which stands for Light Observation Helicopter, getting ready to take off and go down to a place called Dong Tam, which is in the opposite direction from YRBM 21, but I asked them if they could take a passenger to 21 and they said yeah, which was a real thrill since the little helicopter goes about 200 miles per hour. At first, we flew a few feet over the water and then we rose up high over the jungle, cut across a few islands and dropped down on the same field I was put down in originally. This time though, it was no big helicopter and I don't think anybody on the 21 realized right away that I was over there. I had to set around in that village for I guess forty-five minutes to an hour before they sent over a boat to pick me up. While I was there the kids were getting pretty bold. They would run up and grab at my watch and dig in my pockets and things. So finally I had to take out some sheets of paper that I had and I showed them all how to make paper airplanes. They were pretty fascinated with that, so we set around and made paper airplanes until the boat came. Then that afternoon, I got a ride on a patrol boat up to Phouc Xuyen.

I guess my next big incident you could say, was falling off in front of that patrol boat. I was actually pretty damn lucky. They had never had anybody fall off while they were underway and when a lot of people found out what happened, the fact that I had come through okay, they couldn't believe it. What actually happened was the boat was trying to get both engines synchronized so it could level off and run at a higher speed. It was running about forty miles an hour at the time. We were standing on the bow of the boat to try and put enough weight forward so it could level off, when suddenly the boat captain killed the throttle. Since I was furthest forward, I fell off and twisted as I went down. The first thing I though as I was falling off, was the twin propellers in the back. The last time I looked they were turning about 4500 rpms. Anyway, the boat hit me in the back of the head as it passed over me. It hit me again in the back as I was about half way under it and I did a summersault and pushed off the bottom of the boat just as the props passed over me. They came pretty close and I went down to the bottom when I pushed off the boat and stayed down there for a second to be sure it was clear. When I opened my eyes it was pitch black and I thought the boat was right on top of me. So I felt around and swam away and it was still black and I was scared I was under something. I couldn't figure what I was under, so finally I started to go up as I held my hands over my head. It started to get lighter as I rose and I realized that I was just so deep in the canal that it was black. The canal is pretty dirty anyhow. So when I came up the boat was quite a ways pass me. Since I stayed on the bottom for a while they thought they had killed me. When I came up, I was so relieved I had come through alright that I burst out laughing. I shook for quite awhile. Incidentally, that was the day I got those Polaroid shots you sent me. Evidently they were pretty great. I had a lot of guys go half crazy when they saw them; they really think you're something up here. Anyway, getting back to the story, the pictures I thought were half ruined but I was able to clean them up pretty well and fortunately none of the parts showing you were damaged. They were just damaged around the edges. I'll have to admit, I was really lucky to get through all right.

I guess the next big thing was being a witness in a court-marshal. One of the fellows here took a shot at another one of the guys up here, happened to just miss me and another fellow. At any rate, we had to be witnesses at his court-marshal. The outcome of the deal was they busted the guy in rank, fined him some money, and kicked him out of the service with a general discharge. The guy was a nice guy; he was a little hot headed. I don't think he was fit for military service; he got in a number of fights. He worked hard and was nice enough when he could control his temper. I think they were wise in getting rid of him.

The next thing that happened up here that I am going to tell you about is the time I dropped my M-79 grenade launcher in the canal while I was on watch. I felt pretty stupid actually. I had set the M-79, which is like a large rifle, on the edge of our revetment. A revetment is a sandbag protection about three feet high that goes around the side of the ammi to protect us from shell fragments and bullets. Anyway, I set the M-79 on the revetment and was hopping up on the revetment to set down for a while. I had been walking around for about a half hour, and darn if my leg didn't catch on the side of the M-79 and it fell right into the canal. I went and got another M-79 and the next morning I spent about an hour and a half diving for the one I dropped. If you have ever seen a sewer, than you know what our canal looks like. You spend an hour and a half diving in the sewer or our canal; it's the same thing. Sure makes you think twice about doing it again. I got it back. It had been buried in mud but I cleaned it up alright. They were real happy I got it back. An M-79 is a pretty good weapon and to lose one would hurt our small defenses here, not that I think that we're ever going to have to use it. I must confess, at one point I became disoriented while under the ammi and started crying from fear that I wouldn't find my way back to the surface. Thankfully I did. Outside of those small things and listening to the rice grow and killing mosquitoes and bugs, with every bug imaginable here, occasionally wading through tough swamps, I haven't really done much up here at Phouc Xuyen. It is a good place to leave.

"Hello, it's your old boyfriend in Vietnam again, this time without music. Actually it's about three days latter. I am sorry that this tape probably won't reach you by your birthday, there are several reasons. For one thing, we've all been pretty busy trying to finish up the base to give it to the Vietnamese. I've been working with the Seabees for the last couple of days, helping them in their rush to complete the base. Also, there are no postage stamps up here and I found you need postage stamps to mail tapes back home, they can't be sent for free.

So until I can get my hands on some postage stamps, there won't be any tape going out of here, not mine anyhow.

Well how you been? I guess that is a stupid question to ask. I ask it every time I write a letter. Bunch of new things I can tell you about. I guess I already said that in a letter but I thought I might give you a description of our living space around here. Our hooch, so to speak, everything is a hooch in Vietnam. The Vietnamese live in hooches, the Americans live in hooches, everybody works in hooches, I'm getting sick of that word", Ken laughs briefly. "Anyway, our hooch is built on what's called an ammi and I don't know why it is called an ammi, it's actually just a big barge. Our hooch is about eighty-five feet long and the barge is about ninety-five feet long. It's just a standard building. It's got nine feet high walls and a regular pitch to the roof. It's actually about twelve feet high at the center of the roof, looks to be about sixteen feet across. All the way down both sides of the hooch inside, are double racks. I think there are fourteen racks on the sides, and they're all full, and everybody's got their own bunch of boxes and cabinets for their personal things. I have all my gear in two grenade boxes and a cabinet that Rich and I built. Rich is the fellow that sleeps next to me. We have more or less been buddies together up here. We came up together and we stood watches together for a while. Right now I'm standing an ammi watch, which is like a roving patrol. I walk up and down on the ammi with a grenade launcher, a flash light, and some concussion grenades. We throw these concussion grenades into the canal every fifteen minutes or so and it is like a small depth charge. When they go off in the canal they sink down to the bottom and blow up. If there were any enemy swimmers trying to go by underwater or come across the canal underwater, it would bring them right to the surface. So I throw those every so often and shoot grenades out into the fields on the other side of the canal. Probably shoot about twenty M-79 grenades and I throw around fifteen or twenty concussion grenades into the canal a night. It's actually a pretty simple watch; I don't mind it at all. At least I get to sleep in my own rack at night rather than sleeping out on a cot in the tower. And when it rains, even though I get a little wet while I am on the watch, I can come in and dry off and sleep in a dry rack. I really don't mind too much. Anyway, I am getting short up here and it seems to be the custom to give the guys that are short the ammi watch the last week or so they're here. Kind of got side tracked from describing my living quarters didn't I.

Describing my rack will be pretty simple. It's a pipe rack with single wires that go across the bottom to support the thin mattress. There are no springs to sort of speak, although the wires give enough to give the mattress a little spring to it. I have a mosquito net tied up underneath. Incidentally, I'm on the bottom, there's nobody on the top right now. I have the mosquito net tied up to the frame above me, so I keep the mosquito net up all the time and free of mosquitoes. On my left is my cabinet which is also my book self. I'm getting a pretty darn nice library. I've got a small reputation around here for having good books. I have a decent library and I keep them nice, so guys come and borrow books from me and I borrow books from them, it's a pretty nice arrangement. Anyway, I have a rack inside my cabinet for my writing material and my toilet kit and below that I have my two uniforms I wear folded up on one side, and on the other side, I keep my small kit bag with my valuables and so forth in there. It's a pretty nice set up, everything is pretty simple. I really enjoy the simplicity of this place, although sometimes it seems that it gets too simple around here, I would like a little more challenge. You know I always enjoy some kind of hectic life, at least when I lived back in Glendale I did, or it seemed that way. I'll sure be glad to get back to it. Anyway, when I lay on my back in my rack, I look at a poster I bought in Saigon before I came up here. It's a poster of a blond girl. Actually her hair is not quite blond. She looks quite a bit like you standing on a beach with her thumbs in the bottom of her bathing suit with her arms out to one side, just looking at the surf. It reminds me of you, that's why I put it up. Have to tell you, she doesn't have any top on. I couldn't buy one with a top on; besides, it is a little nicer having one with the top off. And then up on one corner of the poster, I have a picture of you. You know me; I always like posters and pictures. Then also on my left up on the wall I have a fan that rotates back and forth. So half the time it is blowing on Rich and the other half of the time it is blowing on me. And that just about sums up my small little world, it is really simple. I can't tell you how simple things are around here. It amazes me you can have life so uncomplicated. Everything seems so far away, all the problems and everything that are back in the world, the world being the United States of course. Anyway, I'll be glad to leave this place. I don't know right now when I will be leaving. I thought I would be leaving on the ninetieth, but we got a few problems up here so I might not get to leave right away. Can't really tell you about them right now, it's all top secret stuff. But I will be able to tell you when I get back to Ben Luc. It's nothing to worry about though, that's for sure. If there was anything to worry about, why, I wouldn't tell you anyway. But don't worry yourself because it is all pretty dumb stuff, stuff that wouldn't interest you anyway. I guess there is not really much more to talk about, I could tell you a little about the fellows that are here. In the rack on my left, on the bottom, is a guy named Dardaz. He lives in the Bronx's, acts like it. And above him is his best friend by the name of Polodori, Joe Polodori. He lives in Albany, New York, so they're really good friends. There both kind of crazy I guess you could say. There's nobody above me. Then on my left is Rich Kaptula and he's from New Jersey. There's nobody above him. Then going down is a guy named Lenny Piper. Piper is from New Hampshire. He's a real nice guy. He's pretty quite, gets along with everybody alright I guess, a little nervous maybe. There's nobody above him either. Across from me is a guy named Myers, he's from Connecticut. He's alright. He's been up here the longest of anyone. He's a radioman. Above him is a fellow by the name of Suber. He's from South Carolina. He's a real nice guy. He gets along with everybody pretty well. Then the next rack down is a guy named Hanson, he's a new guy. I don't know anything about him. Above him is a guy named

Ron Baker and he's from Alabama. He's a real nice fellow. He's married. He got married about a month before he came over. Married a real pretty girl, he's real proud of her, and he makes the water for us. Then the next rack down, on top, is Randy Strickland from Burbank. We got along pretty good earlier but he's the guy I wrote you about that has a lot of nerve problems, I think. He has been jumpy lately and he's been on me a lot, so I just kind of withdrew. I don't talk to him much anymore; it's kind of a shame because I enjoyed his company. Below him is a guy named Thorton. I guess Thorton is from Chicago, I think, I'm not sure. He's got kind of a chip on his shoulder. He's a pretty nice guy when you get to know him if you stay on the right side of him. I had to stand as a witness in a court-martial for him the other day. Actually, I just gave a statement. We haven't had the court-marshal yet. He was to drunk to come on watch, but that's something that happens to almost everybody up here. There seems to only be about five of us that don't drink. I refuse to drink up here in a combat zone. I want my coordination and all my mental faculties in tact if anything should happen. It is one thing to drink a little bit at your house or apartment or at a party. Out here, it is entirely different. I don't think I would feel right doing it.

Anyway, that sums up the guys at our end of the hooch fairly well I guess. The other guys are just average old guys from all over the States. There are a couple of guys from California. I have one good friend that's a Seabee, a fellow by the name of Greg Holmberg. He's a real good surfer. He lives in New Port and went to Orange Coast for a year and Ervin for a year, and then like me, didn't have a definite enough plan set out, so he had to come into the service. He's a reservist too, but he's in the Seabees rather than the regular navy. I would have rather been a Seabee reservist myself. I really enjoy most of the Seabees. I seem to have their kind of attitude. They are all more ambitious and enjoy work more, and work harder than the guys in the regular navy. I'm somewhere in-between. I like to relax when I have a chance to relax, but I don't mind working hard either. I should have really been working with them more than I have, because I've have had more opportunity to work with them. Greg and I talk about getting together someday when we both get settled back in the States. I've been thinking about if I get an apartment, inviting all the guys I've met over here that live in southern California, and having some type of party. I'll just see what happens when I get back, that's all quite a long ways from now. Or it's just a short time from now, depending on your outlook. I like to think the glass is half empty rather than half full. You know the sign of an optimist, is he says the glass is half full rather then half empty. Well situation is just reversed over here. My time is getting short rather than having a long time to go. That's the way I like to look at it. That's actually the optimistic approach.

There's not a lot to say, the weathers deteriorating quickly. We had a lot of sunny weather, even though it is suppose to be monsoon. But the last couple of weeks we have been getting more and more rain, till the point now it rains most of the time, or sprinkles most of the time, with heavy rain in between. I don't mind that so much, because when it rains like that it gets a lot cooler. I have to sleep with a blanket every night, and I don't mind that at all. It's more comfortable that way, I think. Think I'll close for now. I'm going in to eat chow. I'll come back and try and finish this thing up. I want to get this at least ready to mail if I do have the opportunity. So I'll see you for now and talk to you a little later.

I think it is great to get letters, I really do. You don't know what they mean over here. Everything is so completely different that any kind of link from the world we use to have and the things we know back in the United States, is really a welcome link. I guess now that you've got the extra medium of my voice to help you, maybe I could better describe some of the surroundings up here at Phouc Xuyen. First I'll start with the canal. It's called the Grand Canal and it runs from west to east. In other words, it flows from west to east. Directly in front of the base it goes on down out of sight to the west and down into the trees on the east. Down at the tree line to the east, is the village of Phouc Xuyen. It's a pretty small village.

Probably no more than a hundred hooches and four or five stores. However, it's surprising just how much are in these stores. You can get drinking cups, batteries, and several different kinds of pharmaceutical drugs. They're all French, but they are things you don't expect to see out here. I guess you don't expect to see them because everything is really primitive. I doubt whether they have changed their living style in a hundred years, maybe two-hundred.

The addition of outboard motors to their boats, small gasoline motors, I don't know if you can hear one putting by now in the canal in the tape, but they chug back and forth all day long. They carry grain, wood, wicker baskets and furniture and things like that. Just anything they need along the canal. This canal extends for I believe its sixty or seventy miles. We're about thirty miles up the canal from the Mekong River. I believe it's that much; it might be a little less. At any rate, across the canal are just big green fields. They don't seem to cultivate these fields. Further out near the village on the far side of our field, maybe a thousand meters out, there is some cultivation, but right around the base there's nothing, it just grows wild. Everything is green and flat. I guess you can see from those pictures I sent home, just how flat everything is.

Right now I'm setting up in one of our front machine gun towers, watchtowers I guess you could call them. It's about the quietist place I could find to make a recording. Everybody has their tapes and radios on or they're talking all the time, so it makes it tough to get a nice private recording. This is an ideal spot. Right now it's four o'clock on Monday afternoon, 27th of July. I guess that makes it about one o'clock in the morning on Monday morning, same date for you guys. However, I think you're probably asleep aren't you, I hope you are. If not, I've got some questions to ask. Don't worry I'm just kidding. Anyway, its overcast right now, it has been clear, it hasn't rained in a week which is really something. They can't believe it because we're right in the middle of monsoon season and everything is starting to dry out. The exposed areas in the compound are getting dusty and dry and the grass has stopped growing. You can see they're having trouble with the rice up in some of the rice paddies around the village. Even the canal is starting to recede a little bit. We were worried for a while as to when it was going to overflow at the banks. We weren't worried for the safety of the base because we have built the base in such way that it won't be harmed too much by the overflow of the canal. Everything is up on stilts, raised about four and a half feet above any water level that might be reached. However, we still didn't want it to overflow the banks because that would make the everyday struggle a little more difficult.

We have a total of seven towers in the compound right now. I guess that is going to be increased by one. Outside the addition of that one tower, everything is just about complete. We have a boardwalk set up that runs down the front of the base along the canal. We also have a helo pad that sits back about sixty yards on the eastern side of the base. We got a boardwalk that runs to the helo pad and then the ammo bunker next to the helo pad. Then one boardwalk picks up three of the towers. Then there's a boardwalk that runs back to the middle tower in the back and then a third boardwalk that links up with the last three towers. In addition to this, we have two personnel bunkers that sit along the side of the main boardwalk. That's about everything they built here and about everything they're going to build. I guess pretty soon we'll have ARVNs come in here. An ARVN is a soldier of the Army of the Republic of Vietnam, and they refer to these guys who make up this army, as ARVNs. I'm not sure, but I think this will be a combined ARVN and Vietnamese navy base. This is the Vietnamese Brown Water Navy. They refer to it as a brown water navy because all their functions take place on the brown water of the canals and rivers. Right now they're only Vietnamese personnel that are ridding along with the American STAB and PBR patrols. STAB stands for Strike Assault Boat and PBR stands for Patrol Boat River. Outside of that, there isn't much here at Phouc Xuyen. It's a pretty simple and small base. The addition of the helo pad was really something. It really put this place on the map, to so to speak. The two attack helicopters that stay here are called Seawolves, and they load up with rockets and are equipped with machine guns. They also carry a machine gun called the mini gun, and it's got six barrels that rotate as they fire. They can fire 2500 rounds in one minute. If you can see this at night, it's really devastating. We've watched various attacks, off in the distance, where they are firing this mini gun, and it's fascinating to see, because every fifth bullet was a tracer. A tracer is a round that leaves a red trail as it's fired, and this red trail stands out. It isn't just a flash of red; it's an actual visual trail you can see from the machine gun to the target or wherever it should hit. At any rate, with every fifth round a tracer at 2500 rounds a minute it looks like he's shooting solid tracers and they can really do a job on a target. I guess the VC are just deathly afraid of these mini guns and I can see why. At any rate, we are real proud to have two Seawolves here; it really increases the stature of this base quite a bit.

So much for Phouc Xuyen, I'm as tired of talking about it as you must be of hearing about it. Going to cut it short for today and then I will fill in some more tomorrow or the next day or whenever I get a chance to, until the tape is complete. But I'll try and get it in the mail so you get it before your birthday, so long for now sweetheart."

We hear the sound of a motorized sampan chugging off into the distance, fading away, as it moved down the long narrow canal.

When Ken Scott finally did get back to Ben Luc, he received a "Dear Ken" letter from the girl for whom he had made the tapes. She never got to hear them.

Today, Ken lives happily in California with his beautiful bride of over thirty years. They have two grown daughters that Ken is very proud of.

The Professor, Doc Carling and Mr. Fry, visiting An Long

An Long village, west entrance to Grand Canal

ATSB Phouc Xuyen, Plain of Reeds, Grand Canal

ATSB Phouc Xuyen, Grand Canal, STAB ahead

NSA sailors at ATSB Phouc Xuyen, berthing hooch

Seaman Ken Scott wading swamp around ATSB Phouc Xuyen

ACV, last hovercraft patrolling the Plains, ATSB Ben Luc

Mercenary swamp air boat, YRBM 21, Dwight Cabella

Ken Scott on aft twin 60s of STAB, ATSB Phouc Xuyen

Seawolf gunship, Cavalry of the Delta

Children of the River

PBRs leaving YRBM 21

CHAPTER THIRTEEN - BEN KEO

After three days in Saigon at the President Hotel, I returned to the Annapolis to catch a ride to my next duty station. I was picked up by a navy driver in a green jeep and we left Saigon after breakfast, heading northwest on Highway 1 into Tay Ninh Province. We transferred to Highway 13 at Go Da Ha, continuing north. We arrived at a little dirt road off the highway around noon and took a left into a small fishing village.

We passed little huts and shacks on the right as we approached a gated ten-foot-high fence. Hanging on the front gate was a homemade sign painted in the South Vietnamese colors of yellow and red. In the center was a design of a giant slingshot, with a star on the top right. Painted in bold black letters the sign read, ATSB BEN KEO, BUILT WITH GENUINE STOLEN PARTS. Oh-boy... home.

Just inside the base to the left was a small bunker with one American GI dressed in cut-off green shorts and flip-flops. An M-16 rifle was slung over his bare shoulder and the sounds of Jimmy Hendrix played on his portable tape deck as he waved us in. To the right was a thirty-foot-high wooden look-out tower, with a handmade ladder going up the side. Behind the tower in the distance I could see Nui Ba Den, "Black Virgin" mountain.

We splashed through a giant mud puddle just inside the compound as we entered the base. The driver pulled up next to a navy-gray Ford pickup and a Chevy deuce-and-a-half and cut the engine. Directly ahead was a four-foot reinforced sandbag wall, protecting the base from the river. Over the top I could see the antennas of two Tango

Assault Boats. The driver jumped out and skipped over a plank board to the galley, built on an ammi pontoon barge. I grabbed my sea-bag, and a dark-hair, bearded young junior grade navy lieutenant appeared out of the Command bunker coming toward me.

"Machinist Mate Third Class, Christopher, reporting for duty sir," I said, standing at attention and saluting.

"Welcome aboard, Christopher. William Barnhouse," he said, returning my salute. He asked where I was from?

"Virginia, sir," I said admiring his full beard.

"Really, I went to Georgetown University in D.C."

"Wow, no kidding, sir, another Chesapeake Bay boy. You ever go crabbing."

"All the time, right on the Potomac," he responded.

"They said you have refrigeration experience."

"Yes sir, I spent some time on a refrigeration ship." He walked me over to a refrigeration compressor behind the galley and asked me how it looked?

"Looks great, sir." It was another brand new unit.

"Outstanding, come with me." He led me through the doorway of a sandbag bunker.

The sandbags must have been three or four layers thick and the floor was the same red dirt as out in the yard. I jumped another mud puddle in the doorway. There were several radios on wooden tables, with two third class radiomen attentively listening in. Displayed on the wall was a map with a plastic cover over it. Colored marker Xs and arrows indicated appointed positions of boat units on the river.

"Well, Christopher, I don't have to tell you we are the control center for this end of Operation Giant Slingshot. Cambodia is just beyond the tree line across the river, and the fields are Viet Cong strongpoints," he said, describing my new home that I had been assigned to for the next ninety days.

During the Cambodian offensive, Ben Keo was the major Tay Ninh jumping off point for the American-Vietnamese flotilla that sailed up the Vam Co Dong into Cambodia. The men of Ben Keo were responsible for supplying necessities for the operation, which was no small job, considering the nearest U.S. Navy supply base at Ben Luc was more than fifty miles away. The main VC threat recently had come from satchel-carrying swimmers, mortars and rockets.

"So keep an eye out and your head down. We've installed razor wire swimmer nets so don't go jumping in the water."

"Oh no, sir, I wouldn't do that."

"Good. And another thing, it's not safe outside the perimeter of the base, so be forewarned and observe the buddy system; don't go anywhere without somebody with you. You'll be assigned sentry duties and will be expected to make runs for replenishing supplies, understand?" "Yes sir."

"Good. Well, it says here that you spent some time on the YRBM 21 in engine repair and Mike boats."

"Yes sir."

"Well we can put you to work. Tom, get John in here."

One of the radiomen, who wore a cowboy hat, jumped up and left the bunker.

Barnhouse turned to a Vietnamese lieutenant for a moment and another third class entered the bunker with Montana Tom.

"John, this is Christopher. See that he gets settled in and show him around a bit. Oh and John, issue him a sixty."

"Yes sir." Mr. Barnhouse shot me a smile.

"Come on, let's go find you a place to sleep."

As we left the command bunker and stepped out into the compound, I stopped to take it all in. John also stopped as he pulled out a Marlboro and offered me one.

"Thanks, don't mind if I do." I pulled out my Zippo and cupped it with my hand.

"So how long you been here?" I asked.

"A while now. I've lost track of time, to tell you the truth," he said taking a long drag off his cigarette and exhaling it out his nostrils.

"How big is this place," I asked as I walked over to the sandbag wall and peeked over at the barbwire in the river.

"Not big by military standards. I believe it's two hundred feet long and one hundred fifty feet wide."

"Wow, that is small." I looked over and admired the PBR's flying Vietnamese Flags tied alongside one of the ammi barges.

The base was composed of three thirty-by-ninety-foot ammi pontoon barges on water secured to the river bank. An additional five smaller pontoon barges were secured to the three. The ammis were fitted out at Nha Be naval base, which supplied many of the smaller support bases. The roofs of the hooches were strengthened for defense against mortar and rocket attack, and the walls were heavily sand-bagged to afford protection from small-arms fire. The living quarters, galley, food supply and patrol boat repair areas were on the water, while the watchtower, tactical operations center, ammunition bunker and mortar pit were on land. There were twenty PBRs attached to Vietnamese Patrol Group 53 and six Vietnamese heavies had been run aground to support them. Facing the river to the right was a thin ten-foot-high wall separating the base from the small village of Ben Keo. To the left was a duck farm and warehouses for storage of rice, with a small dock for transferring the burlap bags onto the junks for shipment down river to Saigon. There also was a small area for landing helicopters.

The base was operated by two governments, with twenty-five American NSA sailors and twenty or so American advisors attached to Vietnamese Patrol Group 53 and Vietnamese Assault Division 71. Roughly seventy Vietnamese sailors manned the boats and a few Viet laborers from the village worked days in the mess.

John led me over a two-by-twelve plank board walkway and onto the middle barge, helping me with my gear. We stopped for a moment at a small shed that he unlocked. He reached in and produced an M-60 machine gun, which he handed to me, along with several belts of ammo.

"You know how to use this?"

"Yes I do," I now had two weapons. "Good, you're on the M-60 team," he locked the armory back up and led me into the hooch.

"Hey everybody, this is Christopher." Several guys were sitting on crates around an empty wooden spool watching a black-and-white TV suspended from the ceiling. They looked over for a moment, smiling, then turned their attention back to the blond weather girl on the tube wearing a mini-skirt.

The living quarters were filled with racks, mosquito nets and brown lockers. Everywhere I looked there were guns and grenades.

The guys were dressed however they pleased and haircuts and shaves seemed to be optional. I found a bottom rack in the back and off-loaded my gear.

"Come on, Christopher, let's go catch lunch." John raced me across another plank to the galley. I was immediately impressed with the cleanliness of the mess hall. There were six tables with four chairs each up against the walls. An old mama-san was refilling the salt and pepper shakers and placing them on white tablecloths. Up front, trays and clean silverware sat at the end of two tables. Steaming food covered with towels was set out on top.

"Damn, the guys at Phouc Xuyen would kill for this."

"What's Phouc Xuyen," John asked?

"It was another base I was at," I answered as I helped myself to the canned roast beef and instant potatoes.

Just then two second class cooks came out of the back kitchen and greeted us.

"Hey guys, this is Christopher, he's going to be with us for a while."

"This is Paul and Pendola." Both were dressed in greens, with white aprons and boots. Pendola was a little Italian guy and Paul Gaffney was a heavyset red-headed mulatto. They were great people and fun to talk to.

While eating lunch, Paul, who had been at the base the longest, began telling me a little about the departed America river divisions and the history of the base. "When I first got here, River Division 531 and Lieutenant Commander Thomas K. Anderson, Commander of the Tay Ninh Naval Task Element, had just kicked the NVA's butt."

In mid-June 1969, units of River Division 531, and elements of two other PBR divisions, along with six Mobile Riverine units, began transiting toward a small Vietnamese naval base located at the village of Ben Keo on the Vam Co Dong River. Tom Anderson was sent first to investigate if the area was suitable for a further advance base upstream from a series of three bases already established. As previously arranged, he met with Vietnamese Navy Lieutenant Nguyen Trong Phat of the 27th River Patrol Company. Dai Qui Phat had left half his family behind in Hanoi, North Vietnam, and moved south to fight what he called a repressive northern government. He commanded a small contingent of Vietnamese gunboats moored at water's edge of the little village. Phat and his Vietnamese sailors lived amongst the village people and showed Tom Anderson where he could best set up a base.

In the first week of operation, Tom Anderson and his units were involved in eight firefights. On their first night ambush patrol, the boats turned back an NVA Regiment near Ben Soi. Until that first night, the enemy could cross the river quite easily, especially at night. After losing a number of sampans and personnel, the NVA soon realized they had no chance of crossing the river and withdrew. By the last of June all units were assembled, including a barracks barge. A force of thirty PBRs, a couple of Monitors, a Zippo, Douche, several Alphas and a few units from the Vietnamese Navy, 27th River Patrol Company - a total of about fifty boats. One of the Monitors was configured as a Command communications boat and served as Tactical Operations Center.

A contingent of NSA sailors and a few Seabees were sent up from the Naval Supply Center of Nha Be to build the camp. Shortly after arriving, they were introduced to Lieutenant Commander Anderson, who advised them of the importance of their mission, and told them there would be a lot of hard work ahead, and that others were depending on them to stop the Communist. They were instructed to dig foxholes near their guard posts, since there were snipers in the area and the base was rocketed every few nights. A couple of days latter, they were rocketed and the next day they all went back and dug their favorite hole a lot deeper. They erected a thirty-foot tower, with a big starlight scope and a single .50 caliber machine gun facing the Cambodian border, just three miles across the river. They then filled thousands of sand bags, built a communication and ammo bunker, strung barbwire with noisemakers, beer cans, trip flares, claymore mines and a fence with a gate at the road entrance.

During the morning of June 28th, the partially-constructed support base came under intense enemy fire from one-hundred seven millimeter rockets, rocket-propelled grenades, mortar and automatic weapons. At the outset of the attack, Tom Anderson was on board his fully-enclosed command boat. He immediately went on the deck to

212

an exposed position in order to determine the exact source of enemy fire. Under almost continuous attack and in great personal danger, Tom Anderson remained in his exposed position while deploying all units assigned in a strategic manner to spread the return fire and minimize possible damage and casualties. Retaining effective control over his River Patrol Boats and Moble Riverine Force units, as well as Viet Regional Force units, he called in nearby U.S. Army artillery and Navy Seawolf fire support and directed their fire into enemy positions.

Throughout the engagement and into the morning of the 29th as the enemy was repelled, Anderson repeatedly exposed himself to intense enemy fire, directing devastating return fire. In addition, Tom and his men provided medical aid for one Viet sailor and three civilians wounded in the village behind the base and skillfully coordinated the medical air evacuation. Lieutenant Commander Tom Anderson's decisiveness, professionalism and courage under fire had resulted in overturning the enemy attack and minimizing damage to the base.

Tom Anderson was directed to attend weekly Thursday meetings with the Province Senior Advisor of Tay Ninh, a CIA guy who coordinated all U.S. and South Vietnamese forces in the area. Tom expressed his concerns that the Reds were trying to slip men and materiel across the river, so they could attack Tay Ninh. This view was supported by the 25th Infantry Division sources. Tom was able to find out where he could get Army artillery and air support, as well as Air Force assets and even Philippine artillery. He also learned that an Army unit of the 4th Battalion, 23rd Infantry, Mechanized called the "Tomahawks" was based on Black Virgin Mountain, not far away. They had the same engines in their armored personnel carriers as the PBRs and became an engine support. In turn, the Army discovered that the Navy's 40 mm automatic grenade launchers could be used to great advantage on their armored personnel carriers. The two groups became great friends as some of the Army guys rode along on the boats and some of the Navy guys rode the personnel carriers.

There was a Vietnamese fort a few miles upstream, manned by two-hundred Vietnamese Army Airborne and two Green Beret advisors. They were on the side of the river close to Cambodia and were very happy to see the Navy firepower arrive. The North Vietnamese Army, was on the Cambodian side of the border around two thousand men strong, and was making plans to attack and take Tay Ninh City, the third largest city in South Vietnam. The two-hundred Republic of Vietnam soldiers wouldn't have stood a chance. Tom Anderson and his people visited the fort and set up positions and fields of fire where they could station boats if the Army came under attack. They also established radio frequencies between the Army base and their Tactical Operations Center.

In July, the 25th Infantry Division troopers braced for a possible attack on Tay Ninh City. C Company, 4th Battalion, Mechanized, 23rd Infantry drew heavy fire as they began a sweep around Nui Ba Den Mountain. Gunners from the 1st Battalion, 8th Artillery poured in 105 mm and eight-inch howitzer fire while "tropic lightning" mortar men contributed 81 mm mortar fire.

After this barrage, the men of the 4th again moved up the slopes of the "Black Virgin." Again they met machine gun fire, but quickly wiped out the enemy emplacement. When the battle ended, twenty-seven Red soldiers were dead and there were no U.S. casualties.

Elsewhere in the 25th Division's area, sixteen NVA soldiers were killed near "Parrot's Beak," sixteen miles southwest of Cu Chi.

For the rest of the month, most of the activity around Tay Ninh was centered around the Black Virgin mountain. Navy patrol boats assisted the 25th Division in operations, inserting and extracting long-range patrol teams. The sailors also continued patrolling the river and provided convoy escorts. The patrolmen reported an average of ten contacts a night on the Vam Co Dong River.

The Tay Ninh Province Chief, a capable and decisive man, who was a member of the Coa Dai religious sect, contended that the Viet Cong recruiting had been lagging because of the Coa Dai, which was strong and pro-government. Also, the regional popular force troops in the area were of high quality.

At the beginning of August, Seaman Harold Payne was on guard duty in the tower when he noticed two Vietnamese soldiers that seemed to be out of place and pacing the base off. After calling down to let someone know, he was told to keep an eye on them till back up could arrive, but they split up and he eventually lost sight of them.

A few days later, a Vietnamese girl wandered up to the makeshift beer stand in the center of the base and tried to buy a beer from him. Again he tried to notify someone, but she also vanished before help could arrive. Shortly after, a jeep carrying a civilian and two soldiers pulled up and asked him if he could identify this woman. After agreeing, he was taken to Tay Ninh Army Base to meet with a high-ranking Vietnamese officer who then had him escorted down the road in a truck loaded with ARVN soldiers. As the truck drove down the road he saw the girl sitting next to a bicycle on the side, as her eyes met his and the truck came to a screeching halt. Next thing he knew, the soldiers had rushed her and beat her to the ground, almost knocking her teeth out. At first he felt sick, thinking he had sealed the girl's fate and wondered why the soldiers had been so harsh. But as they stripped her down and he saw the C-4 explosives wrapped around her waist, he began to shudder at the thought of what could have happened.

On the evening of August 13th, the North Vietnamese launched their attack with an estimated two thousand men at the airborne base and at Ben Keo. Tom Anderson dispatched boats to the Army base and took up previously determined positions, while other boats were fighting at Ben Keo and downstream. Although exposed to enemy fire, Seaman Payne remained at his post in the tower and assisted in locating the enemy positions and spotting artillery and machine gun fire into those positions. He looked through the starlight scope as the enemy walked straight toward the base under heavy fire, not dodging or running, just walking in a straight line, hardly varying at all. They fought for two nights and two-and-a-half days. The Army helped with artillery and the supply of ammo and .50 cal barrels, which had melted and bent from prolonged firing. The Airborne troops had stacked three hundred NVA bodies near their fort. Some NVA did manage to get inside the fort perimeter, but were held off via hand-to-hand combat. The Airborne sustained several casualties, but the Navy's casualties were considered relatively light. The South Vietnamese sailors that were killed were brought back and wrapped in white sheets with candles placed around them during the night, while their shipmates wept and prayed. The next morning they were taken away. The Airborne tracked between one and two hundred blood trails of wounded and dead being dragged back across the Cambodian border. The battle ended the NVA plans to take Tay Ninh City and they put a price on Lieutenant Commander Anderson's head, dead or alive.

One morning, about 0600 hours, one of the PBR sailors was cleaning up the boat near Ben Keo as they drifted downstream after a long night patrol when he noticed hands and a head coming up over the stern of the boat. It was an enemy sapper with a knife in his teeth. The sailor poked him between the eyes with a swab handle, causing him to fall back into the river. The sailor grabbed a grenade, pulled the pin and dropped it in with the sapper killing him instantly. Vice Admiral Zumwalt heard about this and flew in personally to give the sailor a Bronze Star medal.

In late August, with the major threat gone, about half the forces were pulled out of the area, including River Division 531. The Army said it best when they received the news. Lieutenant Commander Anderson and his men rode to the sound of the guns on water with a spirit the cavalry would envy. River Division 594, under the command of Lieutenant Thomas W. Frenzinger, was brought in and took up the fight alongside Assault Division 15 until April, when Vietnamese River Patrol Group 53 took charge.

"Damn, how'd you remember all that," I asked? Paul stood up smiling and shrugged as he retreated back into the kitchen.

Dear Folks,   August 20, 1969

In two more days, River Division 531 will have completed its portion of the task at Tay Ninh and will be returning to Nha Be. Both the effort and the success in Tay Ninh has been one of the most courageous in our Division's history. So successful was the operation, General Wheeler, Chairman of the Joint Chiefs of Staff in Washington, D.C., during his recent visit to Vietnam, specifically commented on the excellent effectiveness of the operation conducted here by your men. Although it was an extremely difficult, tiring and dangerous job, your sons and husbands provided the key to success by their unending determination and courage.

Today, I will be relieved of command of the Division, turning over the leadership to Lieutenant T. P. McGinley. The leadership of this group of men has been a wonderful experience as each of them has voluntarily done his best to ensure a smooth running division. This is what has made my job so gratifying and I'm sure the same degree of support and dedication to duty will continue with my successor.

I truly regret leaving the division and the associations I have had with the high caliber of men as these with whom I have served. I can only hope that in the future I will have the pleasure of again serving with any or all of the people in River Division 531.

I have respectfully submitted my most sincere thanks and appreciation to all of the units that worked with us for the most outstanding support and cooperation received by the Tay Ninh Navy Element since our arrival in June 1969. I am firmly convinced that the Inter-service and joint cooperation and support has been the single most contributing factor leading to the successful operations enjoyed by the Tay Ninh Navy to date. Furthermore, I feel that the instantaneous and enthusiastic ground, air, and arty responses to enemy attacks significantly reduced the casualty rate which might have otherwise been experienced by my sailors. For this, I am the most grateful.

Again, let me express to you men and your families that you have my deepest respect as sailors and men and I sincerely thank you all for the unbelievable support you have given me during the past year. Well done and God speed.

LCDR T. K. Anderson

At dusk John informed me I had the night watch and walked me out to the look-out tower.

"At night we lock the gate and put an M-60 in the tower. If you see anybody around the fence or gate, they're VC, don't hesitate to blow them away," he said with a dead serious look on his face. We then climbed the ladder and looked out into the dim, fading light at the rice paddies and jungle across the river. It was beautiful. The river appeared out of the dense jungle from the left of the base, and after passing us, cut ninety degrees, moving straight out away from the base, leaving a two-mile visual corridor before again cutting right and disappearing around a bend. The water flowed south to north which was evident by the large green floating plants passing the base. Across the river was a small mud fort in the middle of a huge rice paddy.

"The tree line is Cambodia. You see anything, shoot it. You don't need to ask, it's a free-fire zone."

The tall palm trees looked to be a hundred years old and the jungle appeared as if it could eat you up if you dared to enter.

"This is our starlight scope and it turns night into day." The scope was two feet long and I saw a green field with the top of the rice stems swaying in the light breeze.

"If you see anything suspicious, use the powered phones to call the bunker and report it." There was a hand-held phone in a bag, wired to the radio shack and mortar pit.

"If you need anything, there are people in the pit and the shack. There'll also be one guy roaming. Your relief will show up after midnight, okay? See you in the morning," he said, backing down the ladder.

The boats were leaving to take up their night ambush positions. The sound of the boats engines faded in the distance and the base was alone except for a few PBRs left behind. I watched through the starlight scope as they turned the bend and disappeared down the river. I took my helmet off and sat on it while I hide the flame of my cigarette behind the tower's wooden walls. I wondered who had worn my flak jacket before me. It had peace signs and hippie drawings all over it. Back home, the hippies were protesting our presence in Vietnam and we here fighting were wearing their symbols all over our gear. These were strange times we were living; I bet no other American conflicts were as weird as this one. Twenty-five U.S. sailors in support of a Vietnamese river group in the middle of nowhere after just two weeks of combat training.

218

A little later, I heard footsteps coming up the ladder as I looked over to see another young man climbing up. He had his flak jacket and pot on, with an M-16 slung over his shoulder.

"Hey, how's it going, I'm Dave." He was wearing a hip holster with a Colt 45 in it.

"Pretty good, I'm Chris," I said, admiring his gun.

"See anything?" He took a peek through the starlight scope across to the tree line.

"Nope, everything's quite," I said as the sound of a concussion grenade went off in the river behind me.

"It's okay. Just one of our sentries keeping an eye out for swimmers."

"You see a lot of them?" I asked.

"We caught a couple not long ago."

Then the sailor in the mortar pit dropped a flare projectile in the tube as it opened over the rice paddy and drifted down, slowly illuminating the valley. As it burned out and landed, things returned to pitch black.

"Man I'm too short for this shit," Dave announced.

"How short are you?" I asked.

"I leave tomorrow."

"What the hell you doing up here?"

"Oh what the hell, I couldn't sleep," Dave chuckled.

Dave crawled back down the ladder and I spent the rest of my watch staring out at the tree line and watching the flares drop back to earth until I was relieved to get some sack time.

The next morning Dave put his gun up for auction, and for a few dollars I bought it. The serial numbers had been filed down. I buckled it around my waist, feeling like I'd gone back to the Old West. I wore it everywhere and hung it over my bedpost at night. Normally, we slept in our shorts, with our boots and guns near us. I had grenades on a little shelf over my head and belts of M-60 rounds draped over the rail at my feet. I was finally in the war.

Later that day, I wandered out to the dock and came upon a second class engineman by the name of Webb, working on one of the PBRs. He was a loud, skinny little guy, who appeared drunk most of the time, but we hit it off and became friends. I began a

219

routine of helping him and a Vietnamese sailor by the name of Tin with the maintenance and repairs of the boats. Webb introduced me to some of the other advisors who bunked in the far right hooch with the Vietnamese patrolmen. Chief Ramsey was senior with E6s Kelly and Gray right under him. Most of the advisors were in their thirties and had been in the Navy a while. They thought of themselves as career men; we young sailors called them lifers. For the most part, the American advisors of Group 53 were good guys, but the Vietnamese of the unit were a different story.

It had rained all night as we counted the drops rolling down the tin roof. Everyone put on his foul-weather gear as we prepared for the grave shift watch. I pulled my poncho over my head and left my boots untied. Quietly closing the door behind me, I dragged my M-60 along as I jumped the mud puddles over to the mortar pit and ducked into the sandbag bunker. Seaman John Anderson was there and ready to be relieved, but not before he instructed me in the firing of the mortar tubes. I guess this is what they meant by on-the-job training.

It was quite easy, actually, or at least in our particular situation. The mortar tubes had been set to fire three miles out into the tree line, from where the base had received enemy fire most often. They could be moved easily, weighing under one-hundred pounds each and were usually fired at an angle greater than forty-five degrees, allowing the shells to descend at nearly a vertical angle, breaking through the jungle canopy. You simply pulled the safety pin from the head of the round, yelled "fire in the hole" and dropped it down the tub, while ducking. As it reached bottom, it made contact with a nail that activated the firing device and off it went. From time to time we replaced the nail after it became too dull. The high explosive rounds were quite dependable and their effectiveness was good up to a fifty- to sixty-foot radius around its targets.

The two tubes were primarily used for illumination flares, which helped in warding off attacks and gave us and the Vietnamese firebase eyes out to the tree line. As you pulled the projectiles out of their thick cardboard containers, you noticed little plastic bags of C-4 explosives attached by rubber bands. The number of packets you left on determined how high or far the round would travel. We normally took a couple off and put them under C-rat cans for late night hot snacks.

Behind the 60 and 81 millimeter mortar tubes was a second bunker, containing all the stored mortar rounds, grenades and ammo for the base. Sitting out in the bunker at night listening to the rain was an eerie feeling. No smoking was allowed, but we did it anyway. On the left side and ten feet in front of the tubes, was a four-foot-high sandbag protective wall facing the river. Way too often rounds fell short, barely clearing the wall and leaving you to ponder what would have happened if they hadn't cleared and had been Willy Pete white phosphorous.

There was a tremendous amount of floating plant life, especially varieties of hibiscus, which had dislodged from the fields and banks. The plants would come drifting past the base and had been used to conceal enemy sapper swimmers. At night we pitched concussion grenades continuously into the larger plants, trying to cut off the sappers before they could swim in and connect their satchels to our ammi barges or boats. Even though they might not have been in the water at the time, they were always watching and our alertness deterred them from wanting to attempt an attack.

"I got it Steve, go on and get some sleep" I said as Steve splashed across the compound and into the hooch.

In the early hours of the new day, I raised my head to witness a B-52 air strike. The air force was carpet-bombing the enemy sanctuary five miles up the river across the border. First, I saw the silhouettes of lights projected from the explosions off in the distance, striking in multiple patterns. A second later, the sound of the bombs hitting reached me. Shortly after that, the ground trembled as I realized the impact and destructive force of the thousand-pound bombs. It caused a triple effect like an echo, with each being a split second behind the other. Damn, how could anyone withstand that? The enemy must have men deserting left and right from shell shock.

I had heard about these airmen, flying out of Guam and Thailand, dropping their loads and returning to their bases without ever touching Vietnamese soil. Some, I was told, never received any Vietnam ribbons to wear home on their chest to prove they were there. If I had my way, I'd have given them all a big hug. If it hadn't been for them and the arty boys, the enemy would have walked right over us. I heard the figures and body counts of how many enemy soldiers we were killing, but in my mind it wasn't us, it was those guys. Oh sure, our guys were putting up a hell of a fight and catching groups nightly, but every time the enemy came out in a mass force, the pilots and arty shells made their life pure hell. I was sure glad I was American; I wouldn't want to be under that. Thank you, Lord.

The next day, one of the villagers approached several of us at the front gate with a puppy in his arms. I'm sure it was a crossbreed, but it looked a little like Rin Tin Tin so we traded a case-and-a-half of C-rats for him and proclaimed him to be the base mascot. After saving him from becoming some villager's dinner, we started calling out names to him to see if he would respond to any. After getting nowhere one of the guys said it was a waste of a case-and-a-half of C-rats and the dog's ears perked up. From that day on he became "Case and a Half" We built him a little house near the gate, where we tied him up at nights, training him to be a guard dog and bark at any Vietnamese he saw.

We had one Seabee with us that we called Seabee. Whenever the generator ran out of fuel and the lights started to flicker, you would hear the call "Seabee" go out among the crew and a young blond man would respond "I got it," and jump up, run out and refuel the power generator. Seabee had served up north with the marines early on and had volunteered to go to Ben Keo. He adopted the job of taking care of the generator and was a fixture at the base.

We were awakened in the middle of the night by the siren call to general quarters as I grabbed my M-60 and scrambled out to the dock, readying to fire. A PBR was hurriedly preparing to pull off when my friend Tin waved me over. Not thinking or knowing why, I jumped aboard. Tin informed me that the sentry had seen two swimmers hiding in a floating plant and had thrown a grenade. The PBR headed downriver, and sure enough, there were two bodies trapped in the branches of a downed tree at the bend of the river. It had been a direct hit and both bodies were motionless. Using poles the Vietnamese sailors pulled the bodies free and jumped ashore, pulling them to the beach. Large bladder satchels were strapped to the two sappers. They were wearing black linen cloth diapers, knives and nothing else. They looked like boys to me as the Vietnamese propped them up next to a tree and started celebrating. I knew I should be happy, but I was not prepared for what I witnessed and felt sick about the whole affair.

Why were we killing each other? Couldn't these people see we were trying to give them their freedom? Was our presence here really all that bad? I guess these two VC thought so. Their job was to liberate the South from the Americans. Our job was to keep the South "free". In truth, the people were not the enemy, the governments were. Then the Vietnamese sailors produced a camera and started taking trophy pictures, as if they'd just bagged a twelve-point buck. I knew some of them had lost friends to the enemy, so I tried not to be judgmental, but I could take no more. Tears began to well in my eyes and my heart filled with pain and sorrow as I retreated to the boat. Tin saw my despair and came over to comfort me, asking what was wrong. I didn't want to admit that after being in war for four years, these were the first dead enemy I had seen. They were just young men like us and I was embarrassed by my own reaction as the Vietnamese laughed and took pictures. Eventually we returned to the base. I jumped back on the barge and retreated to my rack with a very sad impression. What war brings with it is not forgivable; I realized the effects of it will be with me the rest of my life. Somehow, I thought, we must learn and teach each other how to live in peace. Future wars should not be fought against each other with weapons, but against hunger, pain, and suffering. We have beauty all around us, yet we are surrounded by horror. Why? Why? Why? Eventually, I was able to fall to sleep.

The next day an advisor, who was a mineman with River Patrol Group 53, explained how dangerous the satchel really was. It weighed more than forty pounds, and if they had been successful, we definitely would have been hurt. Someone might have been killed, and I'm sure that was their intention, along with destroying the ammi pontoons.

The most common method was to use a chemical pencil, which was a soft, thin tube that held electrolyte or acid and a small type resistor. It made a circuit to a detonator/blasting cap that went to a primer cord, which exploded the main charge. The satchel had a bladder with foam in it, which kept it very buoyant, while maintaining up to one-hundred-fifty pounds of explosives. The enemy generally used the bladder because it could be stuck with a knife, causing it to sink in the area where they wanted it to explode. This way the force of the explosion was upward and caused more damage, as the explosion took the path of least resistance to the surface. I started feeling less guilty about the whole event and knew I should be thanking my lucky Stars, but the handling of the bodies by the Vietnamese still bothered me. One possible swimmer was sighted on another occasion with negative contact.

We went back to work as if nothing had happened as Tin and I helped with general maintenance and other duties around the base. The monsoons continued to pour down on us as the base became one big mud puddle and we all stayed soaked. One afternoon we were called into the mess for a lecture from a navy specialist sent out from Saigon to prep us on how to defend the base. He informed us that Intelligence had reported ten-thousand North Vietnamese soldiers headed our way, moving down the Ho Chi Minh Trail. The enemy was expected to make another big push and try to capture Tay Ninh City. The twenty or so sailors in the room became uncomfortable and started to stir in their seats a bit when he explained we would not be able to hold the base. He then described how best and where to cut the fence so we could make our escape through the claymores and concertina wire just before we were to be overrun. The feeling in the room got thick as we all pondered why we were still there and looked at each other with skepticism on our faces. Eventually, the specialist got tired of listening to himself talk and left the mess deck. No one really said much because we all knew we were in trouble the first day we got to Ben Keo. That was the job of the brown water navy, cut the rivers off and find the enemy. If they were going to take the base they were going to have to come out into the open and expose themselves. I don't care how many there were, they would pay dearly.

Thankfully, the big attack never came. Maybe the big bombs caught up to them, or perhaps they split up into small groups and blended into the countryside. We never found out because they never told us much. I'll bet I confused and scared the hell out of everybody back home with those letters I wrote.

Tin invited me to come have dinner and meet his family in his home, and although I was a little worried, I accepted. I had heard stories of servicemen being invited to the Viets' homes and being served fish heads or some other exotic food that might be hard for me to get down. I was very picky and had a weak stomach, but since we had grown close and he wanted me to meet his family, I agreed.

Tin Nguyen and his family lived in a small hut on stilts just outside of the base, down the path near the river. I took off my shoes and stepped up through the doorway. There was just a cloth hanging down to block the sun and keep the bugs out. His wife, Phuong, bowed as she greeted me and introduced me to their small son, Ky Anh, and baby daughter, Hoang Thien. I did not understand what she was saying but I had a pretty good idea and Tin jumped in from time to time, translating. We sat on the bamboo floor at a small table in his one-room house, as his wife passed me a bowl of steamed rice with small silver fish in a brown sauce. Next Tin passed me a small vase that smelled vaguely familiar. Well, what the hell. I had been downwind of this for months, so a little bit wouldn't kill me. I poured nuoc mam over my rice. I believe we said a prayer of thanks to a picture of his deceased father and an urn holding his ashes. I was in their home, and my mother didn't raise her son to be rude, so I went with the program. Holy cow! To my surprise I really liked it. Back home I probably would have used the minnows for bait, but here they were the main course and not half-bad. Tin poured me some homemade rice wine and I held my breath as down it went. His son crawled into my lap and we seemed to become one happy family. I bowed and thanked his wife as she cleared the table and Tin and I adjourned to the doorway to share my cigarettes. Tin was a very nice man and his family was not so unlike mine, except they slept on mats on the floor and had no electricity. Come to think of it, my grandpa used to tell me stories of the good old days when my family lived in the Great Smoky Mountains and ate rabbits and squirrels and didn't have much more than Tin had then.

Tin's wife lit a candle as the sun set and I figured I'd better get back. I thanked Tin for the most enjoyable evening and left him with the remainder of the cigarettes. I also gave his son a couple sticks of gum I had in my pocket. The dinner only seemed to strengthen my relationship with Tin and no one ever called him a gook in my presence again. As far as I was concerned, they were all God's children just like me. However, I was still a little uncertain about those other guys.

Later, my mom sent me a big care package full of goodies. I split them up, giving half to Tin. He lit up like a Christmas tree. I had never seen anyone so happy to get a few cans of tuna fish and potted meat. Whatever he could do for me, he did, and me for him. I taught him everything I knew about the engineering on the boats, and he watched my back in that hostile environment. The other Vietnamese and Americans looked at us funny as they passed each other every day without smiling or speaking, and then Tin and I would walk in, sharing lunch and cutting up like two old friends. Tin eventually got promoted and we saw less of each other as Tin went out on patrols with his men and I stayed behind, standing watch in the tower.

I wanted to find out what it was like to go face the dragon, so I went to the Lieutenant and requested permission to go out with Tin on patrol. Mr. Barnhouse agreed and assigned me to Tin's boat. After dinner we prepped the boats as the advisors went into the Tactical Operations shack to receive their appointed positions and strategies for the night. There would be seven of us on the boat, with Shelly Kelly from Alabama as boat captain of our two-boat patrol. I suited up in my new tailor-made tiger-stripe uniform, donning my helmet and flak jacket and taking along my M-60 and several belts of ammo. We cast off at sunset. I felt a mixture of elation and terror as we sailed up the twisting Vam Co Dong, heading for Cambodia. I looked over at Tin and he shot me back a smile as he sensed my insecurity. Eventually, we split off from our cover boat as he increased his speed, raising the level of their engines, and we cut ours and drifted into a grove of small nipa palm hanging over the river. The crew cut down a couple of branches and laid them over the canopy, concealing our position. Then we settled into quietly listening for movement and waiting for the enemy.

My mind played tricks on me as I caught glimpses of shadows moving. I felt exposed as I looked for flashes from the bank, sending bullets to tear off my head. A warm rain started to fall, relieving the heat and humidity for a moment, then it stopped. The skeeters were buzzing in clouds around us, and dive-bombing down, searching for a blood meal. In the silence of the boat, the dull drone of the mosquitoes was almost deafening as we squeezed bottles of insect repellent over ourselves, saturating our uniforms. I partially hid under the tarp. I can still see their long-legged bodies braced on my uniform, sticking their long needle-like proboscis through the cloth in search of my skin. I pulled my sleeves down and buttoned up but wherever my skin was exposed I started to develop welts. Tin passed me a white anti-malaria tablet and salt pills and I swallowed them.

Half of the crew lay down on the fiberglass deck to rest, while the remainder of us took turns behind the big guns, listening to the jungle sing. Suddenly, the singing stopped and the resting sailors' heads popped up. Then the singing would begin again and the heads would go back down. This went on all night as I gazed up at the stars and fumbled around, trying to open a can of C-rats in the dark. Finally, the morning dew appeared and the eastern light started to blend with the dark, chasing away the fear of night. The Chief started up the boat as we gathered our gear and headed back to the base.

Breakfast had never tasted so good as I wolfed down the powdered eggs and spam and went back for seconds. Tin and the guys sat with me as we joked around and I wiped the lack of sleep from my eyes. One trip was enough for me. I told my friends that I wouldn't be going back. But I never forgot what those guys endured night after night, and my level of respect for them rose through the roof.

In August I received a letter from Steve back on YRBM 21. He said that shortly after I had left, he was ordered back to Binh Thuy Naval Base to take care of some business, and while hitching a ride back to YRBM 21, the Seawolf he was in went down due to transmission problems. One of the door gunners, John Perry, handed him an unopened bottle of rum and told him to wrap himself around it and curl up on the floor. He promised to share it with him if they survived. Steve said it was the best bottle of rum he ever drank.

Then he explained that they got word that Lieutenant Commander Poe of River Division 592/RPG 56 had been killed-in-action. Mr. Poe was killed while trying to get papers for adoption of a thirteen year old VC that Chief Mac had captured. The kid had no family so Mr. Poe was taking him back to Maryland to raise him there. Commander Poe was a great guy and it was a terrible loss. Then Steve informed me that just two nights later they were called to general quarters and Seawolves were scrambled out to Phouc Xuyen. Chief Murphy was leaving Vietnam and going home, his tour was over and he was nearing retirement. Nha Be had sent newly-arrived Chief Grant to relieve him. Chief Grant was just beginning his tour. They were both standing on the pontoon barge, discussing the change of command during their nightly harassment and interdiction drill, when either a mortar round was fired incorrectly, too vertical, or with insufficient C-4 propellant. Although the intent was to hit the opposite bank, the round fell short barely clearing the mess roof and hit the water just a few meters in front of where the two Chiefs were standing. Randy Strickland yelled incoming as the sound of the explosion and shrapnel clattered down on the tin roofs and the towers opened up on the 300 yard free-fire zone. The explosive round was so destructive that it sprayed the walls of the hooches, wounding several of the support sailors and the two Chiefs. When things quieted down a bit, men rushed down to the mess deck, now a triage, to help the Doc, pharmacist's mate, and wounded men. Chief Grant was dead and had been laid on the mess deck floor, while Chief Murphy lay on the table, taking his last breaths, as his men tried to save his life. Ken Scott rushed to the side of his surrogate father, while Doc and others turned their attention to a young newly arrived sailor with his abdomen sliced open. Ken tried to comfort Murphy as the Chief's eyes turned glassy and he drifted away.

Chief Murphy's lungs had filled with blood and he died of asphyxiation. Later his men positioned him and Chief Grant into body bags onto the mess deck floor and zipped them up. There was a moment of reverence as the sailors knelt down beside them and said their goodbyes. After air lifting the wounded, Chief Murphy's men broke down as they carried him and Chief Grant to the helo pad. YRBM 21 was deeply shaken as they removed their bodies from the helo and set them on the deck. Chief Murphy was very popular and was retiring to Hawaii after a long career. Mr. Fry had sat up just the night before, talking to Chief Grant. Now Fry was kneeling down to inspect the bodies of the two Chiefs, as the smell of winter green permeated the air. This left our friend Brown, ranking E5 with very little experience and big shoes to fill. The crew of YRBM 21, and the sailors of the river divisions, took turns visiting the Chiefs' bodies, as they paid their last respects to their departed shipmates. Later, sailors from YRBM 21 volunteered to go out to Phouc Xuyen to fill the billets of the men that were lost. I cried silently as my heart felt it would burst into a thousand pieces from grief. I tried to hold back my tears, but could not. I balled up the letter and pitched it into the river. I hated this fucking war.

A few days later, a grey bus from Saigon pulled up to the front gate and three FNGs, Fucking New Guys, got off, and one sailor got on. All of the new guys were sporting new greens and stuck out like a sore thumb. Radioman Third Class James Dickson Bryant was from Center Point, Iowa, and was taken into the command bunker to be introduced to the lieutenant's staff, where he would become an intricate part of the team. David Thiel, from Detroit and Smitty, from Ohio, were thrown in with me and the rest of the guys out in the yard. We performed manual labor for the base and manned the defensive positions. Mr. Barnhouse had us roll the last barrel of diesel fuel down to the bank for the boats and informed us it was time to make a fuel run.

Thiel, Smitty and I grabbed our guns and jumped in the back of the Chevy deuce-and-a-half, as I planted my M-60 on the roof of the truck. John took the wheel and Wil rode shotgun. We took a left off the little dirt road and headed to Tay Ninh Army base to requisition supplies. The Army was under orders to support us and give us whatever we needed. A few miles down the road, a tank from the Blackhorse Division of the 11th Cav came barreling toward us and then cut right, tearing through the rice paddies and slinging mud everywhere. The driver's head stuck up through the armament in the front of the tank. He was wearing goggles and lovebeads, with an inch of mud caked on his face. The tank's gunner was half out of the top hatch behind a .50 caliber and there were Infantry riding on top, holding on for dear life as they hauled ass into the dense jungle.

229

The block outside of the main gate was made up of boom-boom houses and little bars built of corrugated steel, plywood and cardboard. Parked outside the main gate was an army troop transport truck, with the driver humping a Viet girl in the front seat while an old mama-san sat in the back with her head bowed. Well, that about summed up this war, I guess. We were waved into a large base surrounded with trench lines and defensive bunkers, manned by sentries with machine guns. There were tanks, personnel carriers, howitzers, gunships, hooches, storage buildings, civilian employees and soldiers everywhere. It was actually a small city, divided into different sections.

First, we stopped off at the chow hall to see what they had to eat. There were a large number of black soldiers wearing "Black Panther" wristbands and neck chokers, congregating, slapping each other's hands in the way they greeted their friends. There was also a lot of what we called "Hippie Warriors." These young men wore peace symbols, lovebeads and little round sunglasses, along with their weapons and ammo. They would signal to each other using the victory sign, signifying peace.

After lunch we traveled to a section of the base where the fuel and ammo was stored in bunkers, away from everything else. We looked up at Black Virgin Mountain from the bottom as an army helicopter touched down on top. The army owned the bottom and the top of the mountain and the enemy owned the rest. During the three-day ceasefire for Ho Chi Minh's birthday, the helicopter pilots counted hundreds of Communists sunning themselves on the hillside, shooting the choppers the bird. What a joke that was. It was apparent that the soldiers stationed at the base were well-equipped and good fighters. They had led the way into Cambodia and controlled the surrounding countryside, which had heavy VC movement and was an NVA infiltration zone. I for one was glad they were just down the road a piece. We thanked the army and retreated out the gate, returning to Ben Keo before dark.

A few rainy days later, two SEALs came strolling down the river as if they were bird-hunting, carrying their guns like Davy Crockett, and entered the base. We weren't sure who they were at first, and then they introduced themselves. They informed us that two of the electronic sensors outside of the base in the jungle had detected movement the night before and they were checking it out. We were all surprised, not knowing we had electronic sensors outside of the base. We invited them to our little home-made beer bar and sat down, listening to their stories. One was a good old boy from the South with a heavy drawl. They told us about the NVA camp up across the border, but it was their sea stories that got us laughing as we shared our monthly ration of beer and cigarettes with them. Before we knew it, they had finished off all the beer and were suiting up to leave. I asked where they were going and they told me they were returning to the jungle. Being surprised, I replied. Don't you want to stay for dinner and camp out here tonight? They looked at me funny and said it was unsafe on the base and that every VC in the area knew right where we were. It seemed they felt more comfortable spending the night in the jungle than with us. Besides, all the beer was gone. I understood their logic, but thought them crazy to want to go back out into the jungle. The Southern gentleman looked at me and said, "Crazy is you guys coming down the river in those boats. Hell we can hear you coming a mile away. Nobody even knows we're out there." I thought about it for few minutes and came to the conclusion he was right. Riding down the river in a boat was a little crazy.

Then there was the time a FNG had a birthday and we decided to take him to the skivvy house outside the base. Just about all bases in Nam had one, and we had two. They weren't very big, just little bamboo huts with makeshift bars. A girl with smallpox or something terribly pitting on her skin and her face was terribly pitted, worked in one of them. The guys use to call her crater face and claymore head. I felt sorry for her, but there was nothing we could do. We sat drinking warm Ba Mui Ba beer and cheap cognac while she did her best to talk the birthday boy into going into the back room. After a while he became intoxicated and she succeeded. There was really no back room; it was more like a sheet blocking off a small section of the hut, with a cot. We sat there, listening as she complained and he laughed his head off, so I decided to take a little peek to check on the new guy. I pulled the sheet to the side, and there was this poor girl, straddling the drunken sailor, trying to force this limp noodle into the right spot while he laughed continuously. There was just no way, so I went in, pulled her off, and dragged him back to the base. I did the noble thing however. I reached in his pocket and made sure she got some money for her effort. When we got back to the base he climbed the tower and was going to show us how he could fly. Again, we pulled him down and sat on him till he passed out. We always observed the buddy system and watched out for each other. The enemy was close and spies were everywhere.

We made a run down to Ben Luc one day to pick up ammo and supplies. It took all day to reach the supply base. On the way we stopped at Go Da Ha for a visit and then jumped back on the road trying to make good time and get back from the hundred-mile round-trip before dark. Crossing over the bridge on the Vam Co Dong at Ben Luc, we passed an army deuce-and-a-half coming from the other direction. John was driving as we all encouraged him not to back down from the army truck. There was barely enough room for both trucks, and as we passed each other at full-speed, both drivers' side-view mirrors hit, exploding and spraying us with glass. At first we thought we'd been hit, and then we looked over to see the mirror gone. On all the trips we made we never received sniper fire, but we heard many stories of trucks that had.

Dick Bryant got drunk one night and was walking across a plank between barges and fell in. The rubber truck tires kept the barges from slamming into each other so there was about a four-foot space of water between barges. He had his jungle boots on and struggled back above water, but couldn't quite reach the plank above him. Again he was pulled under, having nothing to hang onto as he struggled up to the barge, feeling nothing but smooth steel; he went under again, reaching up and grabbing a protruding part of the barge with his fingernails. He had been holding on for a little while when Honniger discovered him and yelled out as a couple of us ran over and pulled him out. He was more than a little shaken and rightfully so, as we all realized how close a call it was.

One Sunday evening, a group of us congregated in the lookout tower for Sergeant Pepper's Hour, which was a ninety-minute radio program that AFVN dedicated to playing the new music from back home. It was a big hit with us young guys, since the playlist was much more progressive than normal. We got to hear Janis Joplin,

Cream, Santana and other groups of what was called psychedelic rock back in the States. The song "Fire," recorded by The Crazy World of Arthur Brown played as the lyrics reminded me of the VC. "Fire, I beg you to burn." I looked up and someone passed me a joint and I flashed back in time to San Francisco.

It was the summer of love, and my shipmate Hank, who was a Navajo Indian, and I were on an all-day liberty pass, sight-seeing around the Chinatown district of the city while listening to a pocket radio. Out of the blue, the disc jockey announced that the radio station was in financial trouble and that CCR had volunteered to perform a rare afternoon concert and were donating the proceeds to the station. As soon as we heard it was being held at the Fillmore West Auditorium, we jumped on a bus and made a beeline for the front door. Luckily, we were able to purchase tickets for a few dollars and had time to spare, so Hank ran into a corner liquor store and bought a half-pint of Southern Comfort. We hid in the alley and gulped it down, then followed the line of flower children into the hall. Traveling up the stairs, we entered a large ballroom with all the kids sitting on the floor. The band kicked off the show with Fortunate Son and all the kids rose to their feet, swaying in time to the beat of the music. Behind the stage, three large movie screens flashed pictures. The screen to the left had a beautiful young woman running naked through a tall field of grass, while the screen to the right had Mickey and Minnie Mouse on an afternoon drive in their jalopy. The center screen had blotches of psychedelic colors, pulsating to the beat of the music. Although Hank and I were in our civvies, it was obvious from our haircuts that we were in the military. The next thing I knew, the young man to my right passed me a marijuana cigarette. I looked at Hank and we shrugged our shoulders, took a puff, and then passed it on. I'll never forget watching John Fogerty pick his Gibson Les Paul guitar, or Doug "Cosmo" Clifford, twirling his drumsticks in the air. When the band ended their song, the audience showered the stage with marijuana joints.

Before Nam, most of us knew nothing of such things. We had all joined right out of school with good intentions. There we were, getting stoned with a bunch of long-haired hippies, viewing silhouettes of these young braless women as they danced on the side of the stage.

There was this one little blond-haired blue-eyed girl that smiled at me, and that was all I needed. I was content to sit there the rest of the afternoon and make eyes at her. A few of the kids started to open up and I began to realize they weren't against us, they were against the war. Most of them had family and friends in Vietnam and they just wanted the whole affair to end so their loved ones could come home. Although Hank and I felt a little out of place, we never felt in danger. It was actually the opposite, as if the rest of the kids felt compassion for us and knew we were headed into harm's way.

I was awakened by the ring of the powered phones next to my ear, which could barely be heard over the portable radios blasting "We Got to Get Out of This Place," while the guys in the tower sang along. Picking up, I heard the Lieutenant yelling. "Where's it coming from! Where's it coming from!" "Where's what coming from, sir?" "We're being hit! We're being hit!" I jumped to my feet and peered over the side to see a smoldering hole as a second round hit and exploded in the river. BOOM!

"Holy shit!" I sounded the alarm and men started scrambling around the base. "Incoming, incoming, get to your battle stations!" I yelled, pushing guys out of the tower. A couple of the guys were so stoned that they were stumbling down the ladder, and fell close to the bottom. Dick came running out of the command shack toward the mortar pit and a tremendous explosion behind him sent him flying face-down in the dirt. He had been running so hard that the concussion knocked him off his feet, scraping him up a bit, but his legs never stopped pumping and he was back up running in no time. It reminded me of the Roadrunner cartoon character. I jumped down, made it in and out of the hooch, grabbing my M-60 and was at my position on the ammi firing when the Lieutenant started calling out coordinates over the phones from the tower to the mortar pit. The sailor at the other end of the phones was so loaded that he was laughing and screwing everything up. "Ha ha ha, what did you say, sir, ha ha." One of the other sailors in the pit grabbed the phone and pushed him out of the way. Dick jumped in and started shuttling mortar rounds to the captain of the team, who was nonstop-dumping projectiles down the tubes. THOOUK! THOOUK! The incoming died down as our rounds began penetrating the tree line. By now it was getting dark as Barnhouse had called in the gunships and the Black Ponies began diving on the jungle.

There was no moon that night, but the stars were out. We could hear the OV-10 Broncos, when suddenly the entire night sky lit up with an unbelievable roar as they cut loose with their mini-guns. It didn't sound like a machine gun, more like a constant roar, or someone tearing a sheet in two. A solid sea of red showered down into the tree line, and we were seeing every fifth round. To us, it was utterly amazing; there is no way we could lose this war. Then they fired their rockets and the tremendous noise when they hit was indescribable. Damn, I loved those guys.

After the Black Ponies pulled off, the PBRs went down to inspect the area, but the enemy was either dead or long gone. Mr. Barnhouse lined us up and chewed us out royally. I couldn't really blame him; after all, he would be the one who would have to have written the letters and he wanted to make it home also. I felt we had learned a serious lesson; we could never truly let our guard down. They were always watching and knew when we were partying, and that was a great time to hit us. Sorry sir.

On another occasion while working on the PBRs, we were attacked by mortars and I jumped aboard and made firing runs on a bunker. I was never as scared as the bullets chipped away at the boat and zipped over our heads. The pucker power was a ten, as I made my mind up not to do it again. The day after, Ramsey and Webb came out to the docks and presented me with an old black beret.

The ritual of the black beret and the river patrol forces that wore them had become a navy tradition. First, they would dunk it in the muddy waters of the river. Tradition called for the hat to be dunked and then worn until dry. Then they shaped it as it dried in the sun. It was shaped with an incline on the right side, with the rest of the cap sloping down over the left ear. After the beret was shaped, the Task Force 116 patch was affixed to the right side, opposite that of the Green Berets.

The patch, circular in shape, bears a MACV shield in the upper center, and in the lower portion, a sword crosses two rivers, indicating the force's mission of interdicting enemy traffic on the waterways. Flanking these two symbols are four lightning bolts, representing the rapid reaction capability of the four elements of the Force, River Patrol Boats, SEALs, Minesweeping and LST support craft, and the force air arm, consisting of Seawolf UH-1B helicopters and fixed wing "Black Ponies", OV-10A Bronco aircraft.

In addition to the force patch, the PBR sailors usually wore a collar device to denote rank or rating. Those with fewer than one hundred days left in their tour also wore a grenade pin to denote their newly acquired status as "short-timers". In addition, a blue-and-gold ribbon is worn to show that they have thirty or fewer days to complete their tour. The ribbon comes from a bottle of Seagram's VO whisky. In order to be allowed to wear it, the sailor must first consume the contents of the fifth. On the rear of the beret was a three-inch silk loop, which remained closed until the sailor was in his first firefight. At that time he earned the right to cut the loop. In subsequent firefights, if he comes under a rocket attack or makes his first enemy kill, he could cut the silk strands in the shape of an inverted "V". Wearing the Beret was an absolute honor for me, as I thanked the advisors for their consideration and kindness. The brown water sailors were some of the finest people I ever knew. Serving with them was one of the highlights of my life, and there will always be a special bond between us.

We were sent out on runs with the "water buffalo", a gray water tank on wheels that we used to hold our drinking water. There was a village nearby where we towed it, filled it up and returned it to base. We showered with the river water, but I refused to drink it. Besides our shitters hung over the river and the water pumps for the showers were right next door. I know the river water moved quickly, but something was wrong with that picture, not to mention that every Viet in the area was using the river for the same purpose. Out of the base, down the road a ways, was an ice house, where we traded for a block of ice from time to time. It was made from river water, so it was unsafe, but it was great for putting beer and sodas into a tub and chilling.

Then there was the time the whole base came down with some kind of rash. The Doc got it the worst and couldn't figure where it was coming from. We tried everything we could find to get rid of it, but nothing worked. Some thought it was from the sewage in the water.

Others thought it was Agent Orange or some other chemical floating down river. The patrolmen complained about the sprayings. Said it turned the jungle brown and took away their cover at night. It was designed to eliminate the enemy's cover. I'm not sure what good it did, and I'm not sure how it affected us. I don't think anybody truly knows. We all caught some sort of Mekong jungle rot, especially on our feet, where the skin dried and peeled off. Our bodies took a pounding from the work, the heat, and the humidity, but I didn't know my blood was contaminated until many years later when they told me I had Hepatitis-C.

All the guys had hooch mamas who washed their clothes and shined their boots. Most of the women lived in Ben Keo Village and ranged in age from young to old. The older women walked around with black teeth from beetle nuts, which was some form of mild narcotic. Some of the young women became the guys' girlfriends and did quite a bit more, but they all had to leave the base by nightfall. Mine was a nice young Co (woman) with a twelve-year-old son, who would pick up my things in the morning and wash them on the side of the Vam Co Dong and have them back in the afternoon. Although there was no Boom Boom between her and me, I did become friends with her son.

She would come over and gather my stuff up and I would take the boy in the village for a treat. She didn't charge me very much so I always considered my helping him to be a part of her fee. Besides I liked the kid and thought how it must have been to be in his shoes. Many times the other children would surround me and sort of paw at me, so he became my protector, to speak of. I wore my pistol so I would remove the clip and round from the chamber of my M-16 and allowed him to tote it around as if I were training him to be a little soldier like my friend Tin. He slung it over his shoulder and pulled it down to shoo away the other kids, but I never let him shoot it. When he asked, I told him he was too young, and that he needed to stay a kid a little longer. Someday you will probably have to, I told him, but I hope not. That's why we fight now, so you won't have to. I'm not sure he understood, hell I'm not sure I did, either. I was only a few years older than he when I began this whole mess. If I ever got out of this place I would never leave home again.

Late one night after watch, I got a craving for a hamburger, french fries and milkshake. Right before I left the States to come to Nam, the rave was these skinny hamburgers and fries we got from a place called Kelly's Drive-in. I went into the kitchen and dug out a steak and was chopping it into little pieces with a clever and trying to roll it into a burger, but it just wasn't working. We got all the steaks we wanted from the army but hamburger was non existent. Pendola came into the kitchen and looked at me, shaking his head and walking back out. We had good food at the base and the cooks did a great job, but I was way overdue for some good old American junk food.

Dick Bryant came to breakfast and told us what had happened to him while on ambush the night before. He was a typical sixties kid growing up in Center Point, Iowa. Graduated from high school in 1967 with low grades, had no money, got drafted and was able to enlist in the navy. After boot camp, he attended Radioman A school and then served two years shore duty in Yokosuka, Japan. By the time he got to Ben Keo, he was a Third Class Radioman and good at Morse code. He was assigned to the tactical, operations, command shack along with the rest of the radiomen and was sent out on patrol frequently.

The night before he was assigned to Chief Ramsey's Boat, they were sitting in their appointed position about midnight when the Vietnamese boat officer told the Chief "We go back to base now." The chief said no, that our orders were to stay hear till 0430. Then the Vietnamese officer pulled out a Colt 45 pistol and stuck it in the Chief's face and repeated. "We go back to base now." Chief Ramsey stood there without saying a thing, looking over at Dick. They could both tell by the body language of the Vietnamese crew that the crew would shoot them and dump them overboard without batting an eye. Dick looked over to the Chief. "They're going to shoot us Chief." They broke ambush and returned to the base, as Dick was thankful that the chief didn't do anything crazy. They weren't in the clear till they reached the base and Dick said he was never so happy to see Ben Keo. Chief Ramsey filed reports and heads rolled, but we never trusted the Vietnamese after that and rumors began to circulating that many of them were VC, or at least VC sympathizers.

Not long after, we began to turn over base duties to Vietnamese navy support men and transfer American NSA sailors to other bases, or back home. We had turned over all guard duties except the roaming position, on which we kept one American to oversee the Vietnamese and keep an eye on the base while the few remaining Americans slept. One dark, frightful night it was my turn as I walked to the mortar pit and found no one home. I then climbed the tower to discover both Vietnamese sailors in hammocks, sleeping.

"Wake up! Wake up! No one is watching the perimeter!" I tried to make them realize the danger. "No problem, no VC." Again I tried to convey my orders. "Get up, this is unsafe." Just then, one of the Viets stuck his M-16 in my face and said di di mau (leave). I backed out of the tower, knowing this was not good. I headed to the hooch to get back up, I yelled for the other guys to get up. One of the guys went and got the Lieutenant up. After hearing the report, he sounded the alarm, waking the rest of the base. He then got on the horn to Saigon and took the Vietnamese Commanders into the bunker, where he began chewing their asses.

Most of us stayed up the rest of the night, feeling violated and unsafe. Lieutenant Barnhouse came out of the bunker and summoned all personnel to the center of the compound at 0600. The Vietnamese sailors were standing tall at attention, facing the U.S. Navy, also at attention. Mr. Barnhouse tore into the Vietnamese officers and men, threatening to throw all of them into the brig on court-martial charges if anything like that ever happened again. He then turned and commended the U.S. sailors for a job well done. I was absolutely stunned that Mr. Barnhouse would do that, but it was too late, the damage had been done. Not only did we have the NVA and VC to contend with, now we had to watch our backs for fear of the South Vietnamese. That was it for me. We were winning the war, but for whom. What the hell were we doing in South Vietnam?

"THERE'S JUST NO RIGHT WAY TO DO WRONG"

BM1 James Elliott Williams
BC PBR 105/ River Section 531

Ralph W. Christopher
ATSB, NSA, Det, Ben Luc (Ben Keo)
FPO San Francisco Cal. 96647

Hi Sweetheart

Well I guess it has been a lot of your letters in between my last letter and this one but you know I didn't forget about you. I have been really busy and now I am at another base which is on land. The name is Ben Keo and they use to have it pretty bad. I have to stay here at least three months and I might extend for my last few months if it is good. I had to work to hard at my last duty station and it was dangerous to. Here I mostly stand watches and do security work. It is only about twenty five Americans but we get along good. We are a short distance from Cambodia but I think we can handle anything that comes our way. They found out I was on the river before so they put me on the M-60 machine gun team. I have my own machine gun. I also have a forty five pistol and M-16 rifle. It is kind of funny in a way, we have our own TV, typewriter and things like that, but every where you look there are guns, grenades, helmets and flak jackets. Everywhere I go I wear my pistol. We work with the army a lot now.

Well I can't really tell you a whole lot about everything since I just got here, but I'll let you know more later. I haven't received any mail yet but I hope everybody is Okay.

Tell everybody I send my love and will see them in six months. Take care of yourself and I'll write later.

Love Chris

P.S. I'm homesick and miss your green stuffed bell peppers.

Gate of ATSB Ben Keo, Smitty, Ralph and Thiel

Gate guard post, ATSB Ben Keo, Case-and-a-half

ATSB Ben Keo mortar pit

ATSB Ben Keo compound, mess ammi to left, berthing right

ATSB Ben Keo, Vam Co Dong River, Tay Ninh Province

Ralph with M-60 machine gun

Smitty and Ralph in Ben Keo village

When I returned to Byrd Airport in Richmond, Virginia, in October 1970, I was applauded by over 100 friends and family who came to welcome me back. One was Crystal Gainous, who was one of my lifelines to home. Thanks

CHAPTER FOURTEEN
HOME SWEET HOME

Thiel was slumped over his chair, watching the sweat drip off the end of his nose. There wasn't a cloud in the sky and the Mekong Sun was beating down so hard it was blinding. It was a good time to find a shady spot and take a little nap; instead, he had drawn guard duty at the front gate. Smitty and I were accompanying him in his misery, as we all sat on hand grenade boxes, puffing Pall Malls and listening to Grand Funk Railroad on my eight-track. Suddenly Lieutenant Barnhouse made a rare daytime appearance out the sandbag doorway of the command bunker into the center of the compound.

"Christopher, your orders are here. There'll be a Jeep at 0800 to take you to Saigon." I was stunned as my jaw hit the floor. Someone must have fucked up; I still had three months left on my tour. I had not started my short-timer's calendar; I had not written a letter ... Wow, I was going home! Turning my head, my smile dropped as I noticed my buddies with their heads bowed, as though they were praying. It dawned on me that I would have to leave them in this hellhole with the Vietnamese. They would replace me with a Viet sailor who didn't know shit and probably couldn't be trusted. I felt like a man who had just drawn a royal flush and wanted to hide it from his friends. Damn, why couldn't we all go home together? After covering each other's butts for months, I was leaving early. Thiel lifted me off the ground with a bear hug, "You dog." Smitty wasn't as strong, I grabbed him and we both fought back the tears.

Breaking our hold I wiped my face, realizing I was leaving the very place I hated and feared. I thought I should go pack. I bounced over the plank onto the pontoon and into the barracks. I wouldn't have to wash in that muddy river anymore. The screen door slammed behind me as I entered the hooch.

"I'm going to the land of the big PX, where they got air conditioning and pretty, round-eyed women," I proclaimed loudly.

All the guys were happy as they slapped me on the back and congratulated me. I immediately started giving away all the things I couldn't take home. My tape deck, my Colt 45, my puppy, "Don't ya'll let 'em eat 'im."

The rest I threw in my sea bag as we had a few toasts and cheers. But eventually everyone drifted off to do what needed to be done. Sleep didn't come that night; a thousand things ran through my head, so I stayed up with the night watch, dropping mortar rounds and flares. I climbed the tower one more time to take my last peek through the starlight scope. Star light, star bright, what can I see tonight. Peering over my shoulder, I had the strangest feeling as though death was watching. He was angry, for I had cheated him. Short-timer's fever crept over me in the form that I must be careful. It would truly be ironic to die this close to going home. Grown up, no longer the adolescent, scarred with the memories of a war not understood, memories of a people forced to live in a conflict, memories of the teenage American boys who came to defend democracy, and memories of men who lost their lives. But for some reason, it seemed I was to be spared and allowed to leave. It would not be so for Tin and his men. This was their home, so they would be here till the end. And if for some reason their side didn't win, then their fate was uncertain. I felt like a coward, deserting him. We had trained alongside, knowing this day would come at some point, but it didn't make it any easier. I wanted to turn and run. Instead, I waved as the night ambush went out as if on a stroll - Tin and his men on a potentially deadly patrol.

The morning sun rose and the cooks prepared the usual feast. Men from both groups entered the chow hall, and I shared my last meal with my friends and Tin. I gave Tin most of my field gear, for I knew he would need it over the long haul. I also gave him food for his family, who lived in their hut on stilts. The Vietnamese sailors passed me by, looking at me with contempt. I was sorry to leave my friends, with the enemy within. The Vietnamization program was a flop, and with these men, they would not win.

They all walked me to the Jeep. We smiled and said our goodbyes as I shook some hands and gave some last hugs to the family I was leaving behind. The Jeep pulled out of the fire base and headed down the little dirt road. I looked into the ancient village a final time, at the little huts in a row. Glancing over my shoulder, the village faded from sight in the distance, but I knew it would always live in the hearts of the men who had been there. Not for what was done, or even why, but simply because we'd been there, and men had died. And I knew, and have always known since, that someday, when I am about to leave this world, I will look back in my precious thoughts and revisit this special place that will forever live in me.

"NOT ALL WOUNDS ARE VISIBLE"

GMG2 Ron Laratta
River Division 532

Hi Sweetheart

Well from what they tell me I have nine days left in Vietnam before I start home. They moved my flight date up to the Tenth. They tell me I should be out of the Navy and at home around the fifteenth of October. They are sending twenty thousand of us sailors home. I'm so happy! I didn't save as much money as I wanted to, but as long as I can come home I don't care about the money. I saved about fifteen hundred dollars plus about five hundred worth of stereo equipment and a TV, watch and some clothes. Not bad I guess. Plus I have some money at home.

I received your letter today and it was really nice to hear from you. You asked me if I had a tape cartridge player and I do. That Door's tape you ordered me is really great. That is the type of music I like. Any kind of hard rock. The eight-track is what I am going to get in my car so the tape will really be used.

About buying me records, I really appreciate it and no you aren't buying my love. I have always loved you and I always will. I wish you would forget the one hundred dollars. You don't owe me anything.

Well Rachel I think I'll sign off. Next time you hear from me it will be in person. Take care of yourself and give the family my love.

Love Chris

P.S. Don't answer this letter.

SUPPOSED TO LAND AT TRAVIS AIR FORCE BASE IN CALIFORNIA, BUT WAS FOGGED IN SO WE HAD TO LAND AT SAN FRANCISCO INTERNATIONAL. MANY GUYS STILL IN COMBAT FATIGUES AND WE TOOK SOME SNIDE REMARKS FROM FLOWER CHILDREN HIPPIES IN THE AIR TERMINAL WHICH DIDN'T SIT TO WELL WITH OUR PEOPLE!

LCDR Thomas K. Anderson
CO / River Division 531

Chronological narrative of Task Force 116, October of 1970

10/03/70 LCDR James A. Caldwell, USN, relieved CDR Kenneth A. Hamman, USN, as OINC HA(L)-3 Detachment Four at Ben Luc. In ceremonies at Dong Tam 13 USN RAC of RAS 15 turned over to form VNN RAD 46. Seawolf 306, assigned to HA(L)-3 Det-3, crash-landed at Cau Lau strip. ATR2 Walter R. WINTERS, USN, 4871478, a crewman in the aircraft, was killed. The remaining crew egressed safely. The aircraft was totally destroyed by fire. Cause of the crash was engine failure.

10/06/70, two PBRs of RPG 62 became victims of swimmer sapper attack from element of 95th NVA in the Song Ong Doc area.

10/12/70, Sealord 5, crashed north of Vi Thanh when the pilot executed an auto-rotation into a rice paddy after sustaining an engine failure. All of the occupants of the aircraft egressed safely. The aircraft sustained substantial damage.

10/13/70, in ceremonies at NSAD Binh Thuy, RADM R.S. Riera, USN, Commander Fleet Air Western Pacific, presented to Light Attack Squadron Four the Chief of Naval Operations Aviation Safety Award for fiscal year 1970.

10/14/70, twenty STABs of STABRON 20 stood down at Dong Tam in preparation for transfer to CONUS.

10/15/70, in ceremonies at ATSB Phouc Xuyen, River Divisions 532 and 571 turned over all PBRs to form Vietnamese RPG 63. LCDR Richard G. STRAND, USN, relieved LT Terry H. CAMBELL, USN, as OINC of HA(L)-3 Det-9 aboard YRBM 21.

10/20/70, ATSB Song Ong Doc came under intense enemy attack at approximately 2330 hours. The base received 57 mm recoilless rifle, mortar, machine gun, and small arms fire, which completely destroyed the support base's 10 ammi complex. HA(L)-3 Det-6 scrambles after the first mortar barrage and along with Black Ponies, commenced immediate strikes on enemy targets of opportunity. GMG3 Thomas Steward McGarry, 362448068, NAGV, RPG 62 and RMSN John DeWitt Drake, 563849595, NSA Saigon were killed-in-action. 11 USN were wounded-in-action. No casualties to HA(L)-3 Det-6 personnel were sustained. As a result of the action, HA(L)-3 Det-6 was relocated to the USS GARRETT COUNTY.

10/24/70, Seawolf 305, sustained engine failure, pilot executed auto-rotation to bank of Bo De River, all occupants egressed safely. Aircraft sustained salt water damage.

The following inscription was left on a bronze plaque at the grave of LTJG Gene B. Nickerson.

POOR IS THE NATION THAT HAS NO HEROES. SHAMEFUL IS THE ONE THAT HAVING THEM FORGETS. REST IN PEACE HERO, YOU HAVE NOT BEEN FORGOTTEN.

COLDWATER HIGH SCHOOL
CLASS OF 1963

THE BROWN WATER TOLL - 1970

1/04/70 SN Paul B. Blunt Jr, San Antonio, TX. NSA, Skimmer
Boat (Quang Nam)

1/08/70 EM1 James C. Mitchell Jr, Torrance, CA. UH-1B
Passenger (Kien Tuong)

1/09/70 GMGSN Howard E. Brown Jr, Lebanon, MO. RivDiv-
594, Vam Co Dong (Kien Phong)

1/11/70 LTJG John C. Brewton, Mobile, AL. ST-2, Det-Alfa
(WIA-11/24/69) (Gia Dinh)

1/16/70 FN Nedward C. Estes Jr, Hiram, GA. RivDiv-593, Phu
Cuong (Bien Hoa)

1/21/70 BM3 Ronald S. Athanasiou, Jacksonville, TX. RAD-151,
ATC-151-36, Vam Co Dong, Mined (Tay Ninh)
ENFN James C. Baumer, Huron, OH. RivAssDiv-151,
ATC-151-36 (Tay Ninh)

1/27/70 EM3 Joseph V. Olszewski, Chico, CA. NSA Saigon, Det-
Ben Luc

1/29/70 ETR2 Howard Blandino, Warren, MI. MST-2, Det-Bravo,
Ben Luc (WIA-1/26/70)

2/02/70 ENFN Anthony J. Metzger Jr, Philadelphia, PA. NSA
Saigon, Det-Nha Be (Gia Dinh)

2/06/70 EO3 Patrick A. McLeod, Seattle, WA. NSA Danang
(Quang Nam)

2/07/70 EN3 James A. Niemi, Hibbing, MN. RivDiv-552, ATSB
Tra Cu (Vinh Binh)

2/10/70 LCDR George R. Matthews, South Salem, NY. Staff
Construction Battalion Pacific, Helo Passenger
LTJG Robert G. Browne, Corpus Christi, TX. NSA, Det-
Chu Lai, Helo Passenger
SK3 David F. Schuette, Green Bay, WI. NSA Det-Chu
Lai, Helo Passenger (Quang Nam)
SN Timothy J. Green, Little Rock, AR. NSA Danang, Det-
Chu Lai, Helo Passenger

2/26/70 LT Bernard L Lefever, North Hollywood, CA. NSA Tan
Son Nhut, UH-1B, Pilot

LTJG Henry Hudson Jr, Daly City, CA. NSA Tan Son Nhut, Co-Pilot (Long Xuyen)

ADR2 George A. Young, Robesonia, PA. NSA Tan Son Nhut, Crewmember

CS3 Archie C Wabschall III, Hood River, OR. NSA, YRBM-21, Helo Passenger

EM3 Ronald S. Bay, Phoenix, AZ. NSA, YRBM-21, Passenger

RM3 Frank B. Glendinning, Bethany, MO. NSA, YRBM-21, Helo Passenger

EN3 Robert L. Fallows, Charlotte, NC. NSA, YRBM-21, Helo Passenger

EN2 David P. Hoffman, Florissant, MO. Min Div-113, CTF-116, Helo Passenger

EN2 Norman K. Byassee, Litchfield Park, AZ. RAD-13, CTF-117, Helo Passenger

2/26/70 LTJG Gene B. Nickerson, Coldwater, MI. RivDiv-553, Patrol Off, B-40 (Kien Giang)

GMG3 Donald F. Hartzell, Bethlehem, PA. RivDiv-553, B-40 (Kien Giang)

2/26/70 SM1 Thermon H. Emory Jr, Jackson, TN. RivDiv-514, Boat Captain (Kien Phong)

3/08/70 RD1 Charles E. Brooks, Athens, TX. RivDiv-513, Boat Captain, ATSB Rach Soi, Rach Gia (Kien Giang)

ENFN Patrick Tracy, East Detroit, MI. Harbor Clearance Unit-1, NSA, TAD, ATSB Moc Hoa (Kien Giang)

3/12/70 GMGSN Frank Jacaruso, Spring Valley, NY. RivDiv-593, PBR-756, B-40, Saigon River (Bien Hoa)

3/25/70 ENFN Ernest J. Brown, Wilmington, NC. RIVDIV-552, ATSB Tra Cu (Vinh Binh)

3/25/70 GMMC Robert L. Chavez, Yuma, AZ. NSF, Cam Ranh Bay, MOTU-13 (Khanh Hoa)

EN3 Harold J. Hartwell, Lake Arthur, LA. NSF, Cam Rahn Bay (Khanh Hoa)

3/26/70 EM2 Vince R. Kiselewski, Waltonville, IL. NSA, Cam Rahn Bay

4/03/70 EN3 Edward J. Baker, Rapid City, IL. STAB-12, STABRON-20, B-40, (Ba Xugen)
GMG3 George R. Crabtree, Jamestown, TN. STAB-12
FN Joseph D. Johns, Louisville, KY. STAB-12, B-40
4/07/70 CECN Glen W. Miller, Wilmington, DE. NSA, ATSB Go Dau Ha (Tay Ninh) WIA 04/6/70
4/11/70 SN David C. Case, Wichita, KS. STAB-11, STABRON-20, (WIA 03/18/70) (An Long)
4/13/70 SN Jose Hernandez Jr, ElPaso, TX. NSA Saigon, Det-Sa Dec (Ding Tuong)
4/16/70 PT2 Douglas E. Hobbs, Bakersfield, CA. ST-1-Det-Golf
5/03/70 BMC Oscar A. Day, Hermon, NY RIVDIV-553, Patrol Officer, PBR, (Kien Giang)
5/16/70 BU2 William B. Doucet, San Anselmo, Ca. NSA Saigon, DET- Binh Thuy
5/16/70 PT2 Douglas E. Hobbs, Bakersfield, CA. ST- 2, Det-Golf, CTF-116 (An Xugen)
5/17/70 RD3 Frederick D. Snyder, Moab, UT. CTF-115, CD-11, PCF- 64 (WIA 04/16/70)
5/18/70 SM1 Edward F. Habblett Jr, Natrena Heights, PA. BC, PBR, RivDiv-572 (Vinh Binh)
6/01/70 Lt John M. Mulcahy, Miami FL. Hal-3, UH-1B-1310, Pilot (Binh Thuy)
AMS1 Wilber D. Frahm, Stanton, IL. HAL-3, UH-1B-1310, Crewmember (Binh Thuy)
AOI Lloyd L. Bowles, Quincy, IL. UH-1B-1310, Crewmember
6/07/70 LCDR "Jere" Alan Barton, San Diego, Ca. VAL-4, OV10A, Pilot (Kien Tuong)
6/07/70 EN3 Leonard C. Warnick, Polk, NE. NAGV, RPG-59, PBR-708 (Binh Thuy)
6/12/70 ADR2 James T. Gladden Jr. Wathena, KS. Cam Ranh Bay NAF, (WIA 5/30/70) (Khanh Hoa)
6/20/70 AN Roger L. Porter, Huron, SD. NAF, Cam Ranh Bay (WIA 6/12/70) (Khanh Hoa)
6/23/70 ENC Frank W. Bomar, Miami, FL. ST-1 Det-Golf, UH-1B Passenger (Phong Dinh)

MM2 Richard J. Solano, Palo Alto, CA. ST-1, Passenger,
BM3 James R. Gore, Sunburst, MT. ST-1, helo Passenger
SM3 John S. Durlin, Lake City, PA. ST-1, helo Passenger
EM3 James L. Riter, Phoenix, AZ. ST-1, helo Passenger
FN Toby A. Thomas, Brentwood, MO., ST-1, Passenger
SN John J. Donnelly III, Philadelphia, PA. helo Passenger
SN Thomas R. Brown, St Paul, MN. NSA Saigon, helo
Passenger
HM2 Harold L. Linvill, Reno, NV. CTF-117, RivRon-15,
Staff, Sea Float, helo Passenger
6/26/70 GMG2 William J. Cariveau, Santa Maria, CA. NAGV,
RPG-55 (Phong Dinh)
6/29/70 SN Leroy B. Mudd, West Mifflin, PA. NSA Saigon,
YRBM-20
0702/70 BM2 Calvin R. Gish, Highland, IN. MST-2, UDT-13,
CTF-116 (Phouc Tuy)
7/06/70 QM2 Lanny H. Buroff, Chicago, IL. CTF-115, CD-11,
PCF-40 (An Xugen)
7/11/70 FN Glenn E. Maier, Bismarck, ND. NSA Saigon, YRBM-
17 (Kien Hoa)
7/15/70 BMSN Jerrel D. Scroggs, Beaumont, TX. NSA Saigon,
ISB (Rach Soi)
7/21/70 DCFN Scott F. Wemette, Malone, KY. USS Askari, RAD-
53 (An Giang)
8/04/70 LCDR John R. Poe, Laurel, MD. CO/RivDiv-592, Staff/
RPG-56 (Gia Dinh) (WIA 8/01/70)
8/06/70 ENSC Lloyd A. Murphy, San Diego, CA. NSA Saigon,
Det-ATSB Phouc Xuyen
BMC Andrew C. Grant, Flint, MI. NSA Saigon, Det-
ATSB Phouc Xuyen
8/06/70 LT Kenneth W. Tapscott, Charleston, SC. NAVFORV
NILO, Song Ong Doc (An Xugen)
8/20/70 SN Wayne W. Mullin, New Bedford, CA. NSA Saigon,
Det-Nha Be
8/23/70 QMC James R. Hunt, Columbus, IN. RAD-53, PO/ASPB-
153 (Go Cong)

9/03/70 FN Gary L. Ruff, Benton Harbor, MI. NSA Saigon, Det-ATSB Tra Cu (Vinh Binh)

9/15/70 LTJG William A. Pedersen, La Canada, CA. Hal-3, Det-6, UH-1B, Pilot (An Xugen)
ADJ2 Jose P. Ramos, McAllon, TX. Hal-3, Det-6, UH-1B, Crewmember (An Xugen)

9/18/70 BM3 Luco W. Palma, Tewksburg, MA. UDT-13, Det-Hotel
HM3 Lawrence C. Williams Jr, Port Author, TX. UDT-13, Det-Hotel, CTF-116, hostile

9/22/70 EN3 Johnny C. Jones, McKinney, TX. RivDiv-572, ATSB Phouc Xuyen

9/27/70 ST1 Freddie L. Tapper, Hobart, IN. IUWG-1, Staff, Cam Ranh Bay (Khank Hoa)

10/03/70 ATR2 Walter R. Winters, Hal-3, Det-3, Cau Mau (Vinh Binh)

10/06/70 GMG1 Edward W. Withee, Madison, ME. NAGV, RPG-55, PBR (Kien Giang)

10/18/70 RD1 Frederick L. Nutter, Zanesville, OH. Com. RIV Pat Ron-5, Staff, CTF-116

10/20/70 RMSN John DeWitt Drake, Stockton, CA. NSA Saigon, Det-Ben Luc, TAD, ATSB Song Ong Doc (An Xugen)
GMG3 Thomas S. McGarry, Springville, TN. NAGV, RPG-62, ATSB Song Ong Doc

10/25/70 QM1 Joseph P. Jurgella, Stevens Point, WI. PCF-59, Cat Lo, CTF-115

11/04/70 EN3 Bruce C. Hunt, South Pasadena, CA. RAD-153, ATC-153-2, CTF-117, (An Xugen)

11/11/70 SN John E. Hollis, Apple Springs, TX. USS Benewah, APB-35, CTF-117, (Kien Phong)

11/29/70 EN2 Robert E. Young, Orlando, FL. NSA Saigon, Det-ATSB Kien An, Hostile

12/01/70 EN2 Walter D. Lambert, Angelton, TX. USS Hunterdon County, AGP-838

12/07/70 BMC Paul Colwell, Toulouse, KY. NAGV, RPG-58, Rach Gia (Kien Giang)

12/19/70 LT Richard H. Buzzell, Arlington, MA. Hal-3, Det-3, UH-1B Pilot (An Xugen)

LTJG Antonio O. Ortiz, Pirtleville, AZ. Hal-3, Det-3,
CTF-116, Crewmember
AEC Johnny Ratliff, Washington Court House, OH. Hal-3, Crewmember
ADJ2 Robert E. Worth, Big Lake, TX. Hal-3, Crewmember
12/27/70 EN2 Esteban V. Rochez, New York, NY. NSA Saigon, Det-ATSB Ca Mau, LCM-920

In 1998, at a reunion of Game Warden sailors, Admiral Zumwalt gave a moving speech; informing us we had accomplished all of our missions and had won our part of the war. He also added that after the fall of Saigon in 1975, many of the South Vietnamese sailors whom we had trained had fought on for many months until overtaken or escaping to the Gulf of Thailand and the South China Sea. The Vietnamese sailors who were captured were held in chains and tiger cages in rehabilitation camps for nearly two years. After being released, they were treated as traitors and struggled to find work. Some are still living in Vietnam today. A few made it out and live with us in the land of the free.

WE SPENT MOST OF THE LAST CENTURY IN A LIFE OR DEATH STRUGGLE WITH "THE EVIL EMPIRE" THE SOVIET UNION. THAT SNAKE IS D-E-A-D, WITH A STAKE THROUGH ITS HEART. VIETNAM WAS ONE OF THE BATTLES IN THAT WAR. WE WON THE WAR

MM2 Sam Eaton
NSA / YRBM 21

EPILOGUE

The following was written after visiting the Black Wall in our Nation's capital in July of 2003.

I sat in front of the panels to the west, where the men who were lost in 1970 were named. After watching and speaking to class after class of American youth, it became evident to me that it was not only a place of mourning, but also one of duty, honor, and sacrifice. In memory of what it was like "back then" I share the following thoughts.

After service, many veterans marched home to the sound of name-calling, being spit on by the misguided and confused, who knew not what these silent heroes had endured or given. Most of the veterans returned and went on to lead, utilizing the lessons they had acquired. Some struggled with nightmares and demons as a continuing curse. A few were wounded deeply and left us too soon, for their bodies had been torn and their souls had been stolen.

They asked, and still ask, not for pity or opinions of what was done in Vietnam, but only for love and what they have rightfully earned. Be not afraid to thank them, for it is long overdue, and soon they will be gone.

If you are able to visit the Black Wall, don't be ashamed to reach out and touch their names, even if you have not known them, for they are our brothers and sisters and should not be ignored or left alone. Let no one convince you that the sacrifices of these young men and women were in vain, for they knew not the fullest reasons why they had fought or had given to all Americans. Be not afraid to weep or acknowledge your love, for your actions preserve their spirits. They live now in the wind that blows Old Glory and in the free sun that brightly shines.

And if you choose to leave a flower or memento from the past, then we thank you and know you care and understand.

Their names are now numbered among the roll calls of ranks which fought under Washington, Roosevelt, and Truman and will live for generations to come. They will continue to serve as a reminder to our great people... one Nation, under God, Indivisible, with Liberty and Justice for All.

ACKNOWLEDGEMENTS

Thank you to my teacher and mentor Bob Cawley, for showing me how it is done and inspiring me to be myself.

To Wildon Bleiler, for his inspiring words, devotion, and editing expertise.

To my musician friends, Larry Jenks, Dave Chase, Edd Grell and Roger Latorre of the SUN SPOTS, for helping out.

To my old hippie buddy, Buttons Boggs, for her gifted artistic ability, her compassion, and her dad, who built ships for the United States Navy.

To Larry Bissonnette, for his warmth and steadfast convictions, who guided and counseled me, and along the way became my friend.

A special thanks to Dwight Cabella, Ken Scott, John Perry, Dempsey Bumpass, Dave Staercke, Don Rypka, Richard Schiep, James Bryant, Paul Wayne Cagle, Steve Watson, Ken Dunwoody, James Watson, Harold Payne, Sam and Bac Eaton, Ralph Fries, Henry Livingstone, Ken McGhee, Keith Bettinger and to all the Veterans who supplied bios, unit books, military records, hometown and Navy news articles, letters and pictures, and their hearts, souls and memories to me. I am forever in your debt.

To the United States Navy who released declassified war records to me and wished me well. I am, and will always be, proud to have been a sailor.

Lyrics used by permission of Joe McDonald from the song, "I FEEL I'M FIXING TO DIE RAG", copyright Joe McDonald, a United States Navy Veteran.

I love you Grandma and Grandpa, Mom and Dad, Pat, Aunt Rachel, sister Jo Ann and brother Phillip. Thank you for having the insight to save my letters and pictures and stand by my side in that time when many questioned my motives.

TO THOSE WHO GAVE, SO FREEDOM MIGHT LIVE

Ralph performing at the Rolling Thunder reunion in Las Vegas,
Nevada, 2002, with Randy Linder's Tribute to CCR, featuring
the Midnight Special Band. Shown playing his base guitar
Delores, named in honor of his mother. Ran5327@aol.com

Ralph Christopher during a visit to Bellingham, Washington
to honor Art Nordtuedt, Bob Moors and their crew in 2004.
Thanks for building the boats that severed the Communist
lines, and made it possible for many of us to return home.

ABOUT THE AUTHOR

After Ralph Christopher served in Vietnam with the United States Navy, he returned home to Virginia and attended classes at Virginia Commonwealth University. In 1982, he graduated the Musicians Institute of Technology in Hollywood California. He was the oldest student in his class. He is now a veteran performer and recording artist of over thirty years. He lives with his family in Nevada and works with young adults, music, and Veterans affairs.

"BOATS OF GLASS, BALLS OF BRASS, BLACK BERETS FOREVER"

LT Fred McDavitt
CO / River Section 531

Printed in the United States
44043LVS00004B/43-102